IMAGES
of America

RECOLLECTIONS OF PIERRE PART AND THE BELLE RIVER

On the Cover: Oleus "Junius" Templet raised his cattle for his meat market. Templet is pictured in the back of his house with the cattle. He could always slice up a good steak and ground meat for customers. His cattle and meat market were his life. (Courtesy of Dorothy "Dot" Theriot Templet.)

IMAGES
of America

Recollections of Pierre Part and the Belle River

Geneve Daigle Cavalier and
Tre' Michael Caballero

ARCADIA
PUBLISHING

ISBN 978-1-4671-2797-4

Published by Arcadia Publishing
Charleston, South Carolina

Printed in the United States of America

Library of Congress Control Number: 2017957369

For all general information, please contact Arcadia Publishing:
Telephone 843-853-2070
Fax 843-853-0044
E-mail sales@arcadiapublishing.com
For customer service and orders:
Toll-Free 1-888-313-2665

Visit us on the Internet at www.arcadiapublishing.com

Contents

Acknowledgments

I would like to take this time to say that my first book, Images of America: *Pierre Part*, was a huge success! To everyone who helped me until now, I cannot thank you enough; you have helped me touch so many people's lives by allowing me to pass down generations of stories. It is always my hope to put a smile on your face and a fond memory in your heart, because the greatest gift we can ever receive is what our ancestors left behind. May this book serve to spread wisdom and joy to the younger generation, give them a reminder that everything works out, and prove that one day they will have enough stories for their children to fill a book.

Thanks to my family for always supporting me and to my biggest supporter, my mother, and now my guardian angel, Mary Ann "Marion" Gaudet Daigle, who passed on October 10, 2016. She was so happy I started this book, and I couldn't wait to show her. She helped me so much, telling me anything and everything she could. Knowing that her memories are with me brings me immense joy.

INTRODUCTION

Our little town of Pierre Part went through plenty of hard times. People were very poor and had extremely little. Their houses had cardboard walls adorned with moss and mud in order for the makeshift building to stand on its own. The city repeatedly went through natural disasters, wrecking everything they had built with their own hands. Tornadoes, floods, and raging hurricanes were forces to be reckoned with. But the people were rich at heart even in the hardest of circumstances. We should cherish all that our ancestors did to make this place what it is today. Most of the citizens had to leave Pierre Part to find jobs and comfortable living conditions, leaving children and family behind, or find other solutions to make do. Most of the work was seasonal, so for parts of the year, families continued to struggle financially. Still, we can appreciate everything our ancestors taught us, including their language, Cajun French. The ancient Louisianan tongue was something passed down through generations, but it is slowly fading out as our schools are teaching our children different French. The older generations are passing, and the younger generations are not teaching nor speaking to their children in French like many before them did.

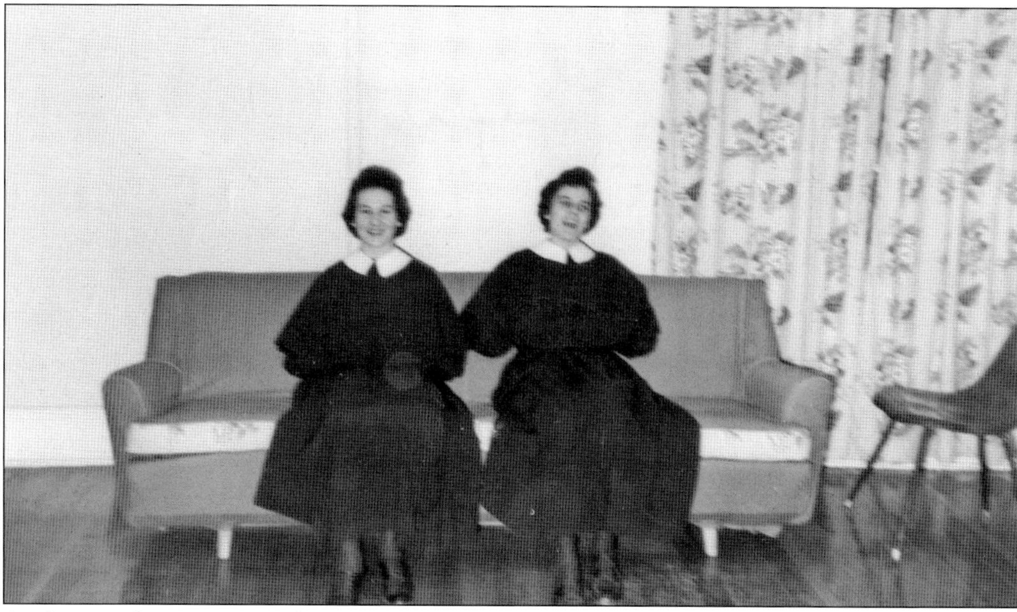

At the age of 19, Lucy Templet and Laura Nell Breaux Pipsair wanted to become nuns. They went to the convent in Covington. It is believed they are pictured here on the sofa in the convent. There is a lot of work to do to become a nun. It is a calling from God. (Courtesy of Wildy Templet and Hilda Templet.)

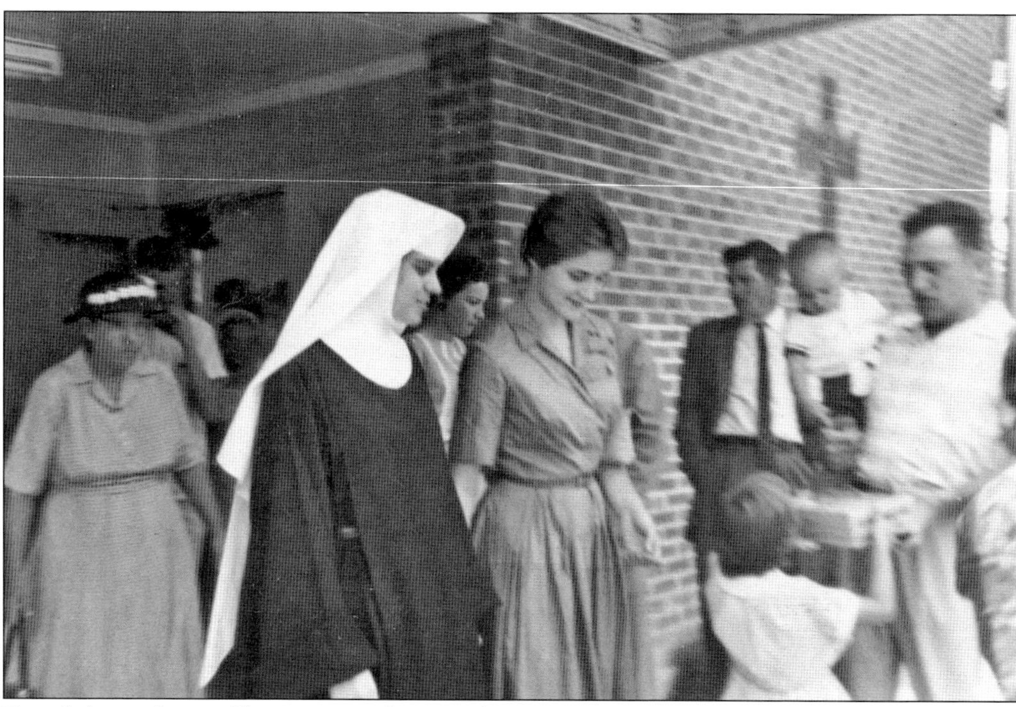

From left to right are Clemence Landry Templet, Lucy Templet Castigne, Laura Louise Woodruff, and Dan Dantini holding his child, Allen Milbian. They are just coming out of a ceremony at the convent in Covington, Louisiana. (Courtesy of Wildy Templet and Hilda Templet.)

One

Churches and Events

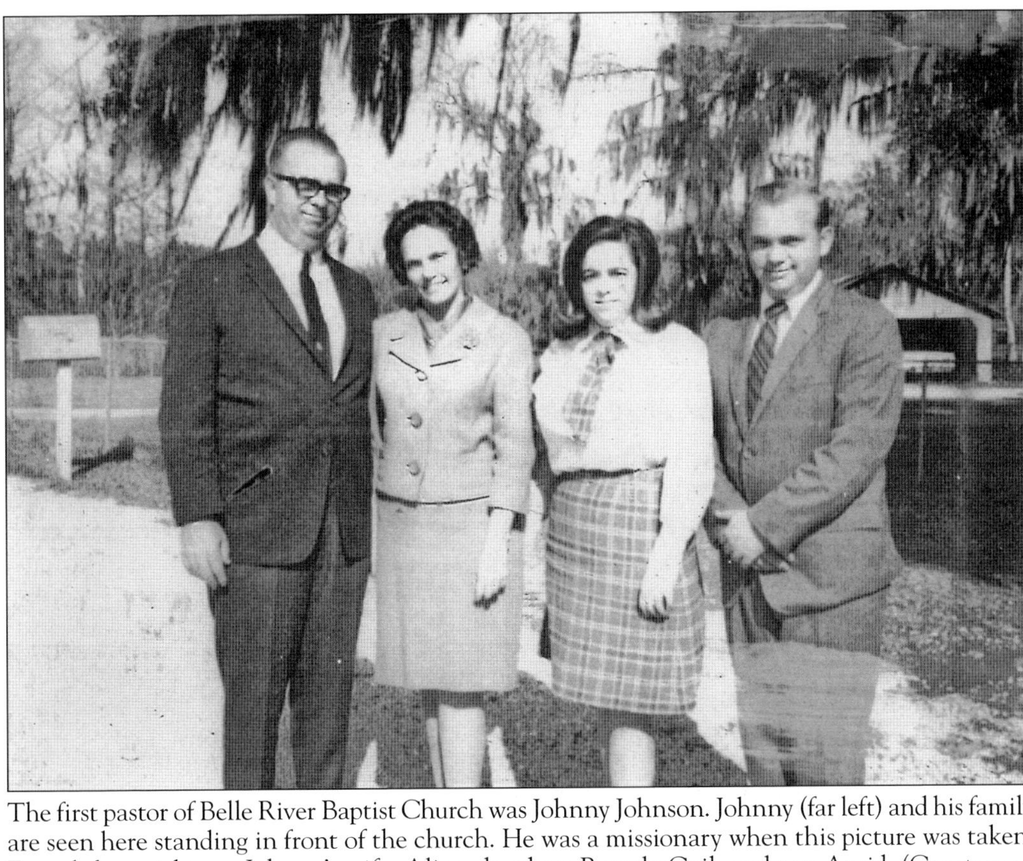

The first pastor of Belle River Baptist Church was Johnny Johnson. Johnny (far left) and his family are seen here standing in front of the church. He was a missionary when this picture was taken. From left to right are Johnny's wife, Alice; daughter Beverly Gail; and son Arvid. (Courtesy of Ann Cavalier Landry Cavalier.)

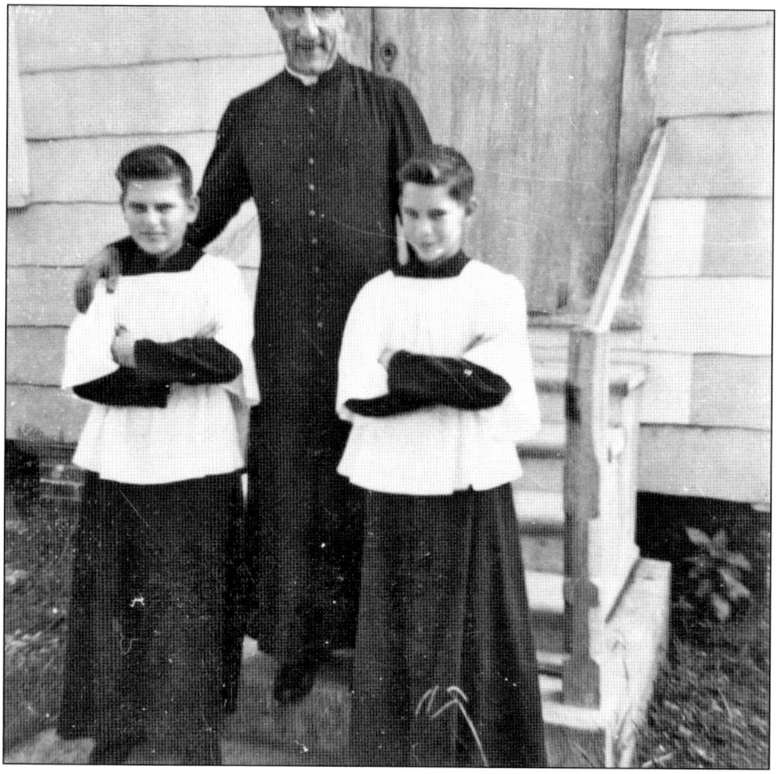

It was always an honor to be an altar server. In the past, the role was filled by young boys. It is not known if these boys had just finished mass or if it had not started yet. From left to right are Michael "Mike" Berthelot, Fr. Romeo LaPierre, and Harris Mabile. (Courtesy of Leonard Mabile and Regina Duprus Mabile.)

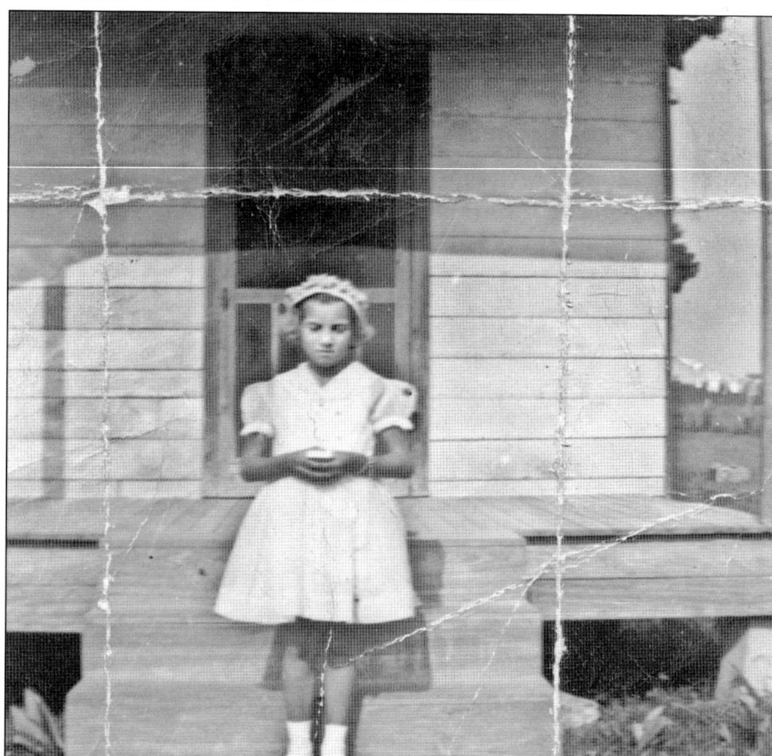

Dressed all in white, Hilda Crochet Albarado Sagona make her first communion in July 1955. She is standing in front of her house after communion. This house was where the gym and therapy place is today. (Courtesy of Odile Crochet Landry.)

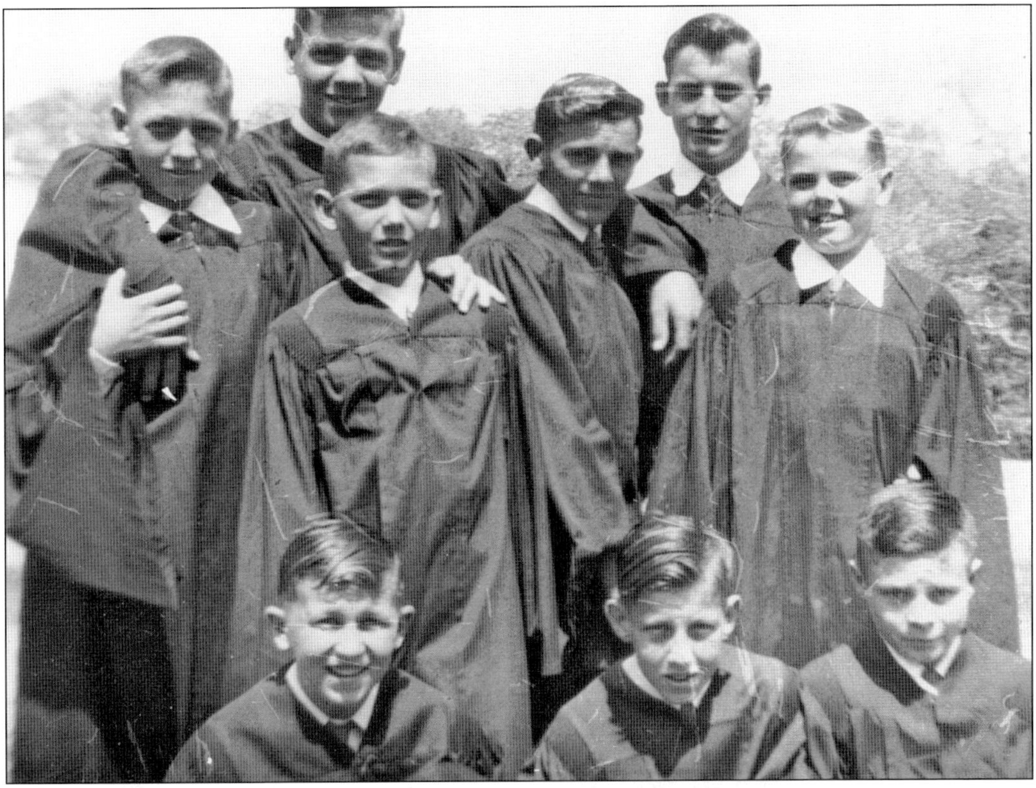

These young men went to Assumption Church in Plattenville, Louisiana, to make their confirmation. From left to right are (first row) Harry Landry, Lee Gaudet, and Herman Mabile; (second row) John McCarthy, Carol Mabile, and T.J. Blanchard; (third row) Russell Gaudet, Alvin McCarthy, and Calvin Blanchard. (Courtesy of Cecile Guillot Mabile.)

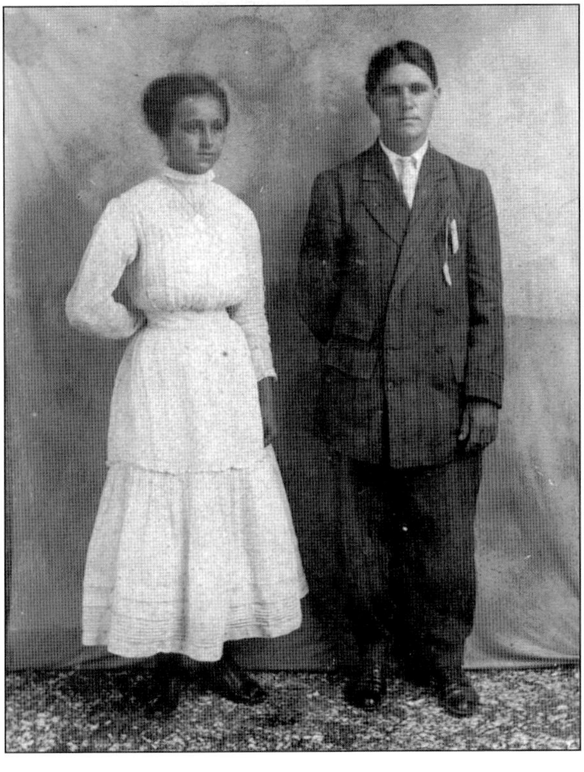

Cyrile Alexandre Daigle and his wife, Pauline Crochet Daigle, were married on September 28, 1911. He was born on April 6, 1892, and she was born on February 7, 1893. They had 10 children. Trasimond "Nonc Trasimond" Martin Daigle and Aurela "Ma-Dell" Landry were his parents, and Paul Crochet was her father. (Courtesy of Dave Daigle Sr. and Tilsey Fryou Daigle.)

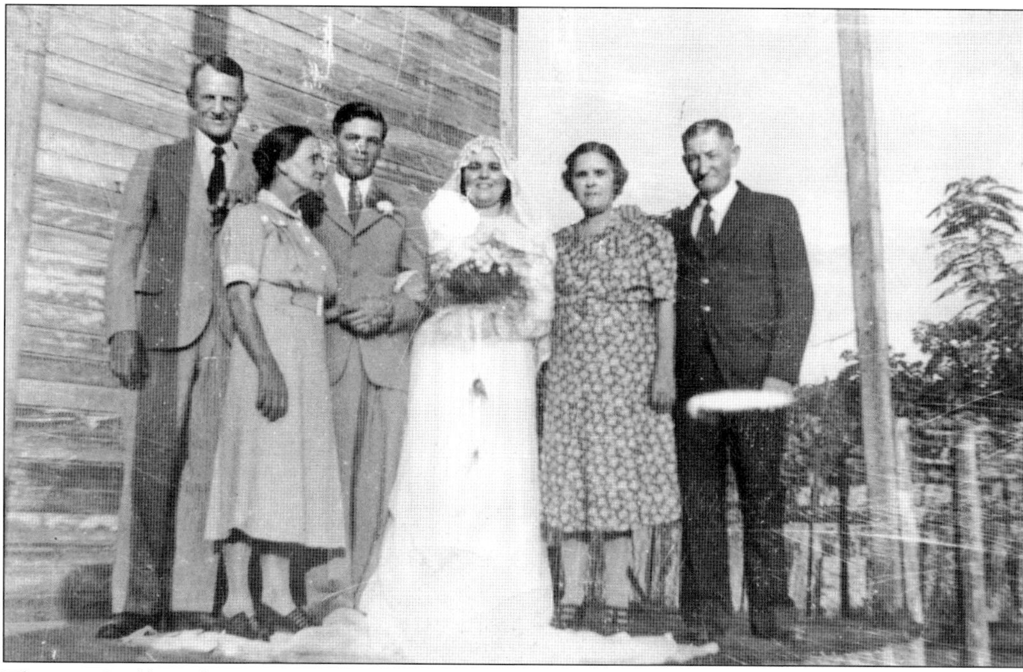

Therese Guillot Theriot and Phillip Theriot are standing with their parents at their wedding. From left to right are Leonie Theriot Sr. and Georgina Crochet Theriot; their son Phillip and his wife, Therese Guillot Theriot; and Bernadette Templet Guillot and Oilbert Guillot. (Courtesy of Brenda Landry Templet and Norbert Temple.)

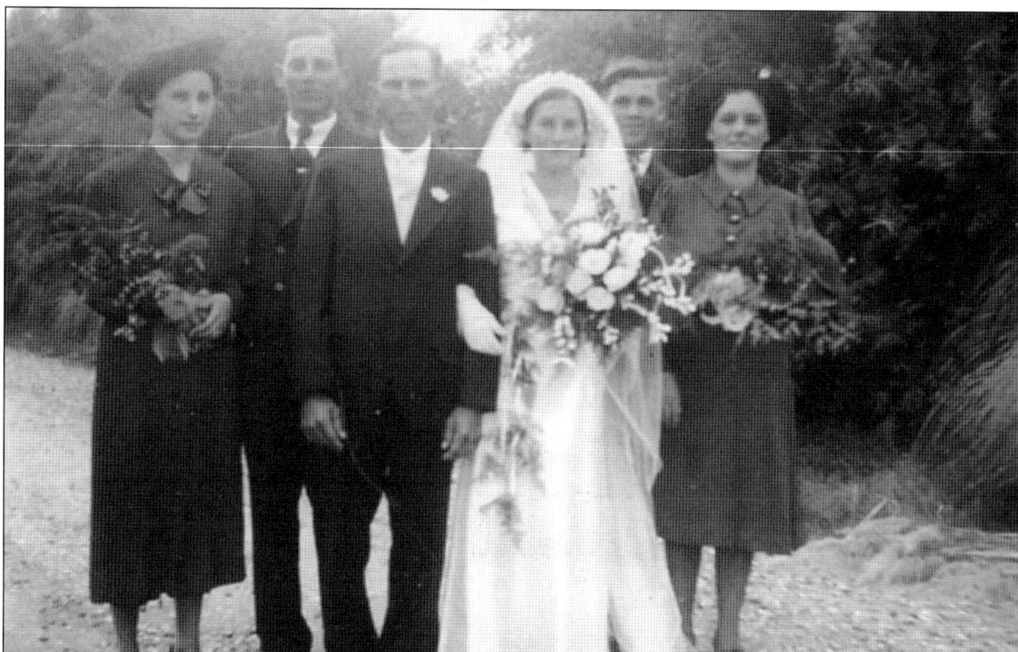

From left to right are Mildred Richard, Jim Blanchard, groom Claude Blanchard, bride Rosa Guillot Blanchard, her brother-in-law Phillip Theriot, and her sister Therese Guillot Theriot. (Courtesy of Cecil Blanchard Mabile.)

Claude Crochet married Frances Daigle Crochet. Frances lived to be 92. Claude was born in 1914. They had a large family of 16 children. (Courtesy of Tonya Crochet Olivier.)

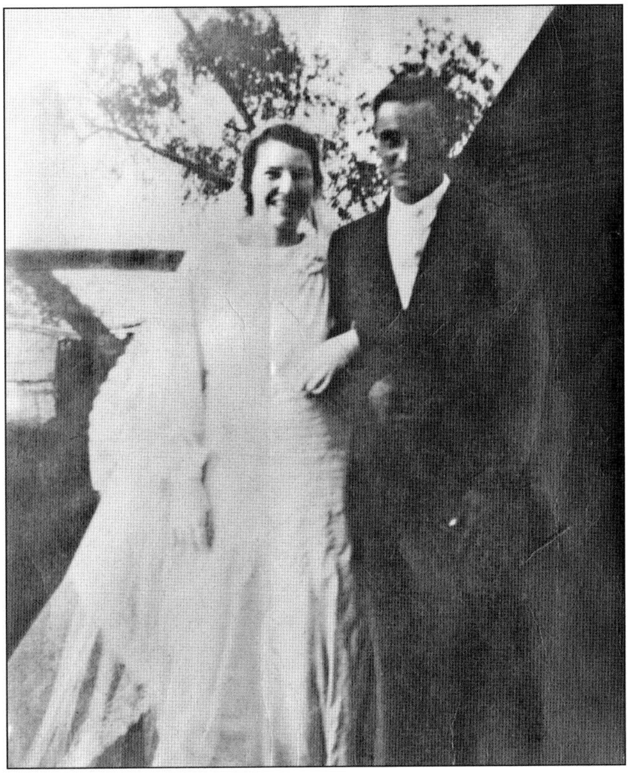

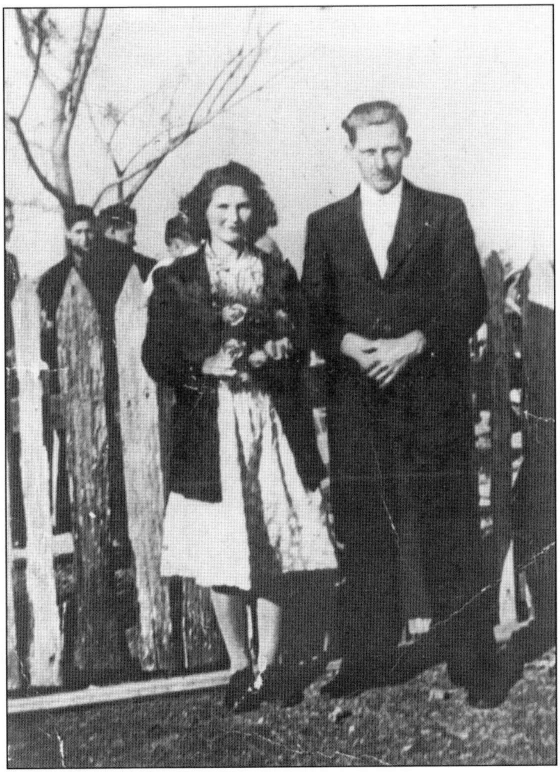

Leonita Mabile Blanchard is pictured on her wedding day; she married Alfred Blanchard. They had two daughters, Nancy Blanchard Charlet and Sally Blanchard Breaux. (Courtesy of Nancy Blanchard Charlet.)

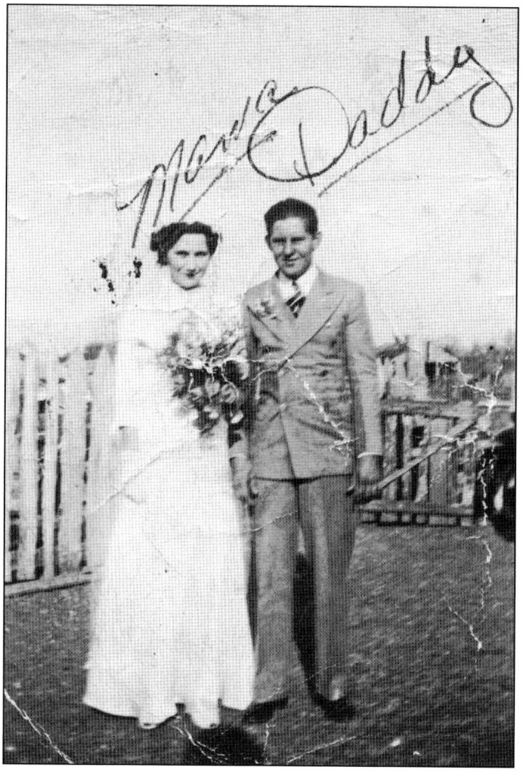

Regina Dupuis Mabile and Leonard Mabile are pictured on their wedding day, February 3, 1942. Regina and Leonard were blessed with nine children. (Courtesy of Leonard Mabile and Regina Dupuis Mabile.)

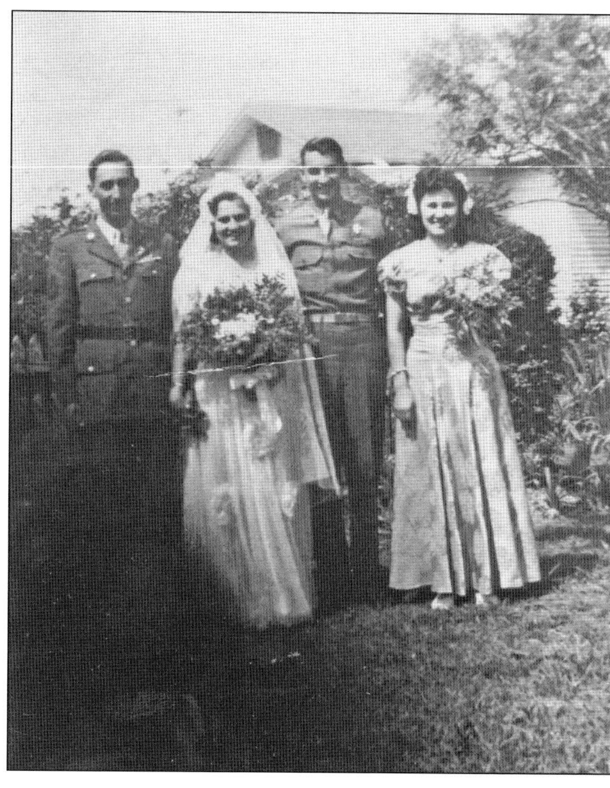

From left to right are LeRoy Matherne and his wife, Bessie Ruiz Matherne; Irvin "Black" Gauthreaux; and Vernice Matherne Theriot. LeRoy and Bessie were married on April 9, 1945, in Pierre Part. This picture was taken at the home of Paul and Christine Breaux Matherne down the bay. (Courtesy of Nadine Theriot.)

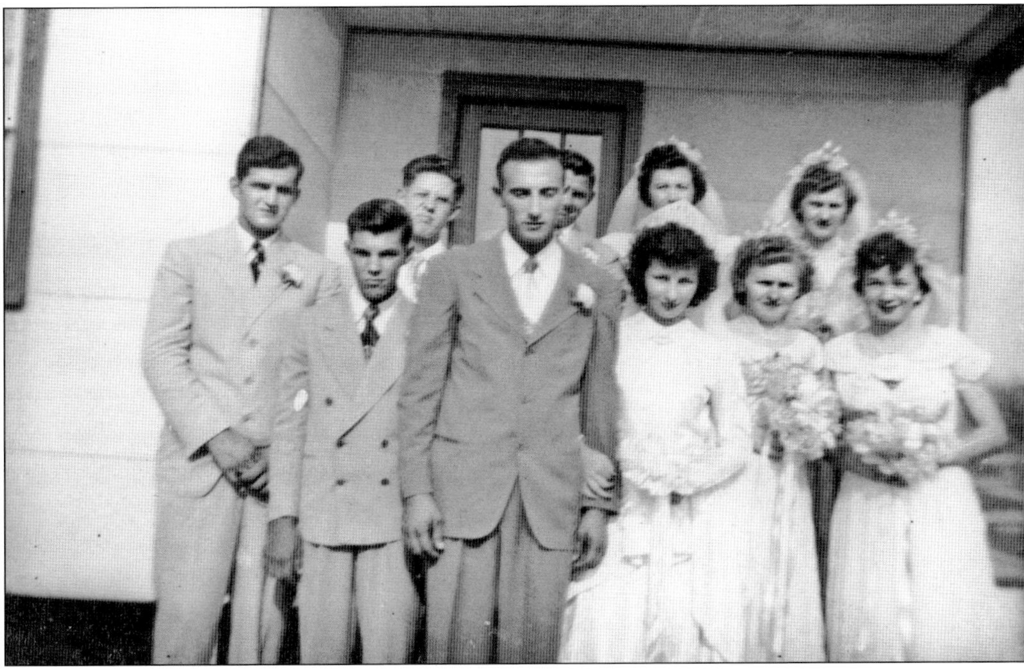

Floyd and Ann Blanchard were married on Wednesday, August 23, 1950. From left to right are (first row) Wilfred Blanchard, Floyd, Ann, Virgie Giroir, and Winnie Blanchard; (second row) Eugene Mabile, P.J. Blanchard, Dudley Mabile, Beatrice Blanchard Tullier, and Lucy Verrett. (Courtesy of T.J. Blanchard.)

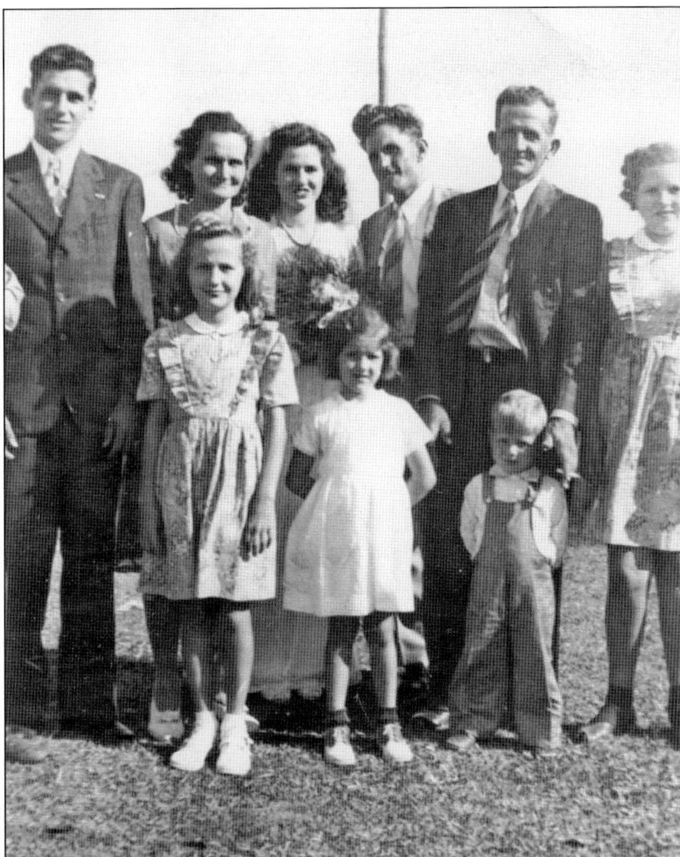

Steve Berthelot and Verna Mabile Berthelot are pictured on their wedding day. From left to right are (first row) Edith Mabile Blanchard, Vivian Mabile Cavalier, and Joe Mabile Jr.; (second row) Joseph Mabile, Ada Blanchard Mabile, Verna, Steve, unidentified, and Delta Mabile. Steve was born on February 10, 1922, and passed away on October 22, 2007. Verna was born on July 23, 1926, and passed away on July 11, 2002. (Courtesy of T.J. Blanchard.)

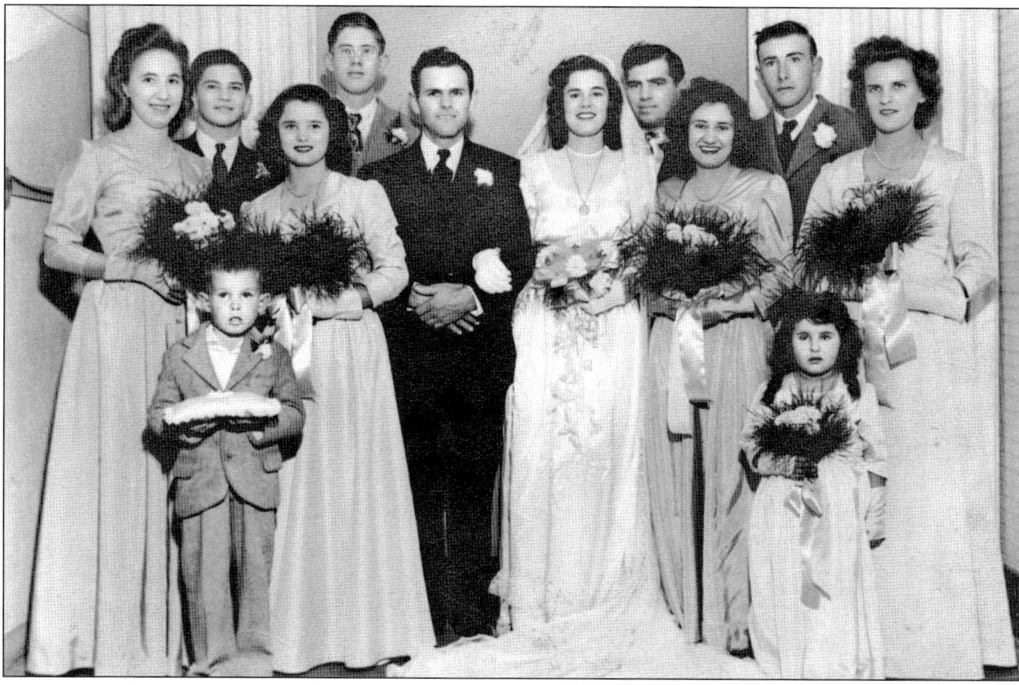

Rumsey and Margie Blanchard Rodrigue are pictured on their wedding day with their wedding party. From left to right are (first row) Alton "Pete" Landry Jr. and Betty Blanchard Boudreaux; (second row) Pearl Matherne, unidentified, Rumsey, Margie, Voilet Blanchard, and Annie Rodrigue; (third row) unidentified, P.J. Blanchard, "Junior" Aucoin, and Floyd Blanchard. (Courtesy of T.J. Blanchard.)

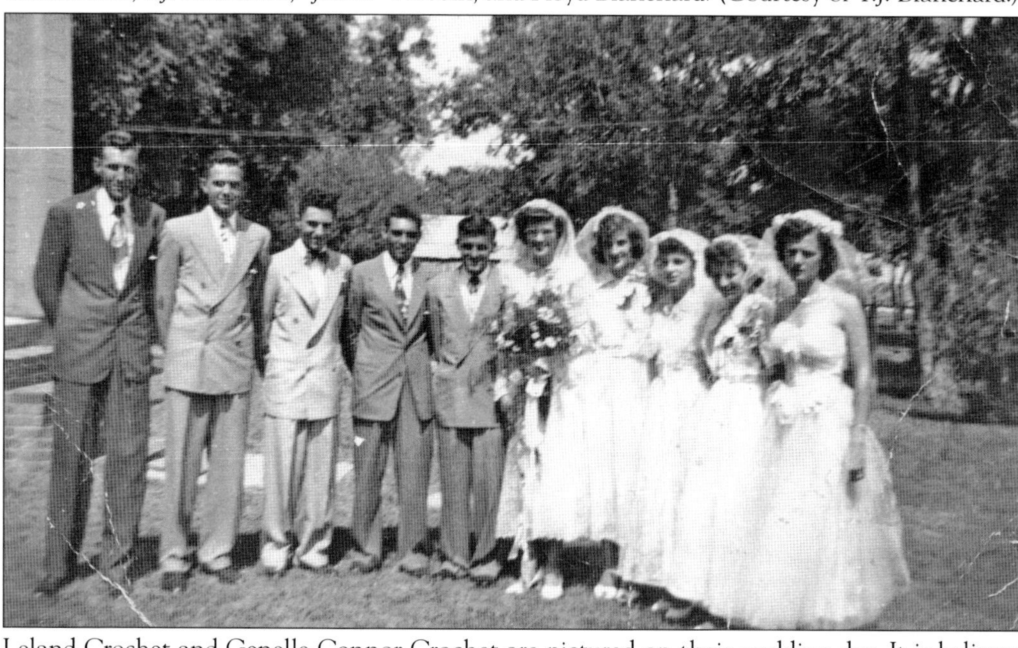

Leland Crochet and Genelle Connor Crochet are pictured on their wedding day. It is believed that their wedding party included Alex Crochet, Maude Crochet Landry, Mickey Dugas, Faye Boudreaux Bertrand, Johnny Bowdoin, Cliff Connor, and Greta Bowdoin Johnson. (Courtesy of Odile Crochet Landry.)

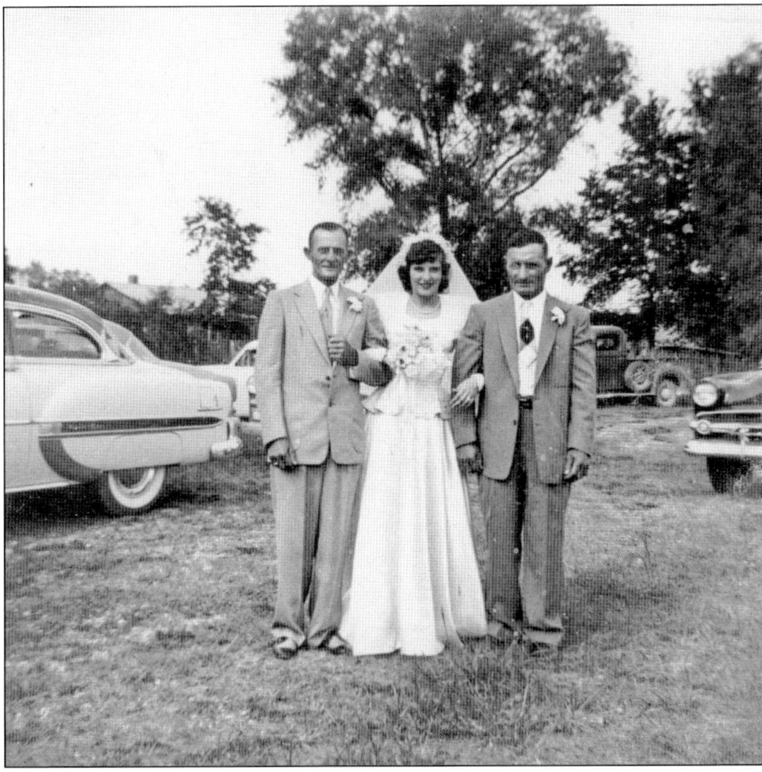

The wedding day of Geraldine Landry Fryou and Gerald Fryou was June 1, 1955. Geraldine is pictured with her father-in-law, Pete Fryou (left), and her father, Rene Landry (right). (Courtesy of Dave Daigle and Tilsey Fryou Daigle.)

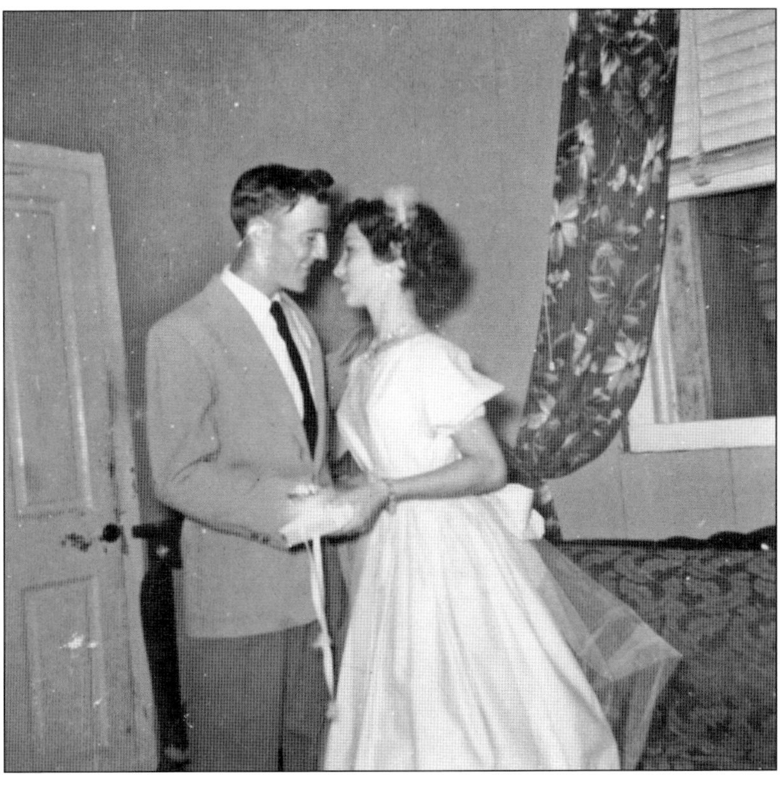

Doris Cavalier Hebert and Ernest Cavalier were married on August 9, 1958, at Belle River Baptist Church in Belle River. Doris was just 15 years old. They are pictured in the church. Ernest died in 1974; Doris died in 2009. (Courtesy of Elise Cavalier Cavalier.)

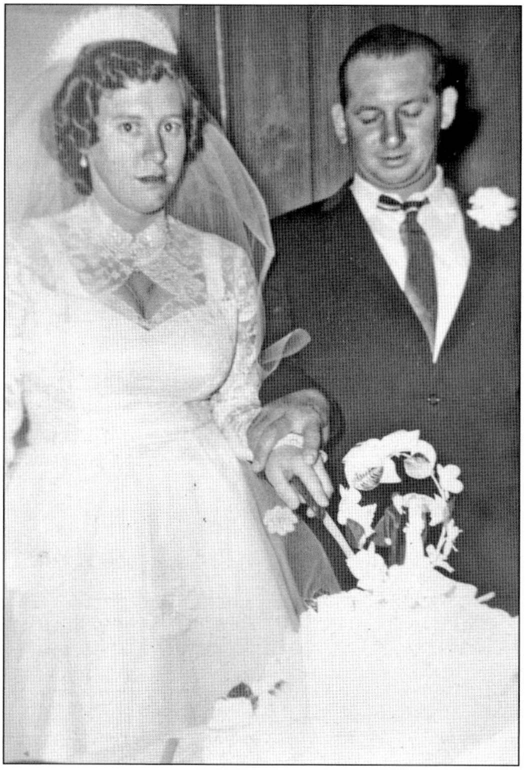

Lassie Mae Pipsair Gros and Lovelace Gros Sr. have just been married and are cutting their wedding cake. The couple was married for a little over 30 years when Lassie Mae died in April 1988. Lovelace died in February 1996. (Courtesy of Carol Gros Charlet.)

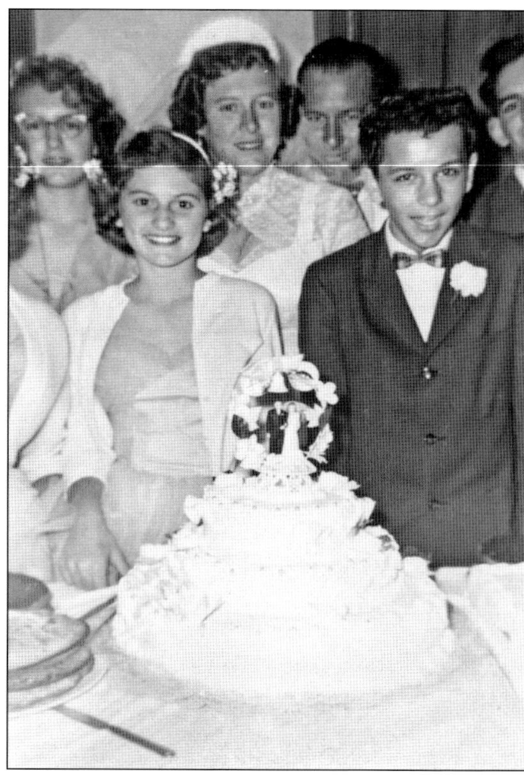

It is a happy day at the house of Joseph and Nobie Leonard Pipsair, parents of the bride. This was a reception honoring Lovelace Gros Sr. and Lassie Mae Pipsair Gros. Pictured with the cake are, from left to right, (first row) Ruby Daigle Pipsair and Roger Leonard; (second row) Mary Louise Pipsair Blanchard, Lassie Mae, Lovelace, and his father, Leon Gros. (Courtesy of Carol Gros Charlet.)

Chester Blanchard Sr. and Mary Louise Pipsair Blanchard were married on November 22, 1958, at St. Joseph the Worker Catholic Church. They are pictured in front of the church. (Courtesy of Carolyn Guidry.)

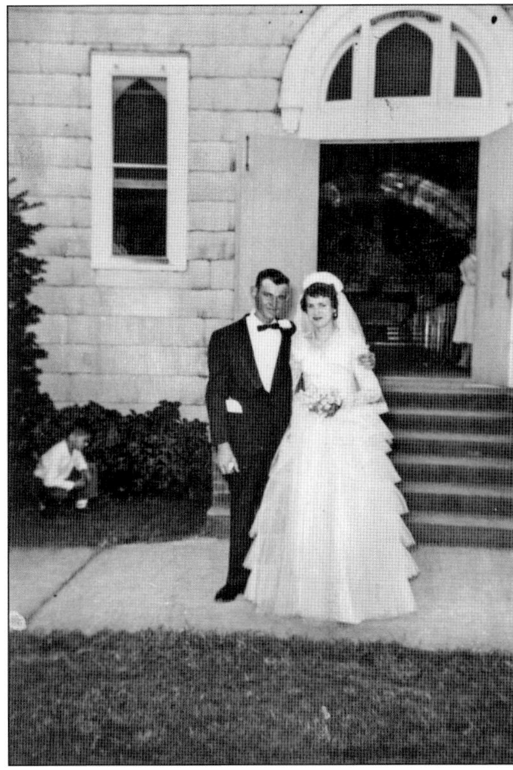

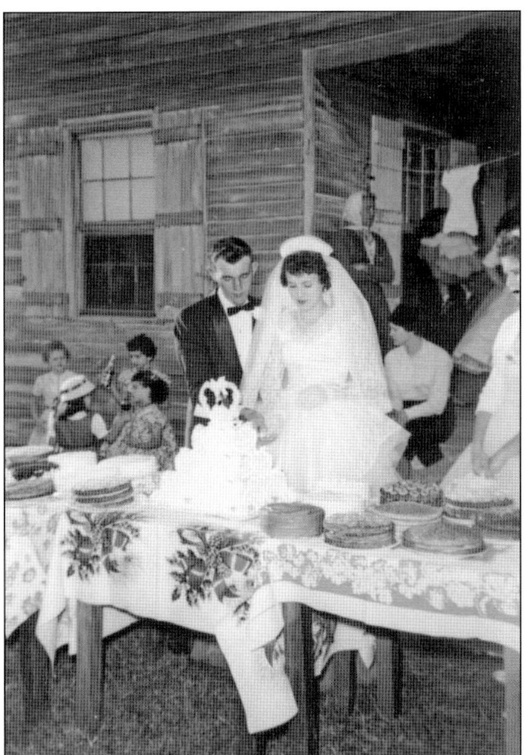

Many receptions were held at family houses. Chester Blanchard Sr. and Mary Louise Pipsair Blanchard had their reception in Belle River at the house of her parents, Joseph and Nobie Leonard Pipsair. (Courtesy of Carolyn Blanchard Guidry.)

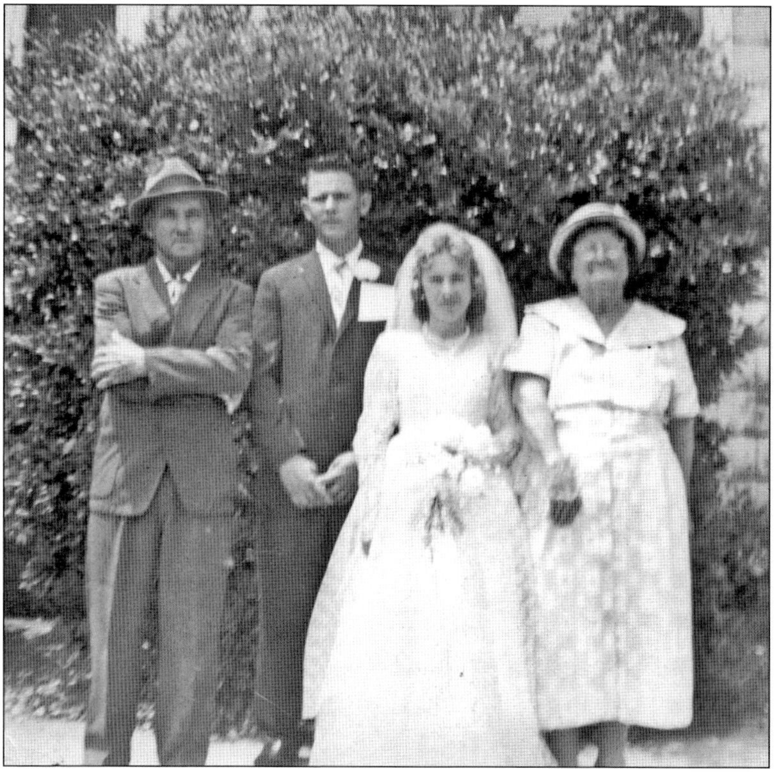

In May 1962, Shirley Templet Landry married Alvin Landry. She is pictured with her grandparents. From left to right are Henry Rivere, Alvin, Shirley, and Lorena "Gram Nana" Landry Templet. Henry was Shirley's mother's father, and Lorena was her father's mother. (Courtesy of Brenda Landry Templet and Nobert Templet.)

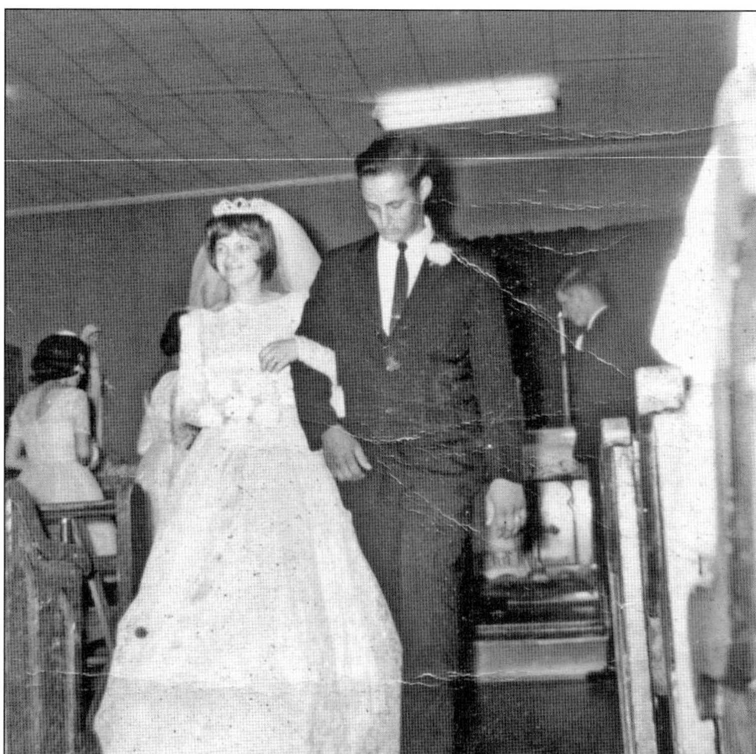

Charles Crochet and Geraldine "Jean" Carline Crochet were married in August 1965. They had three children, Tonya Crochet Olivier, Rachel Crochet St. Germain, and Dean Crochet. Charles passed away on September 24, 2008, at the age of 64. Jean passed away on June 28, 2016, at the age of 71. (Courtesy of Tonya Crochet Olivier.)

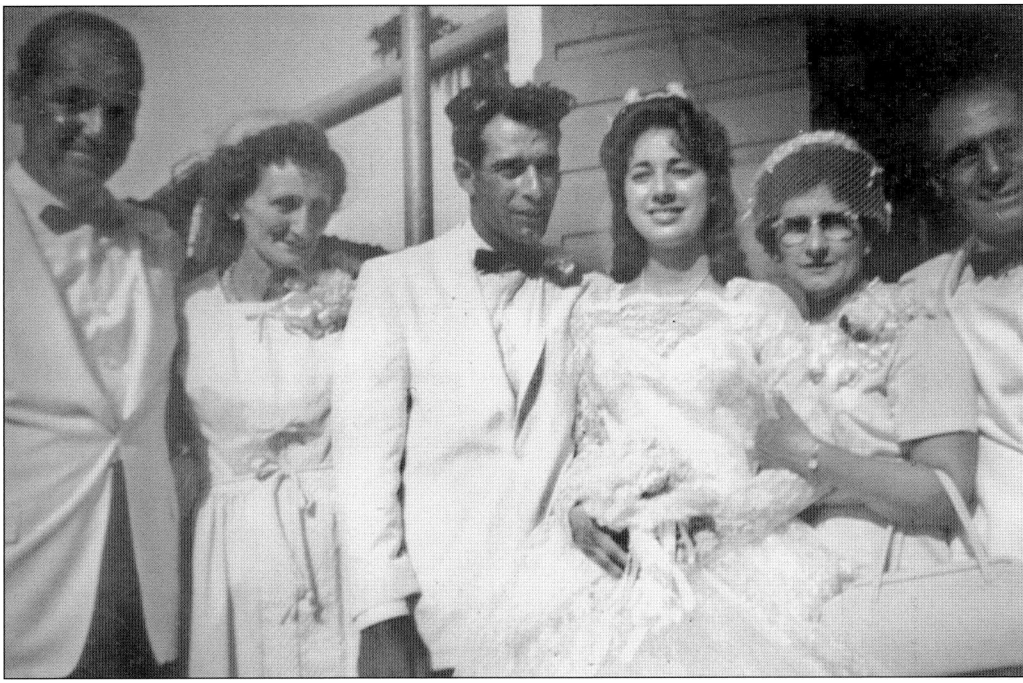

This is the wedding of Gustave Joseph Gaudet and Sarah Leonard Gaudet. Joseph and Sarah were married on May 2, 1964. Pictured above are, from left to right, Rene Leonard Sr., Grace Gauthreaux, Gustave Joseph Gaudet, Sarah Leonard Gaudet, Jean Rivere Gaudet, and Joseph Gaudet. Jean and Joseph are the parents of Gustave. Rene and Grace are the parents of Sarah. Below are, from left to right, Phillip "Junior" Richard, Susan Russo, Edward "Tookie" Breaux, Linda Gros McCarthy, Gustave, Sarah, Willy "Cheyenne" Gros, Kathern Blanchard, Alvin "Bago" Rivere, and Ruth Landry Templet. (Both, courtesy of Gustave Joseph Gaudet and Sarah Leonard Gaudet.)

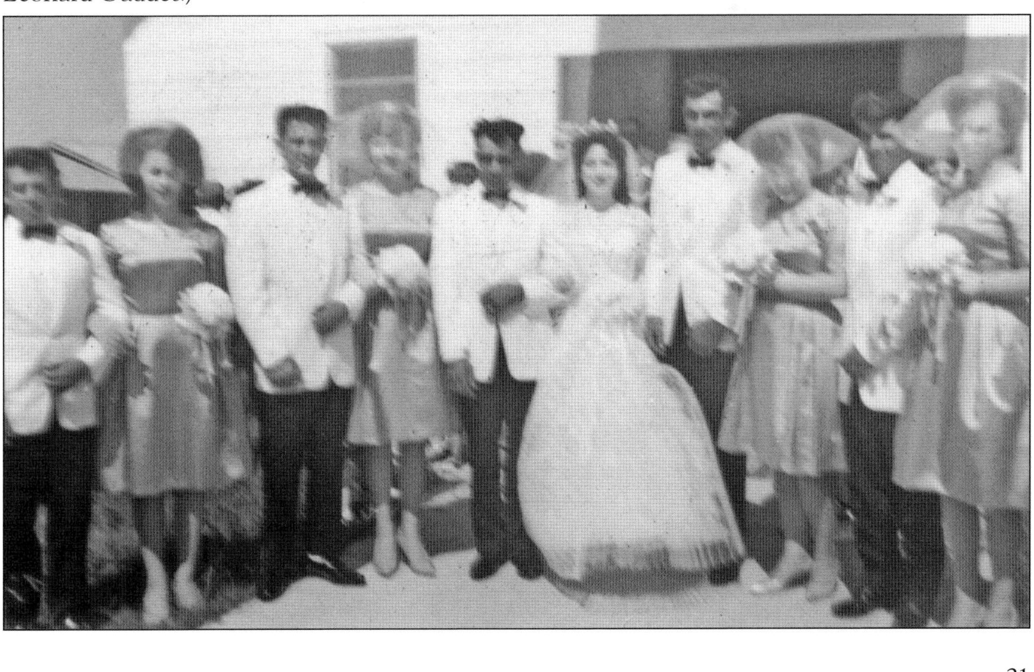

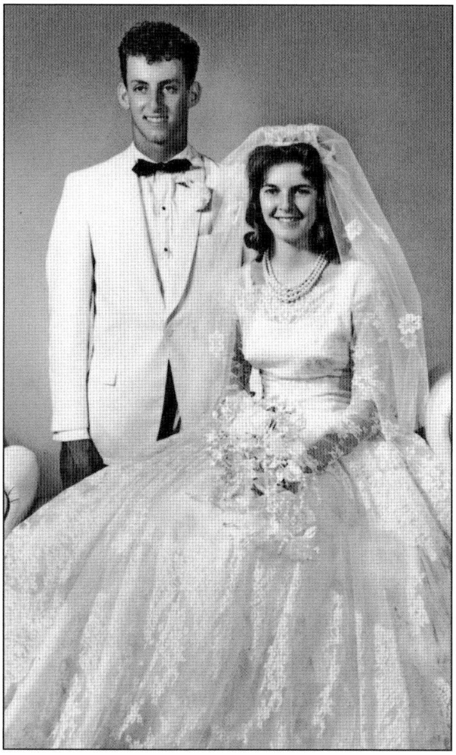

Lawrence Cavalier and Rita Mae Hebert Cavalier Metrejean were married for three short months when Lawrence went to Brusly McCall to duck hunt in a pond. Lawrence killed a duck and got in the water to get the duck, and he drowned. No one knows why he did that, because it was a very cool and windy day. (Courtesy of Brenda Landry Templet and Nobert Templet.)

On January 18, 1969, Georgina Himel LeBlanc married Dudley LeBlanc. Georgina (far right) is pictured with her bridesmaids (from left to right), her sister Sadie Himel Crochet McCalaster, Doreen LeBlanc Landry, and maid of honor Clara Blanchard. The LeBlancs have been married 48 years and have two daughters and one son. (Courtesy of Tonya Crochet Olivier.)

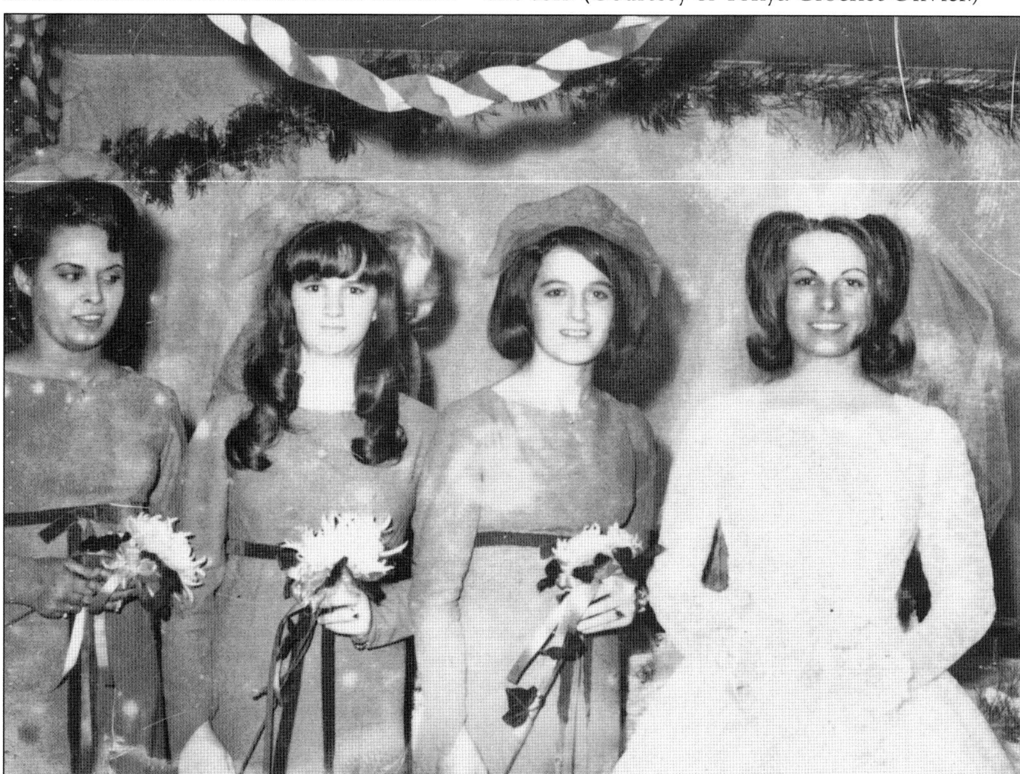

Two

School Days

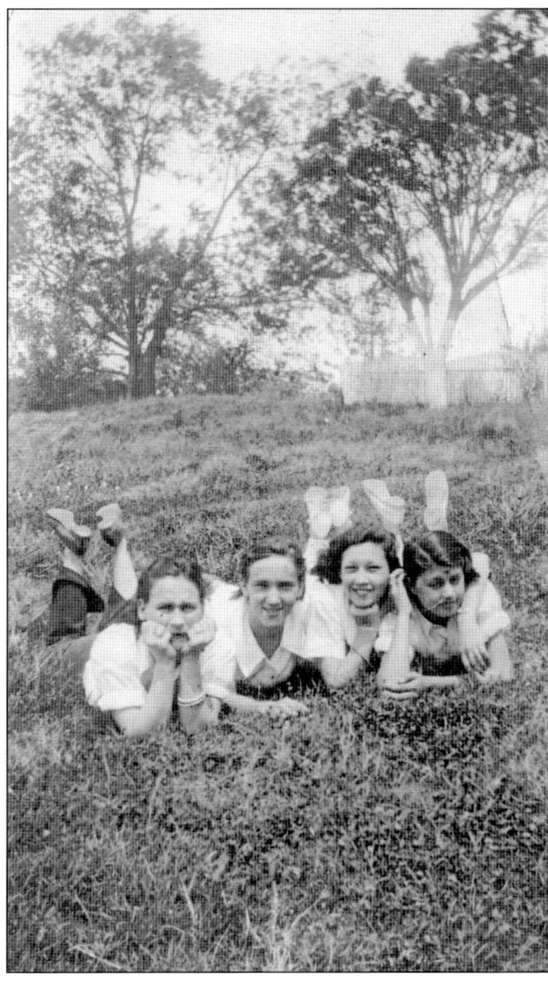

The teachers of Pierre Part School are pictured in April 1936. From left to right are Eloise Memuet, May Boudreaux, Camille Smith, and Atrice Guillot. They are enjoying their time lying in the grass. It is not known if they are at recess or if this was taken after school. They look young to be teachers. (Courtesy of Wildy Templet and Hilda Templet.)

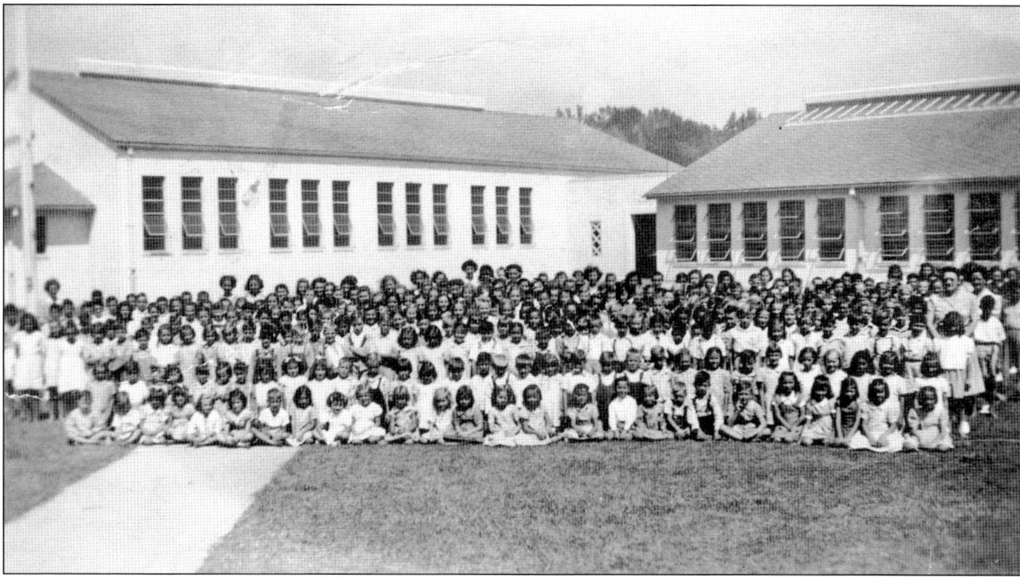

The whole school came out for this 1942 photograph at Pierre Part School. Many photographs of the school were taken this year; a man came around taking them. It is hard to recognize anyone because the photographer had to stand far away from the students. (Courtesy of Alice Alleman Cavalier.)

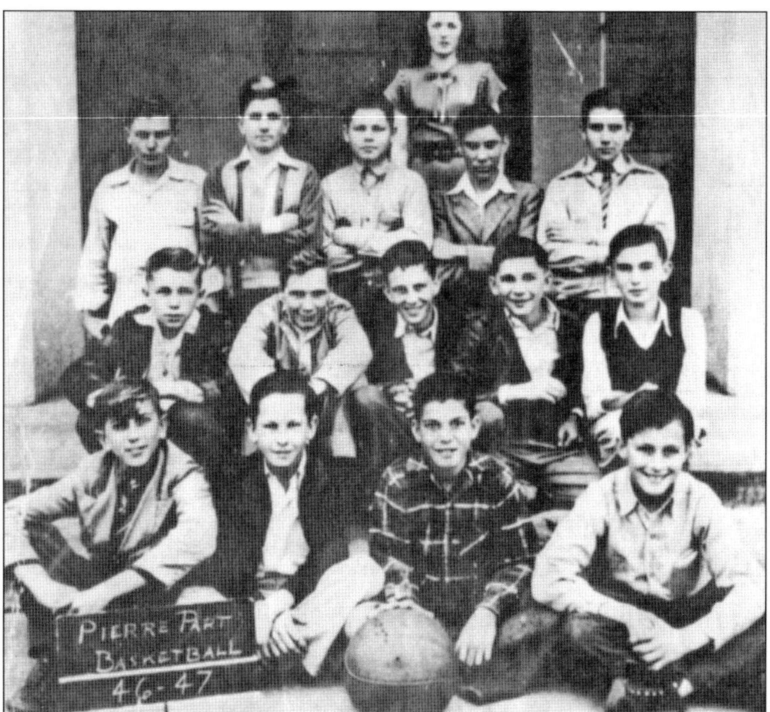

The 1946–1947 Pierre Part basketball team is, from left to right, (first row) Eldridge Comeaux, Benny Landry, Oswald Guillot, and Alex Crochet; (second row) Reuban Sedotal, Jimmy Cavalier, Stephen Theriot, Harold Hebert, and Donald Daigle; (third row) Laury Templet, Leonard Breaux, Jerry Landry, Ervin Miller, and Laury Perera; (fourth row) coach Joyce Daze Faucheux. (Courtesy of Joe Daigle and Marion Gaudet Daigle.)

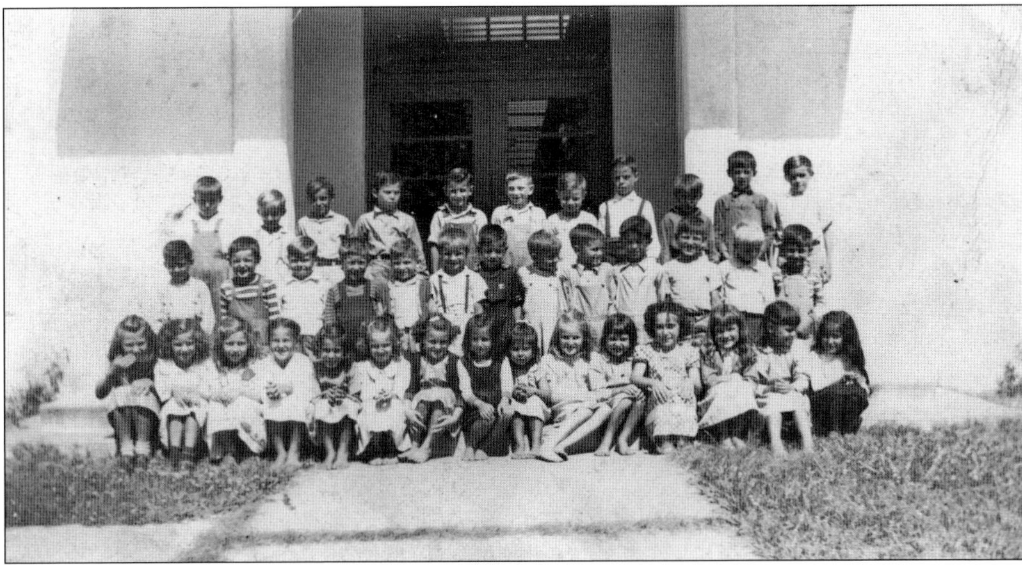

This is the second- and third-grade class at Pierre Part School. From left to right are (first row) Betty Richard, Mildred Blanchard, Nelida Landry, Laura Nell Breaux Pipsair, Mary Ann "Marion" Gaudet Daigle, two unidentified, Dora Blanchard Hebert, three unidentified, Ethel Breaux, and three unidentified; (second row) Logi Guillot, unidentified, T.J. Blanchard, Earl Matherne, Ridley Guillot, and the rest are unidentified; (third row) unidentified, Nootie Hebert, two unidentified, Robert Pipsair, two unidentified, Leo Aucoin, and three unidentified. (Courtesy of T.J. Blanchard.)

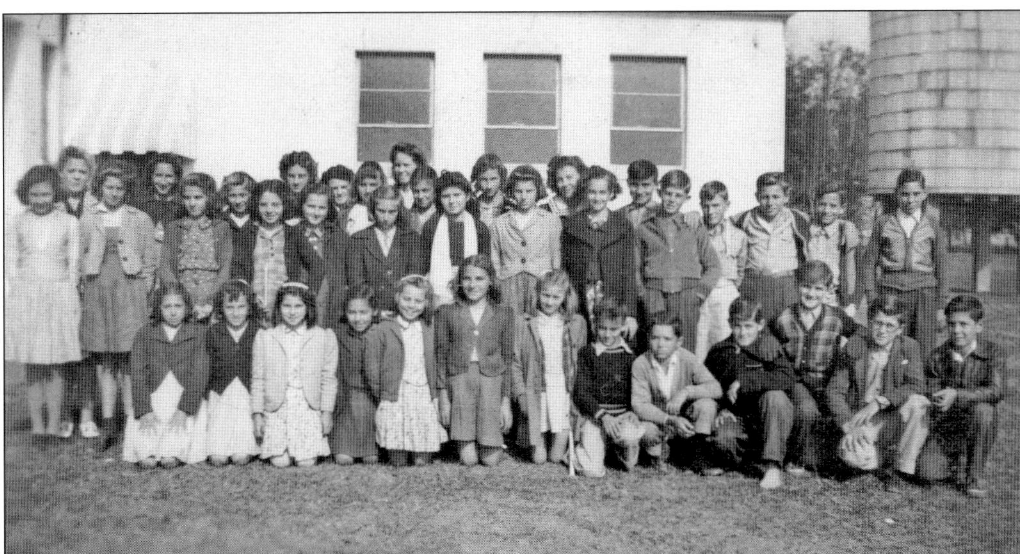

These students are pictured in 1942 behind the gym at Pierre Part School; it is not known who everyone is. P.J. Blanchard, Edna Blanchard, and Floyd Blanchard were among this class. It had to be a little chilly, because the children have coats on. (Courtesy of T.J. Blanchard.)

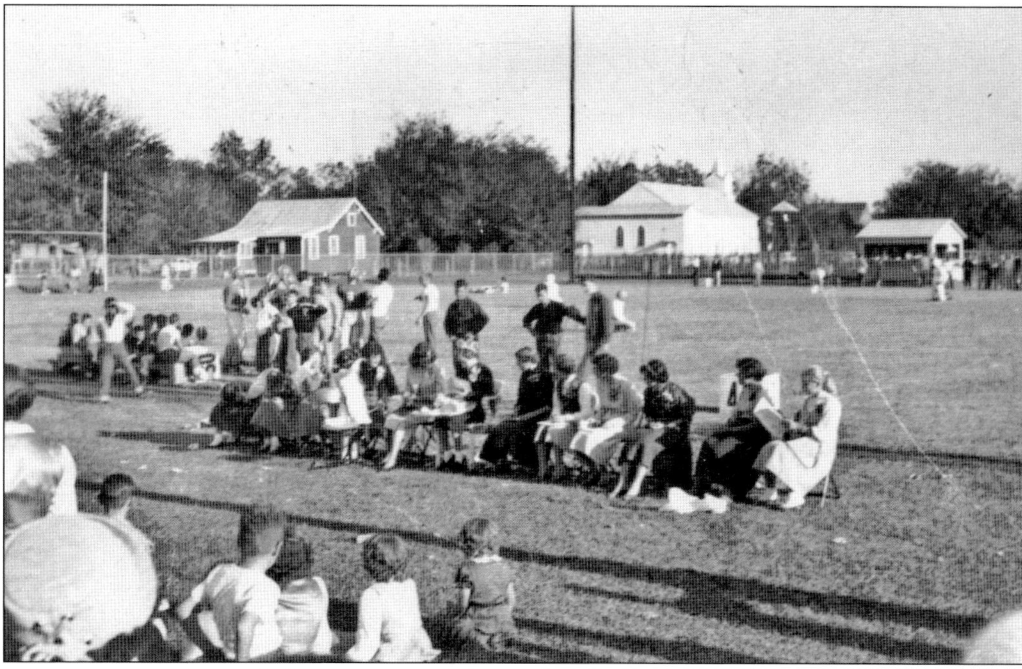

All eyes are on the football game at Pierre Part Elementary School. It is not known who they were playing. The way the girls are dressed, it could have been a jamboree game. The men, all dressed in suits, are announcing something. One girl has a crown on her head and is opening a present. (Both, courtesy of Wildy Templet and Hilda Landry Templet.)

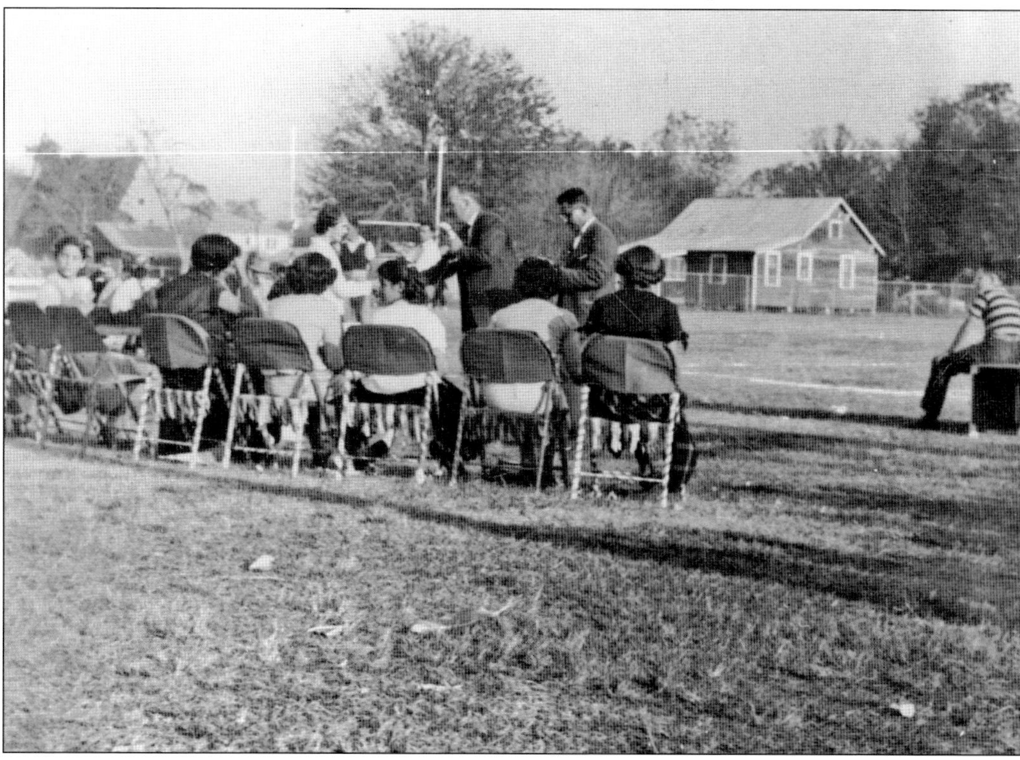

In the backyard of Pierre Part School are Elaine St. Germain Landry (left) all dressed up and Barbara Ann Landry Coupel. This picture was probably taken in the late 1950s. (Courtesy of Wildy Templet and Hilda Landry Templet.)

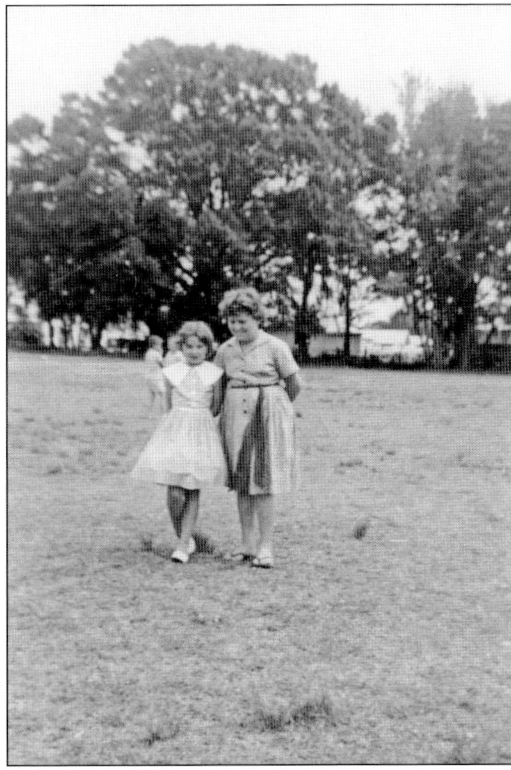

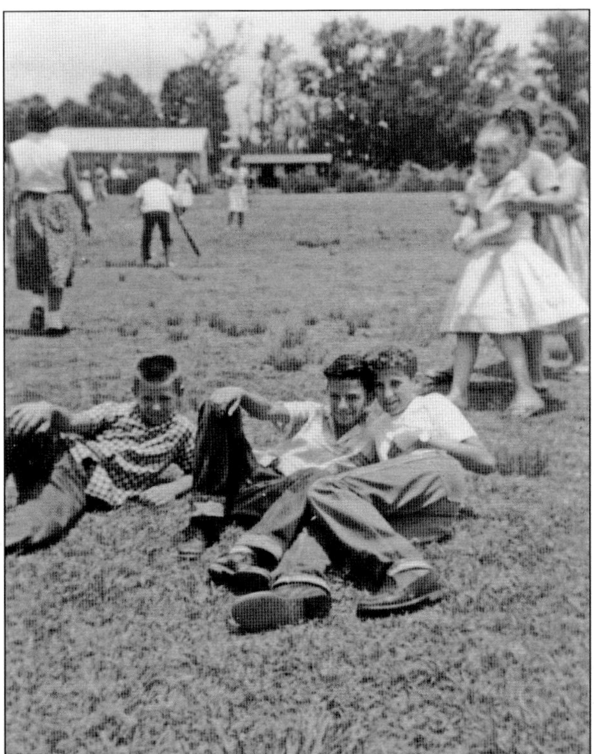

At recess, everyone enjoyed playing with friends; these kids are all having a good time. The girls on the right look like they are trying to see who will go talk to those boys on the ground. The girls are, from left to right, Carolyn Landry Hebert, unidentified, and Margaret Theriot. The boys are, from left to right, unidentified, Henry Blanchard, and possibly Aubrey Verette. (Courtesy of Wildy Templet and Hilda Landry Templet.)

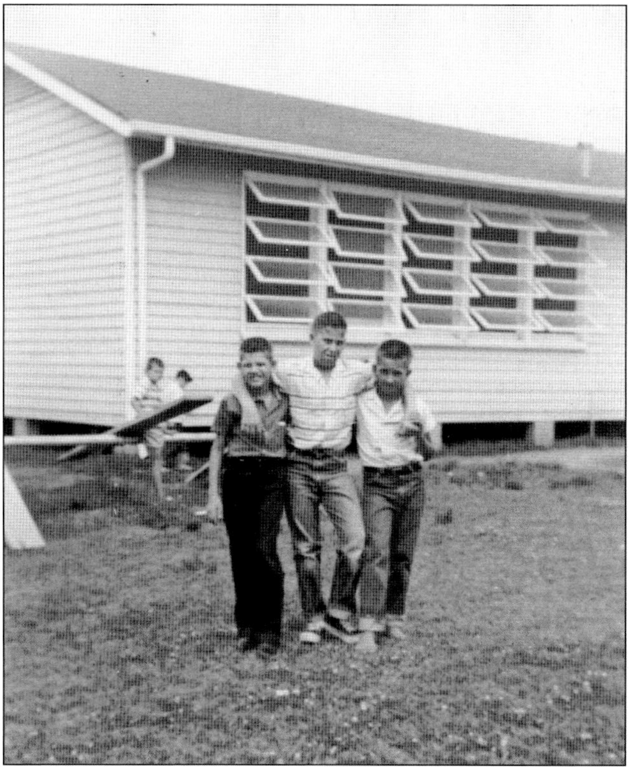

In the mid-1950s (from left to right), Neal Richard, Phillip McCarthy, and Roland Theriot are at recess at Pierre Part Elementary School. The boys on the seesaw are unidentified. (Courtesy of Wildy Templet and Hilda Landry Templet.)

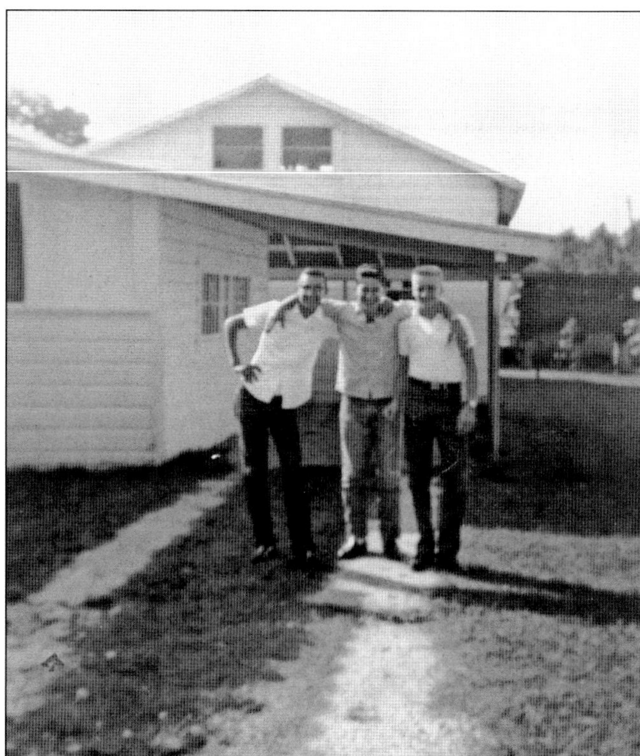

This picture may have been taken in the early 1960s behind the cafeteria. From left to right are Raleigh Landry, Gerald Theriot, and Eddie Theriot. (Courtesy of Wildy Templet and Hilda Landry Templet.)

Jarvis Breaux and Dianna Landry Peltier are pictured at Pierre Part Elementary School in the mid-1950s. Back then, the school's water came from a cistern, as can be seen in this picture. Every house had some type of cistern to supply water. (Courtesy of Wildy Templet and Hilda Landry Templet.)

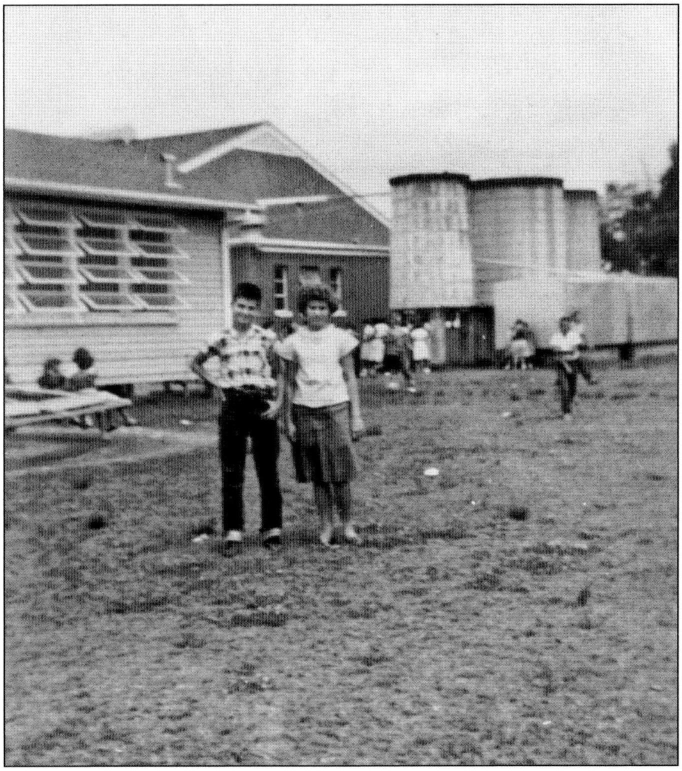

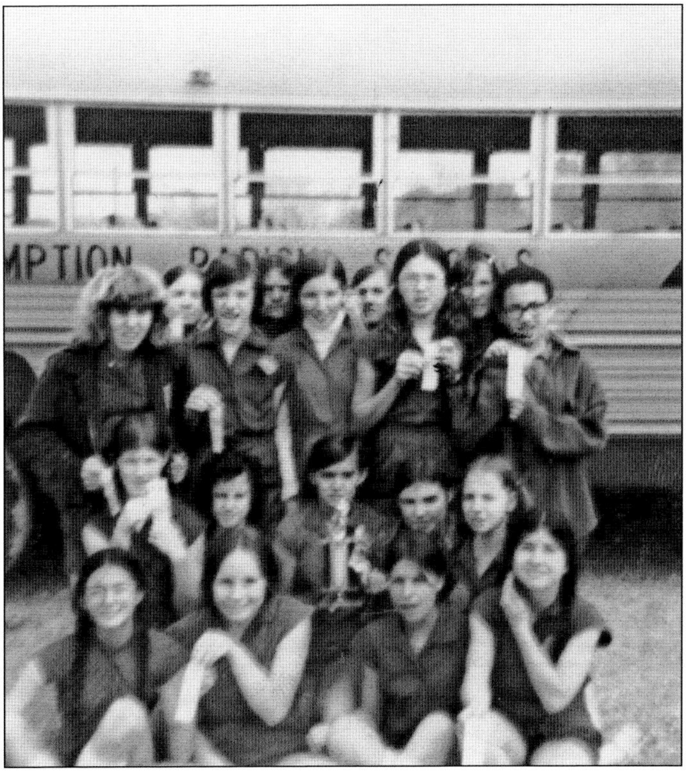

The 1974 championship-winning Pierre Part Elementary School volleyball team is, from left to right, (first row) Gail Alleman Richard, Vicky Crochet, Veronica Gaudet, and Belinda Landry Hayden; (second row) Juanita Hebert Cavalier, Melissa Bernucheaux Gautreau, Geneve Daigle Cavalier, Meryl Mabile Borne, and unidentified; (third row) Ilene Metrejean, Georgetta Cox, Lenette Templet Berthelot, Darlene Cavalier, and Gail Landry; (fourth row) Brenda Landry Templet, Darlene Aucoin Hue, unidentified, and Belinda Blanchard LeBlanc. (Author's collection.)

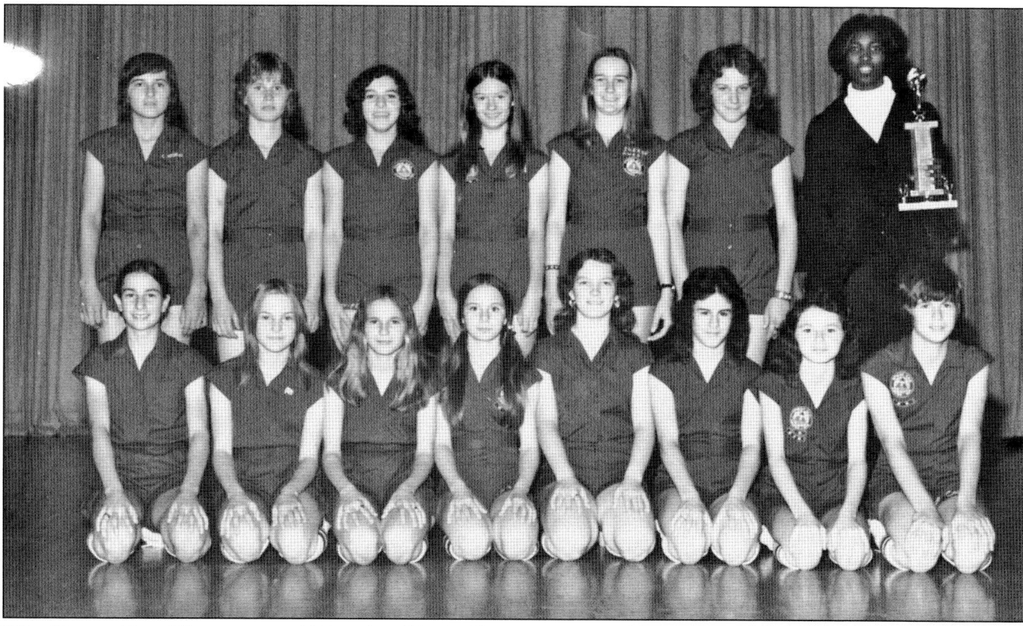

The Pierre Part Elementary School volleyball team is seen here. From left to right are (kneeling) Rhonda Comeaux, Angie Landry, Matilda LeBlanc Gautreaux, Judy Blanchard Landry, Brenda Landry Templet, Melissa Bernucheaux Gautreau, unidentified, and Lisa Mabile Templet; (standing) Clara Hebert Blanchard, Glenda Mabile, Jennifer Metrejean Landry, Patty Aucoin Templet, Sherry Aucoin Breaux, June Guillot Womack, and Coach Colmen. (Courtesy of Wildy Templet and Hilda Landry Templet.)

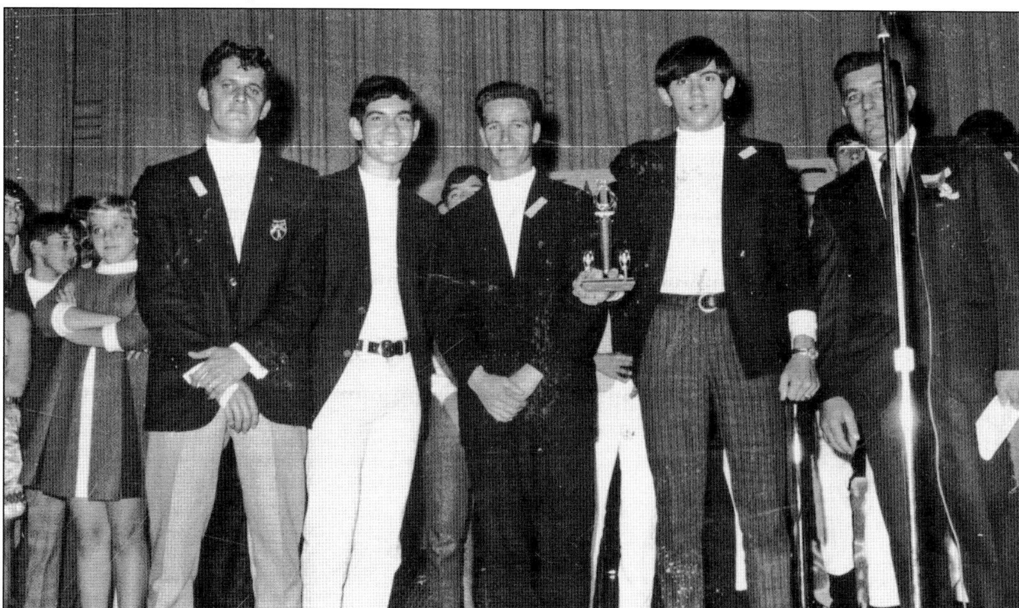

In 1968, a battle of the bands was held in the gym of Pierre Part Elementary School. Coming out in first place was Apogee Soul. The band is, from left to right, Norbert Blanchard, Armond Courville, Ned Blanchard, and Larry Courville. Announcer Alex Giroir (far right) handed Larry the first-place trophy. (Courtesy of Wildy Templet and Hilda Landry Templet.)

Three

Industry

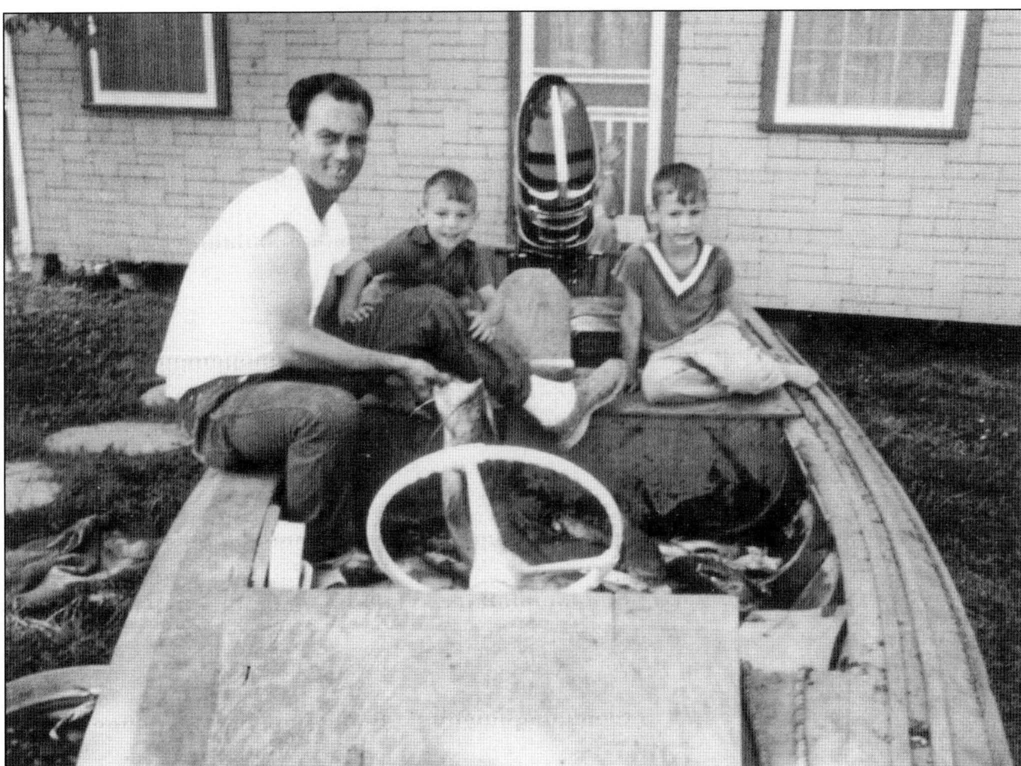

Jimmy Gaudet returns home from fishing and shows his boys Carl and Darrell his catch of the day. The bigger the catch, the more excited the boys got. It was a good day for fishing, by the looks of the boat. (Courtesy of Jane Landry Gaudet.)

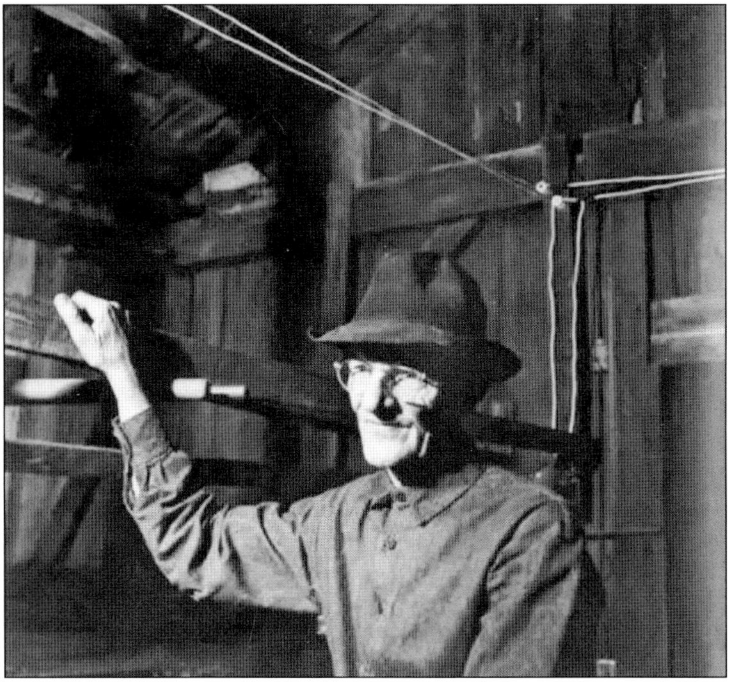

Leonie "Papere" Theriot Sr. is pictured in the cooking area of his syrup mill around the 1940s. His six sons, René, Leonie Jr., Phillip, Ned, Weekless, and Eno, as well as others, helped to run the mill. Papere named the syrup Golden Glow and sold it all around the area. It was first sold in 60-gallon barrels but was later sold in smaller, labeled cans. When Papere stopped making the syrup, Leland Theriot took the name Golden Glow and opened his own syrup mill. (Courtesy of Nadine Theriot.)

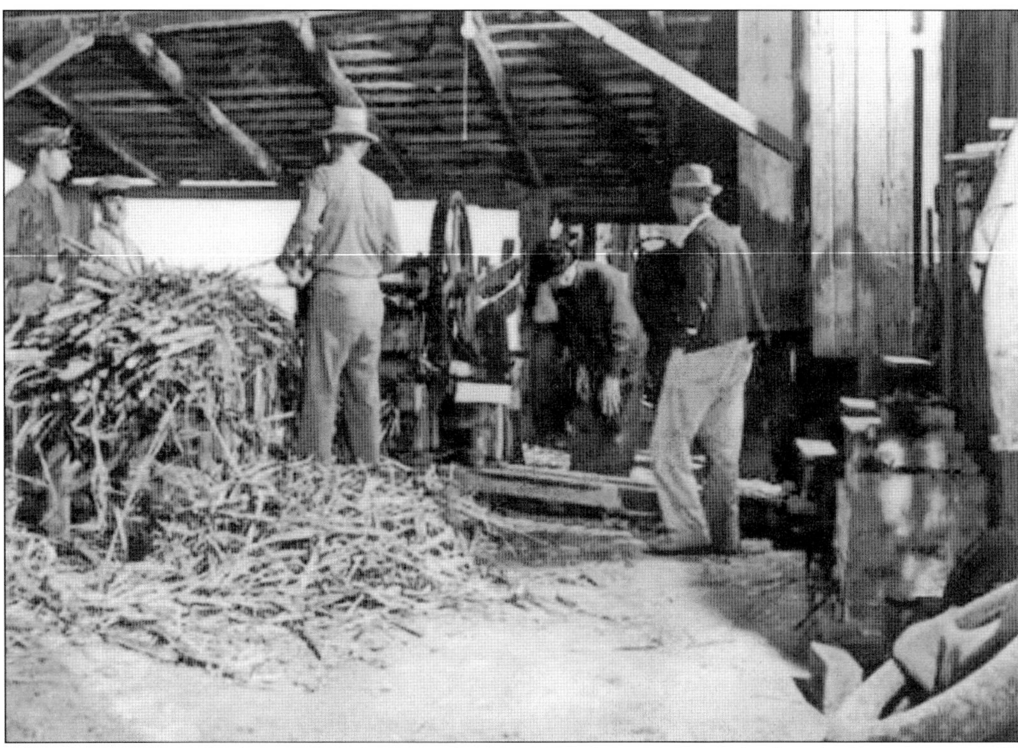

This syrup mill, called a *sucrerie*, belonged to Leonie Theriot Sr. He had to feed only two stalks at a time into the machine to squeeze the juice out. An old McCormick tractor was used to run the machine. At lower right is a small brick oven used to burn sulphur to clean and purify the cane juice. (Courtesy of Nadine Theriot.)

Leonie Theriot Sr. is pictured in his syrup mill pouring sugar cane juice from one vat to another. A long-handled spoon was used to scrape the foam off the top of the syrup. Cooking the syrup was a long and tedious job that was done for 24 hours. Paddles, skimmers, and strainers were used. (Courtesy of Nadine Theriot.)

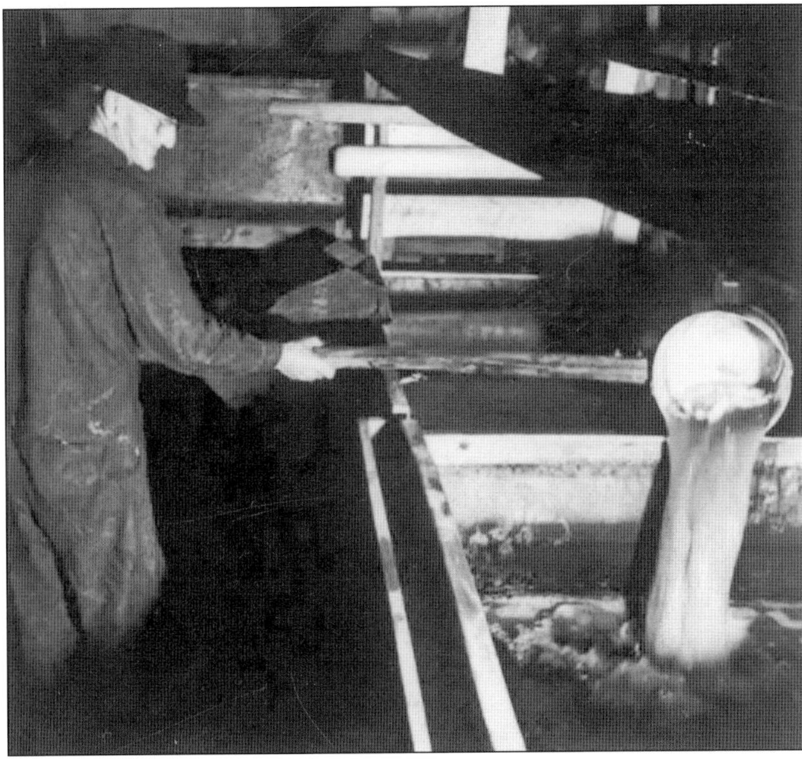

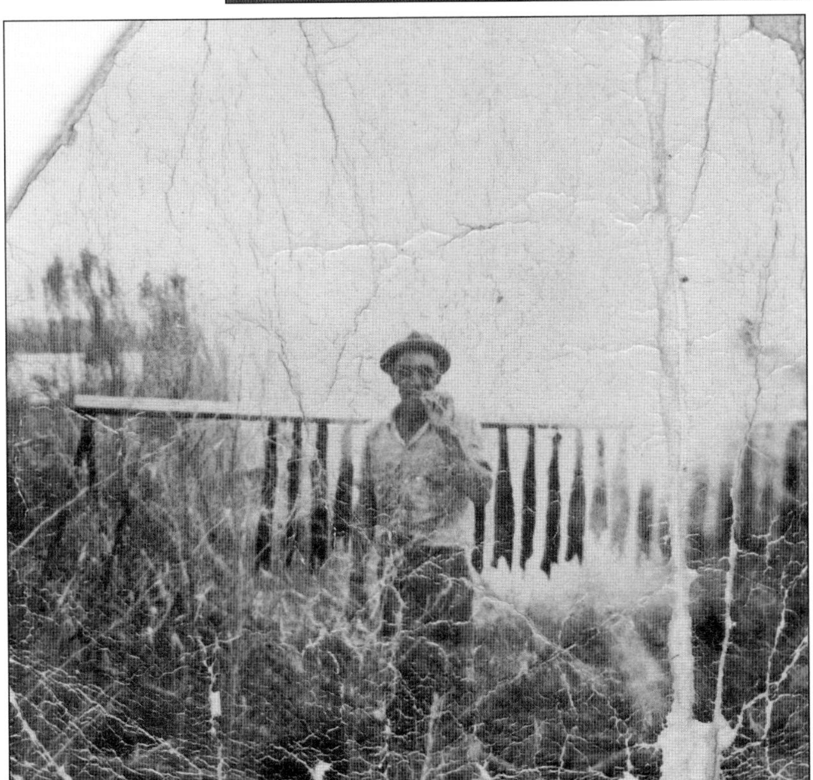

In the past, many people had to travel to make a living. Joseph Gaudet leased land in Bayou Penchant to hunt and trap for fur. Here, Joseph is trying to dry his furs during a cold and rainy winter. He would set a fire in a bucket for the smoke to dry the furs before stretching them. (Courtesy of Gustave Joseph Gaudet and Sarah Leonard Gaudet.)

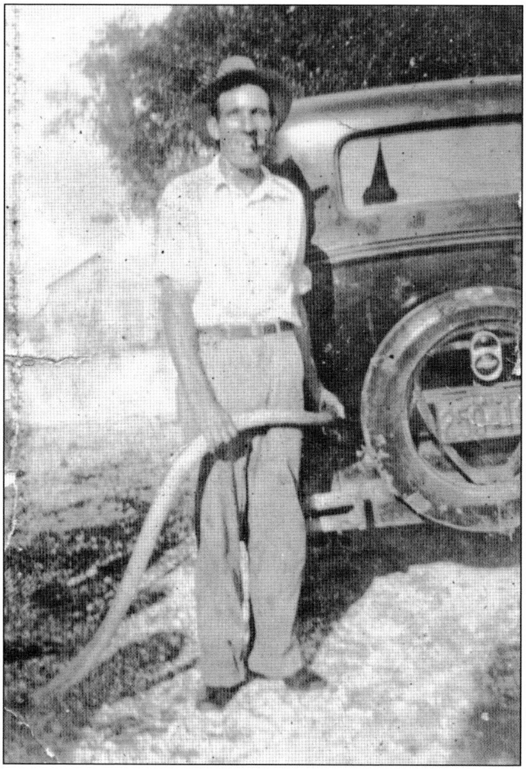

Knotts Seafood Factory was along the bay next to the old bridge in 1933. Daily Alleman worked for the Knotts, helping out in the factory and pumping gas. He is pictured pumping gas at the station. (Courtesy of Alice Alleman Cavalier.)

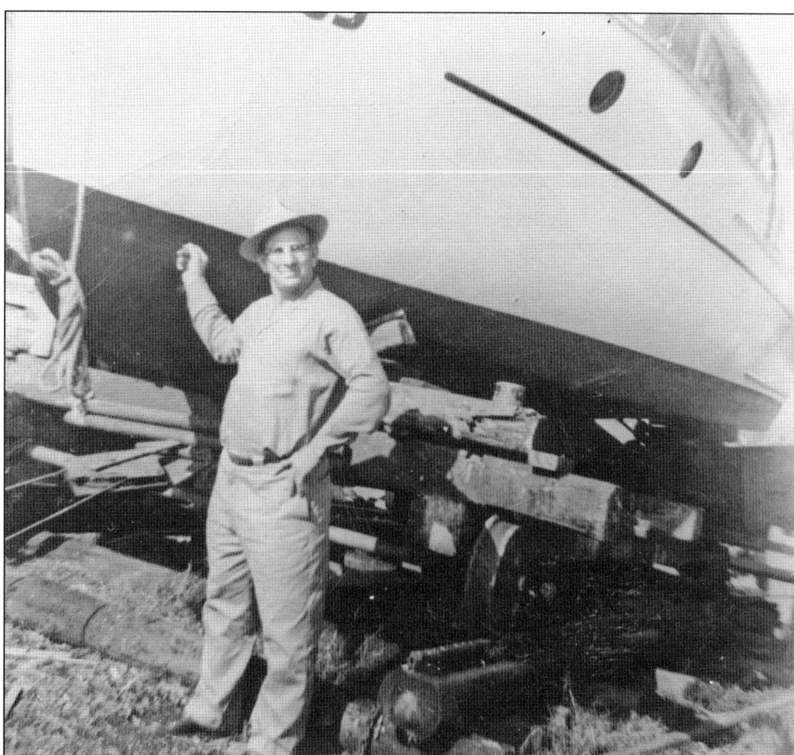

Dudley Landry made a boat lift to work on boats. He fixed many boats in his time. It was easier to repair the bottom when the boat was on the lift. He could work on them from the inside or the outside. Dudley is pictured in 1959 in front of a boat he had just repaired. (Courtesy of Jane Landry Gaudet.)

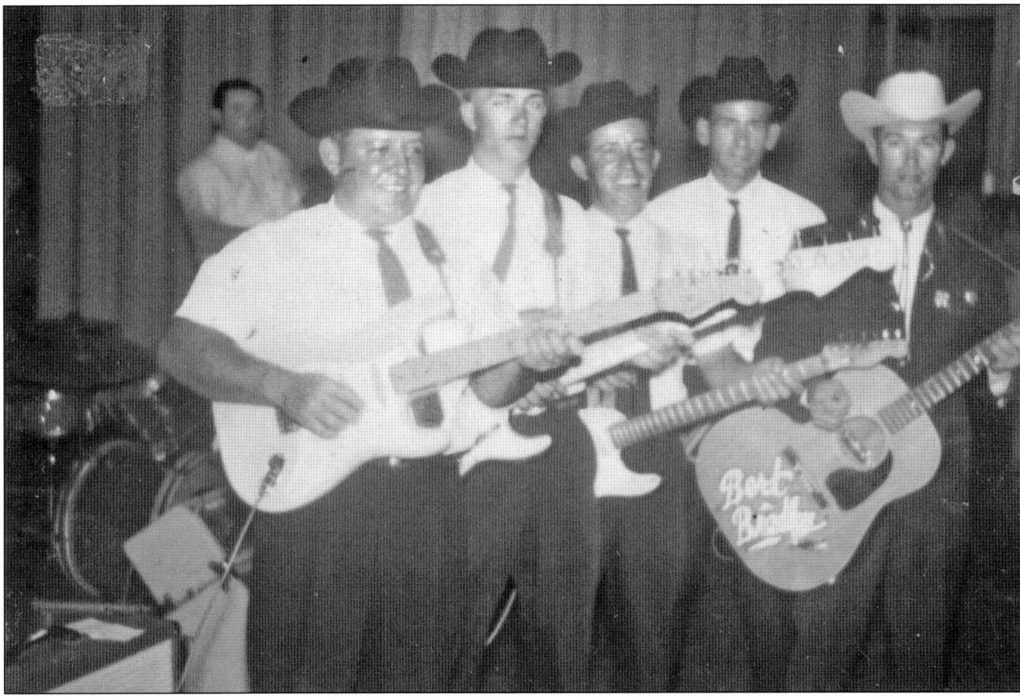

Men with music in their hearts love to play music. Bert Bradley only had to say "I need a player tonight," and if they could, they were there. From left to right are Gerald Richard, E.J. St. Germain, Golen Richard, Clarence Domingue, and Bert Bradley. (Courtesy of Diane Richard.)

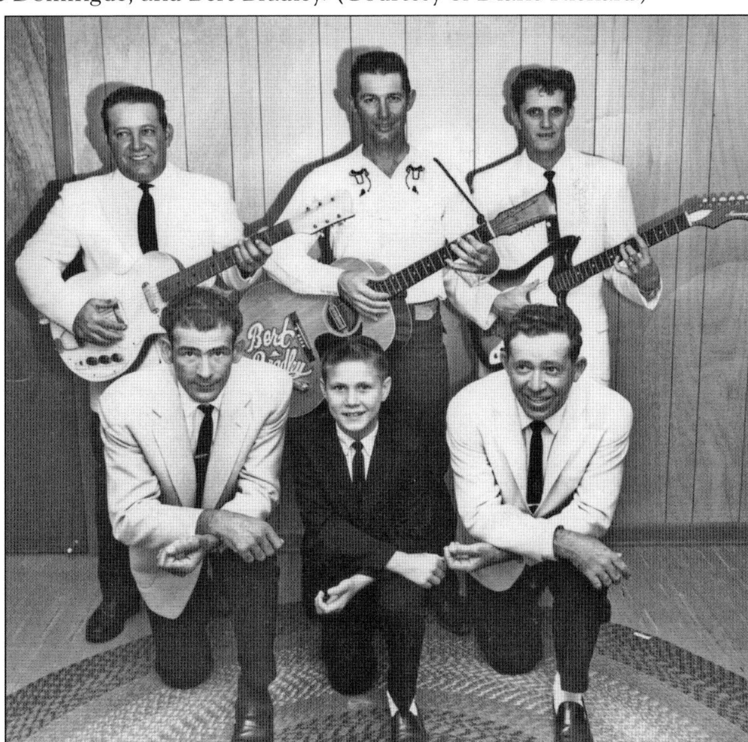

When a player in Bert Bradley's band had to work, Bradley would invite other musicians to play with him. From left to right are (first row) Clarence Domingue, Nelson Blanchard, and Golen Richard; (second row) Gerald Richard, Bert Bradley, and Norbert Blanchard. Gerald and Golen would play with Bradley when they did not have to play with the Richard Brothers. (Courtesy of Diane Richard.)

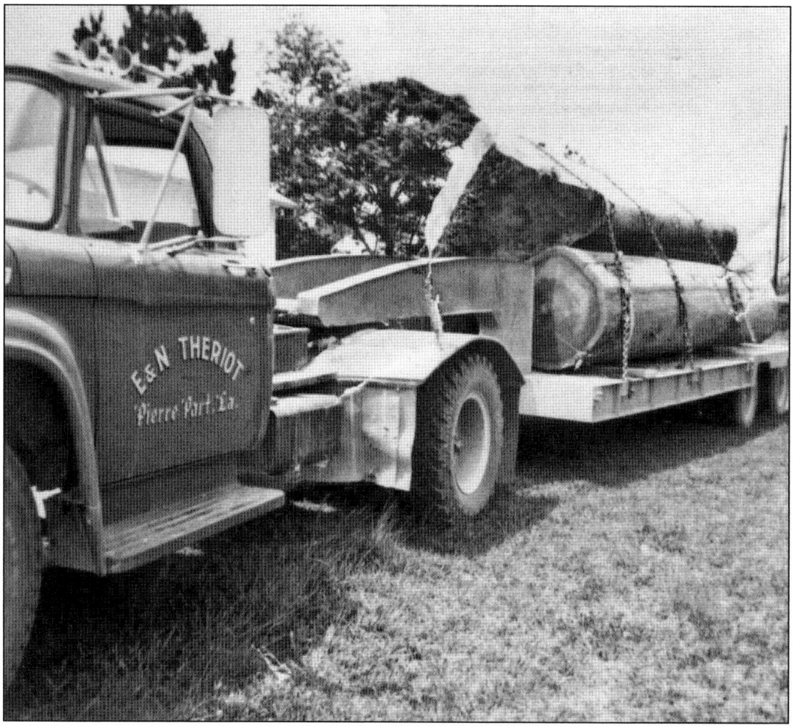

Eno and Ned Theriot owned the E&N Theriot truck, pictured in May 1967 with a low-boy trailer. The truck was used to haul sugarcane, but off-season, it was also used to haul cypress logs, houses, trailers, and equipment all around the area. Pictured below are Ned Theriot (left) and Wilton Blanchard. (Both, courtesy of Nadine Theriot.)

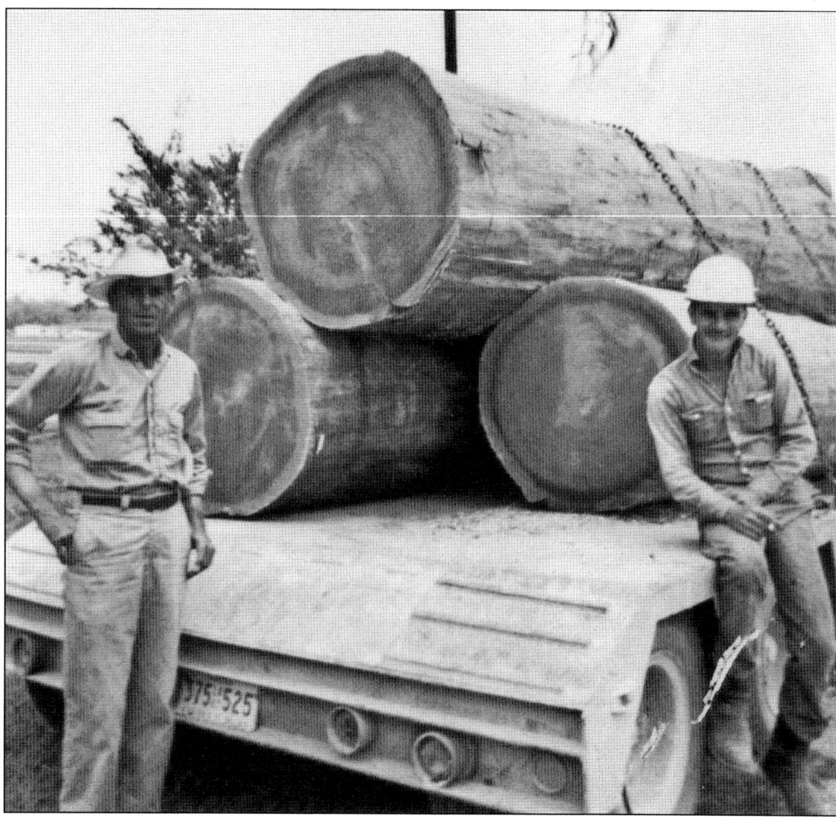

Around Christmas 1967, Floyd Cavalier and Abner Leonard are working on the dredge boat *Manchaca* for Fred Settoon. Abner's son Sterling Leonard (left) and Floyd are holding ducks they killed. The *Manchaca* was working in Alabama. (Courtesy of Alice Alleman Cavalier.)

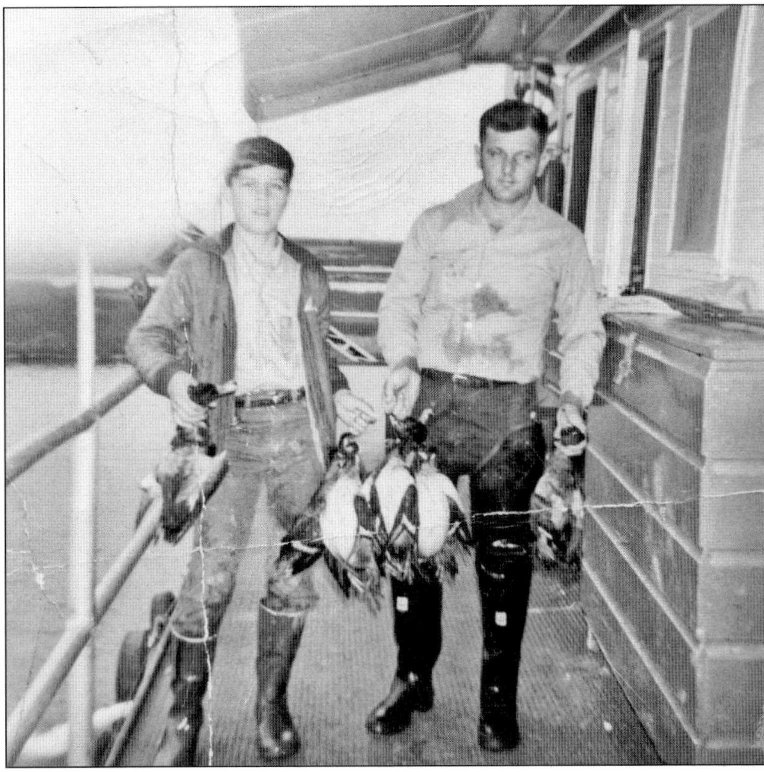

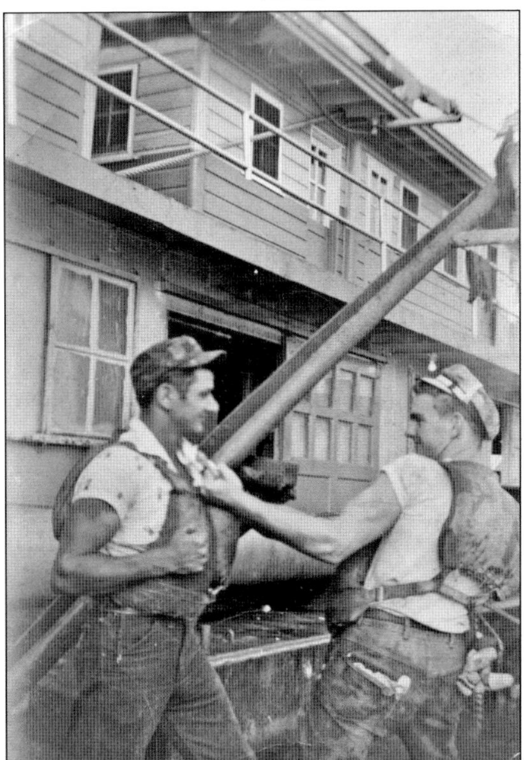

When the dredge boat was not working, there was a lot of playing around. Men went to work on the dredge boat for weeks at a time. The boat is docked in this picture, and Floyd Cavalier (left) and his brother-in-law Jerry Daigle are having a little fun. For safety, they always had their life jackets on. (Courtesy of Alice Alleman Cavalier.)

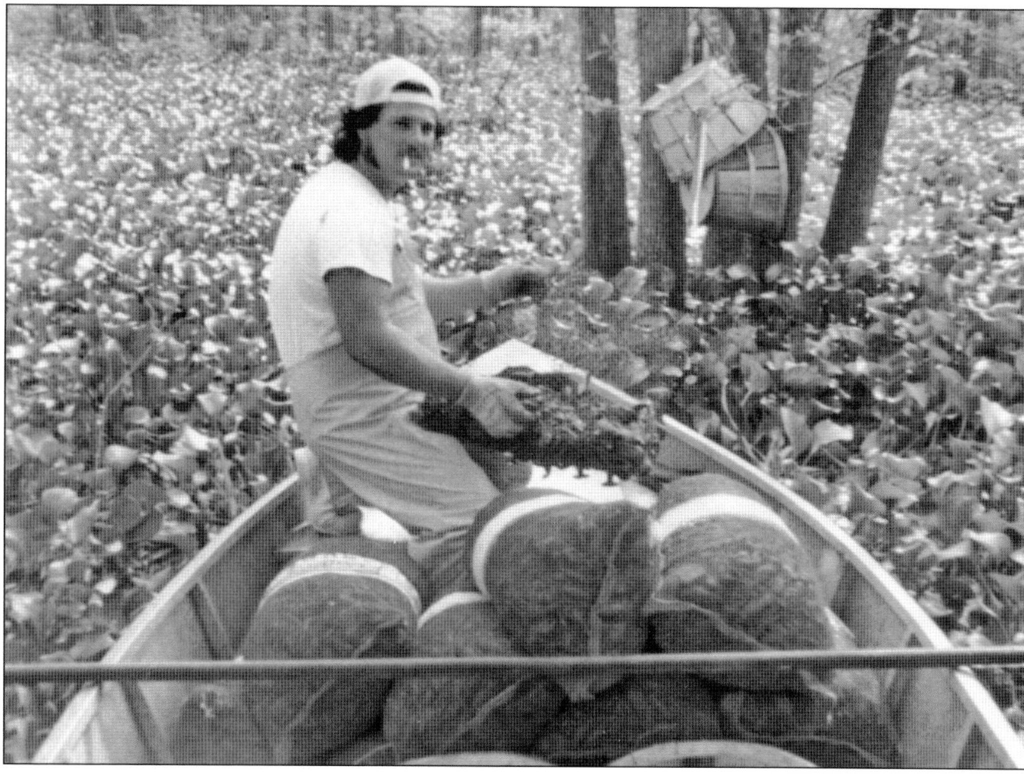

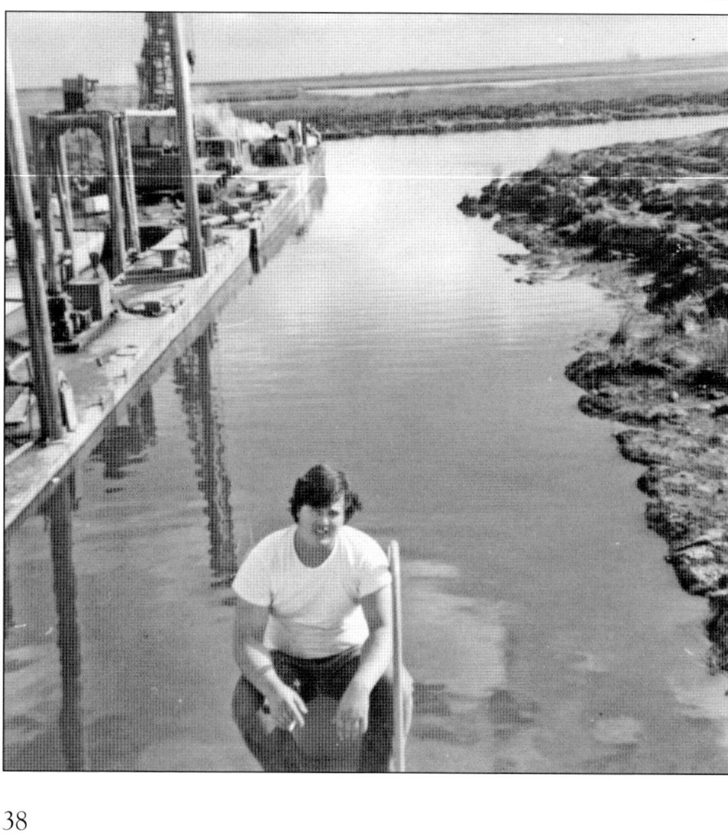

Crawfishing was a way of living for many people and still is today. Douglas Cavalier, seen here at the age of 24, loved to crawfish. He was a very good fisherman. Judging by the sacks of crawfish, either he was having a good day or he ran a lot of traps. (Courtesy of Isabell Rivere Cavalier.)

In 1970, Fred Settoon had work in New Orleans for his boats. Douglas Cavalier and his uncle Floyd Cavalier worked on the *Miss Shirley P* tug boat. Douglas (pictured) was a wheel man and Floyd was captain. (Courtesy of Isabell Rivere Cavalier.)

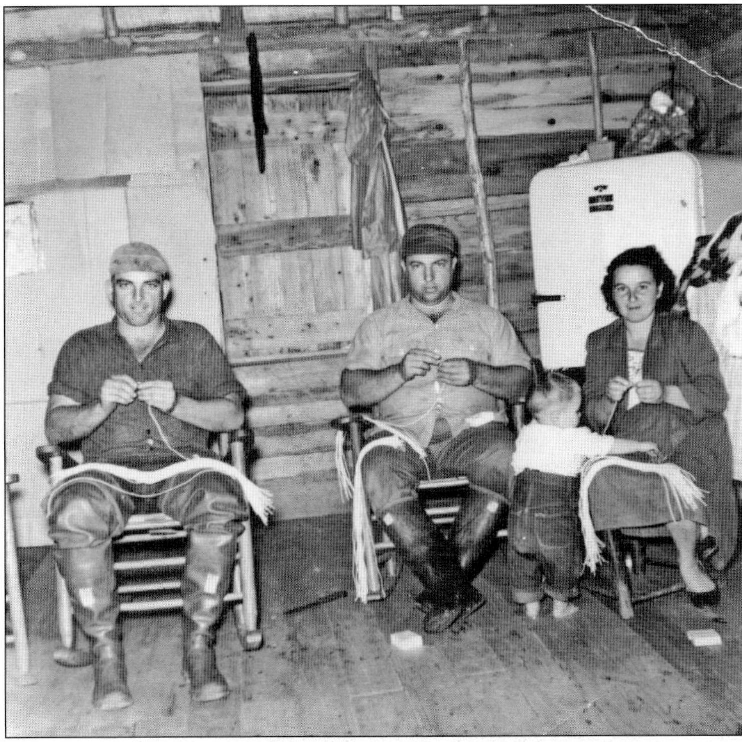

"Grandma Alice" Albarado Cavalier's kitchen was the place the family liked to be. From left to right are Albert Cavalier, Wilfred "Buck" Cavalier, and Elise Cavalier making fish lines to catch catfish, *choupique*, garfish, *gaspergou*, and anything else they could hook. At the age of about two, Ronald "Ronnie" Cavalier tries to help them. (Courtesy of Elise Cavalier Cavalier.)

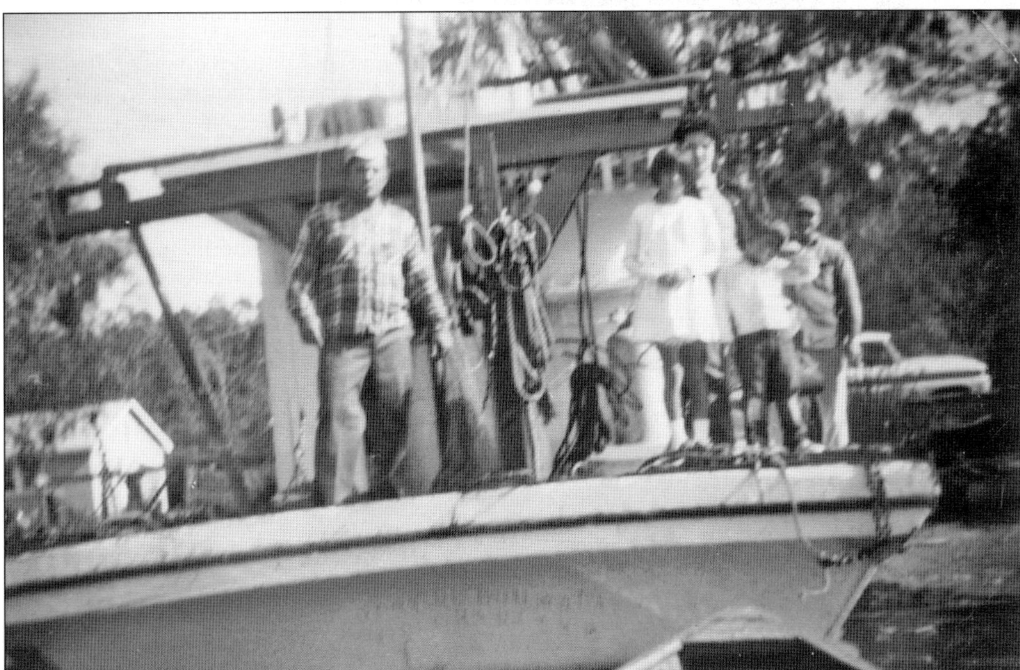

Joseph "Joe" Daigle and Melvin Hebert bought a shrimp boat in November 1968. Showing the boat to his children are, from left to right, (first row) Joe, Rebecca "Becky" Daigle, and Kevin Crook Daigle, (second row) Jean Rivere Gaudet and Melvin. (Courtesy of Joe Daigle and Mary Ann "Marion" Gaudet Daigle.)

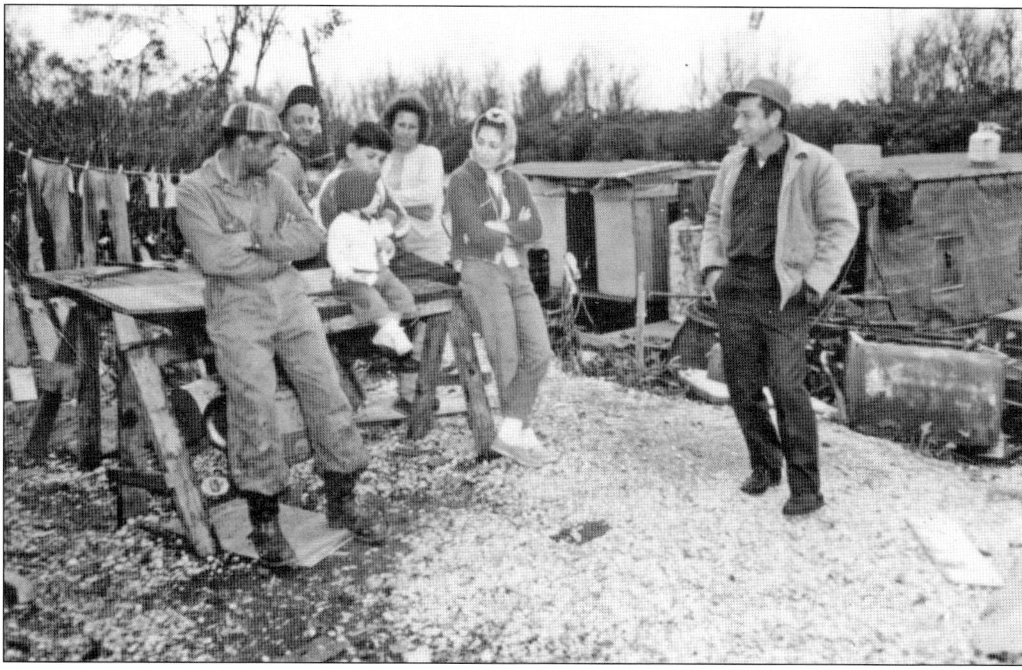

At Bayou Penchant, Gustave Joseph Gaudet and Sarah Leonard Gaudet spent many winters at the camp trapping and hunting. Pictured above in 1967 are, from left to right, (first row) Joseph, Joann Gaudet Leal, Sarah, and Woodruff "Bosco" Dupre; (second row) Sullivan Gaudet, Noeline "Pokeen" Dupre Richard, and Nolan "Pat" Richard. Pictured below is baby JoAnn Gaudet Leal and, behind her, Pokeen showing her nutria fur, Doreen Richard at right, and Nolan Richard in the background. (Both, courtesy of Gustave Joseph Gaudet and Sarah Leonard Gaudet.)

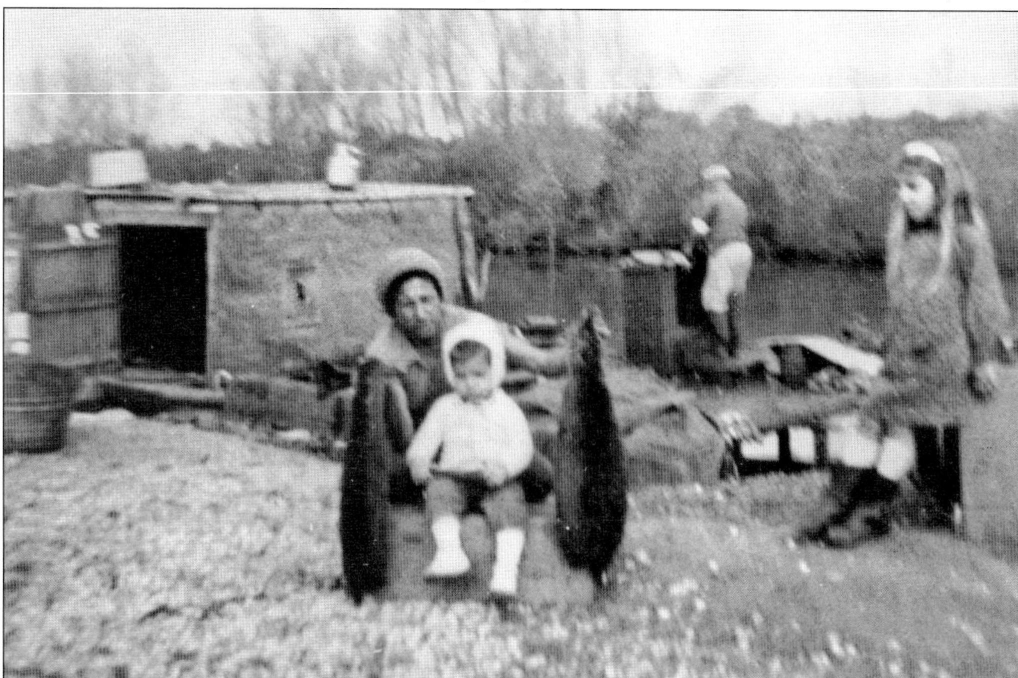

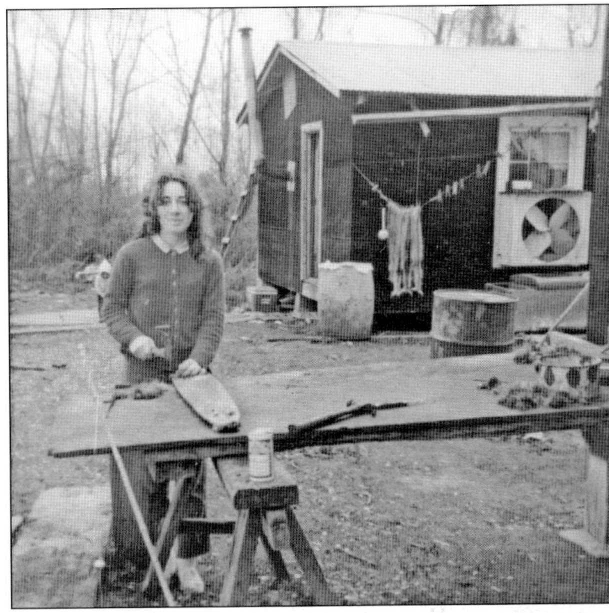

Sarah Leonard Gaudet stretches nutria fur on a board to dry. Sarah and her husband, Gustave Joseph Gaudet, worked hard and long hours. Trapping for fur was done in the winter. Nutrias brought in very little money, so they had to have many of them to make it worthwhile. (Courtesy of Gustave Joseph Gaudet and Sarah Leonard Gaudet.)

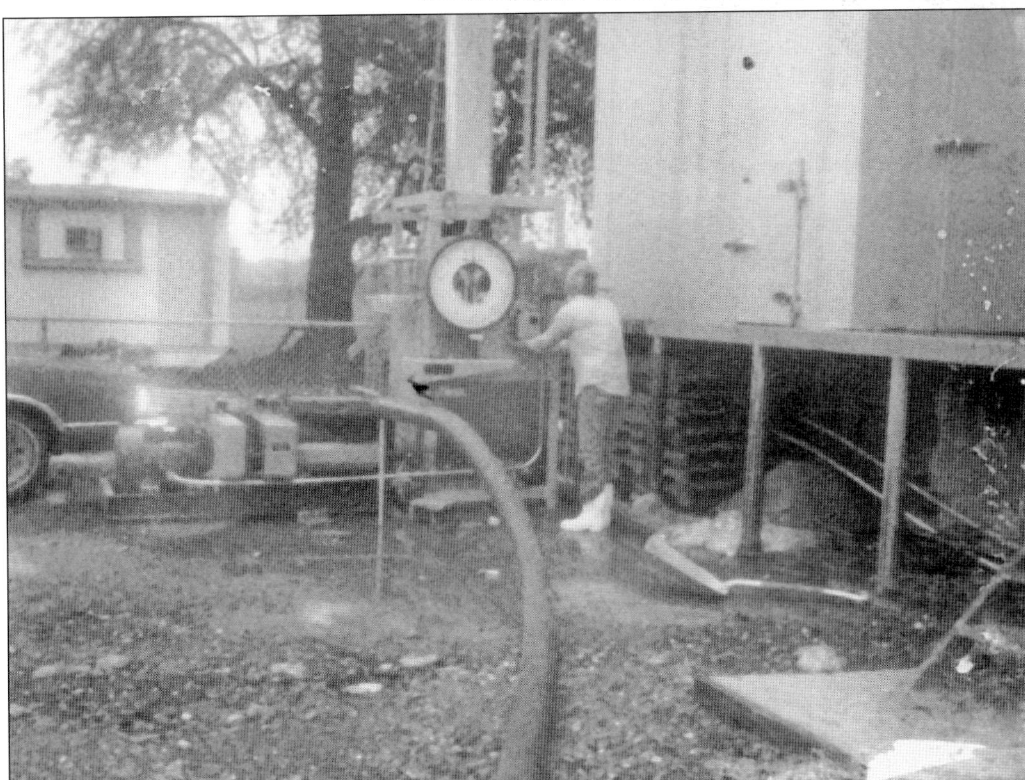

In 1983, Bateman's Ice opened its second location. The ice plant is in Belle River. Owners Jerry "Bo" Bateman and Marie Lobell Bateman moved next door to the ice plant. Bo is pictured running the ice machine to load a crawfish truck. The long hose was put in the back of the truck, and the ice was sprayed into it. People can still get ice from the Batemans today. (Courtesy of Marie Lobell Bateman and Jerry "Bo" Bateman.)

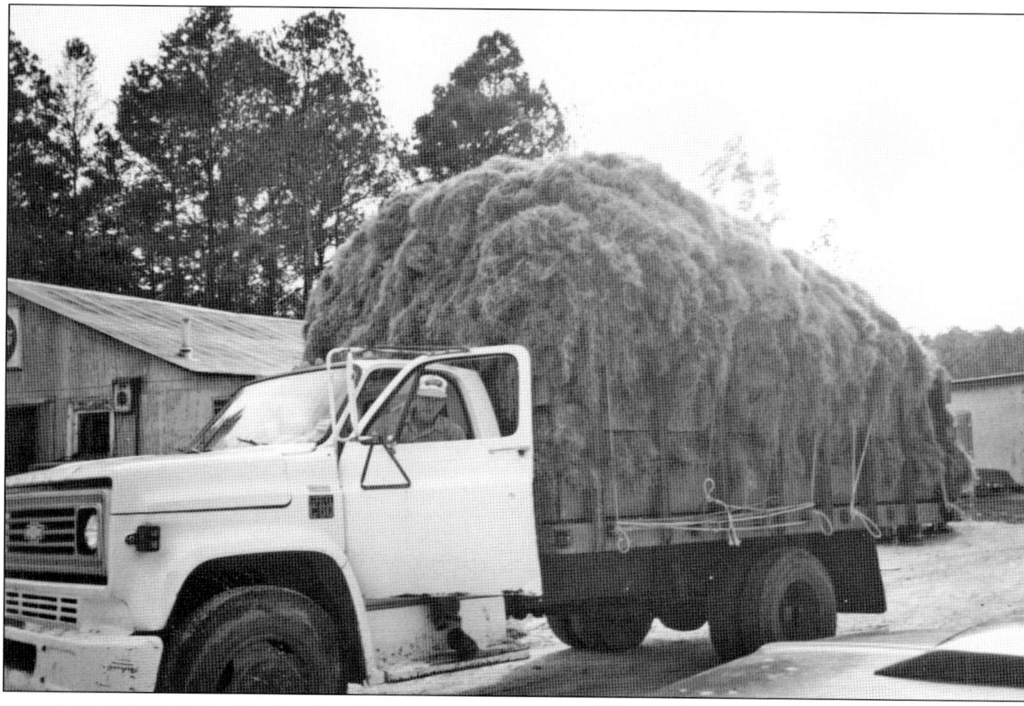

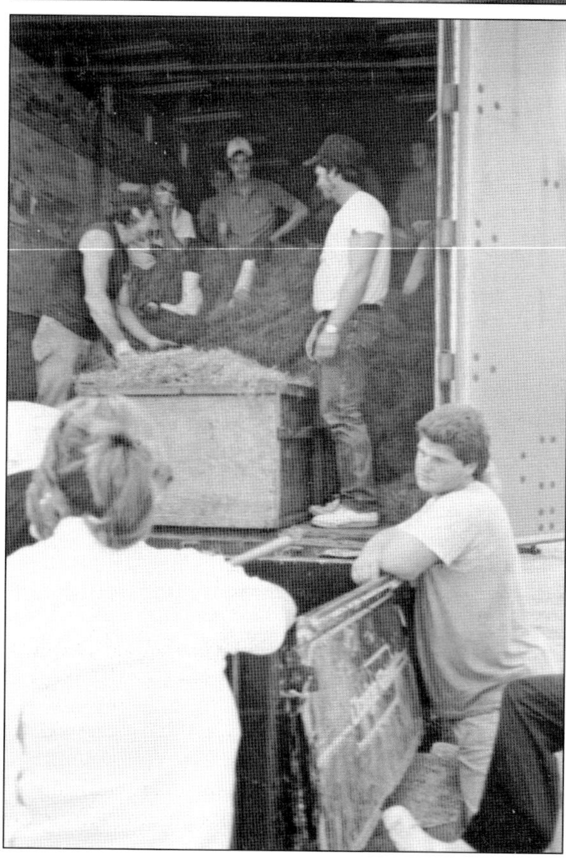

This is the truck that came to Wilbert Hebert's to pick up moss he had bought. Moss was treated, bagged, and sold to craft stores everywhere. In the early to mid-20th century, it was used to make mattresses and pillows and to cover holes in walls. (Courtesy of Brenda Landry Templet and Norbert Templet.)

Moss picking is an old trade that is no longer done in this little town. Pictured are buyers picking up moss from Wilbert Hebert. It is unknown if the buyer was Jessica from Texas or Lawrence Duet from Labadieville. Wilbert bought moss for many years. This picture was taken in November 1989. It is believed that Adam Morales is the one sitting on the moss in the truck. Jimmy Duval Jr. is standing on the right, and Thomas Landry is inside the truck. The rest are unidentified. (Courtesy of Brenda Landry Templet and Norbert Templet.)

In the 1989 crawfish season, Wilfred "Buck" Cavalier and his wife, Elise Cavalier, are in their boat, returning to their camp. Buck and Elise had picked up some of their crawfish traps to move to another place. Greeting them with his back turned is Alfred Rivere. Herman "T-Boy" Cavalier Jr. is swimming in the water. (Courtesy of Elise Cavalier Cavalier.)

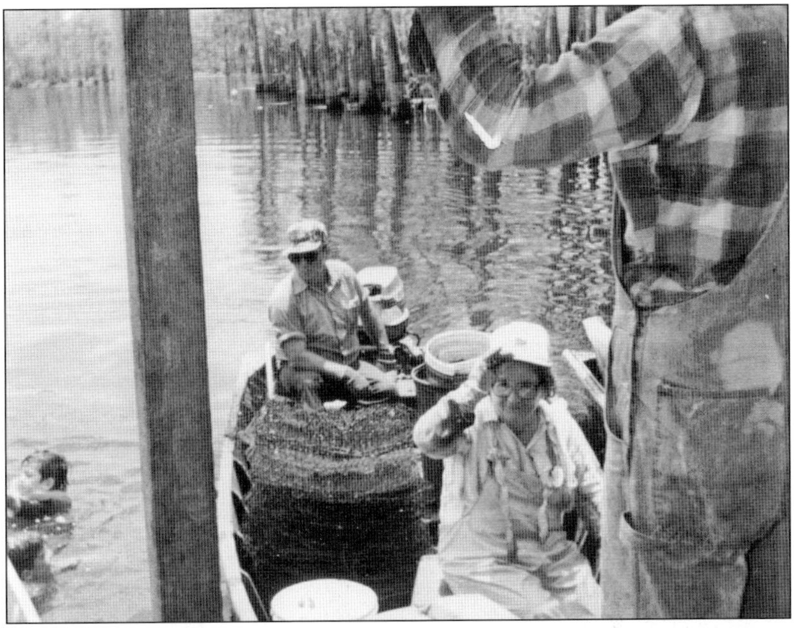

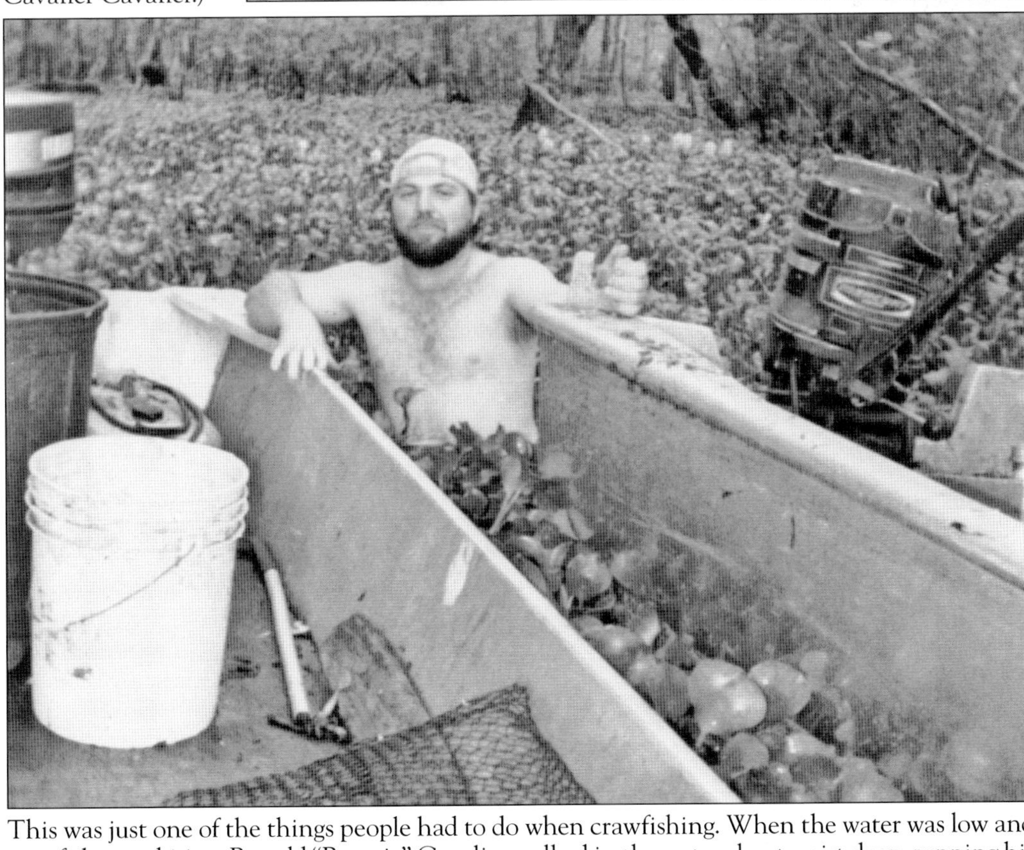

This was just one of the things people had to do when crawfishing. When the water was low and crawfish were biting, Ronald "Ronnie" Cavalier walked in the water about waist-deep, running his crawfish traps and pulling his boat. Here he has stopped to rest and pose for a picture. (Courtesy of Elise Cavalier Cavalier.)

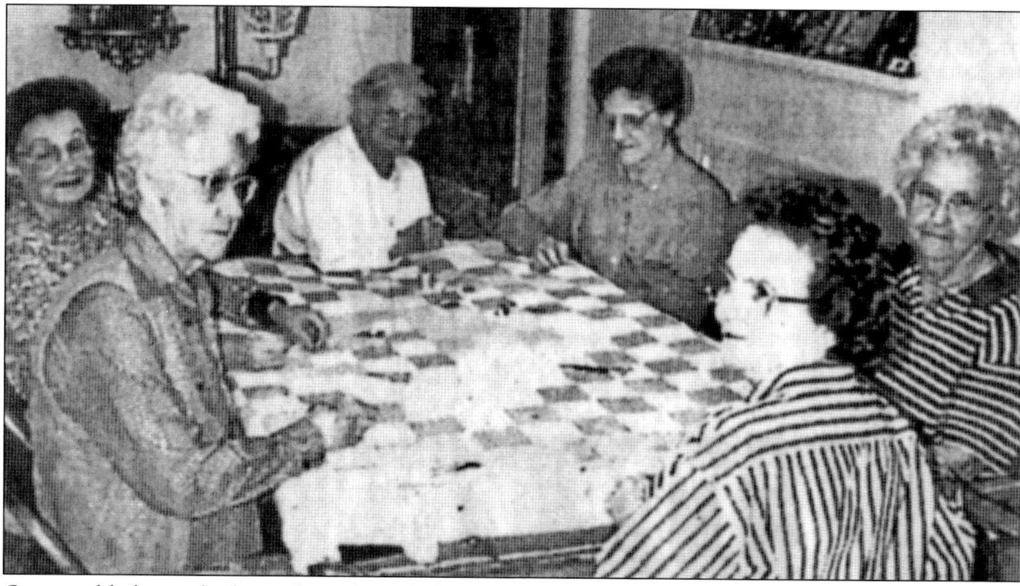

One could always find a quilt in these ladies' hands. They loved to sit around the quilt. From left to right are Inez Rodrigue, Levie Gaudet Theriot, Leonite Mabile Blanchard, Anne Metrejean Mabile, Regina Dupuis Mabile, and May Metrejean Landry. (Courtesy of Leonard Mabile and Regina Dupuis Mabile.)

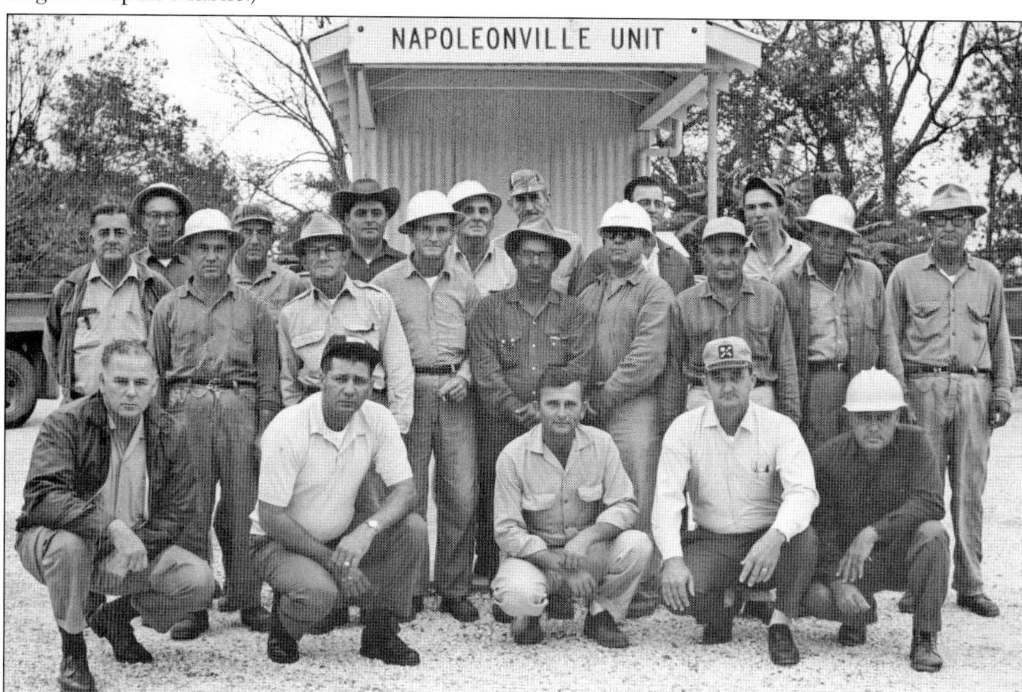

Gang 530 of the Louisiana Department of Highways Napoleonville Unit is pictured in 1979. Lovelace Templet is fourth from left in the second row. He retired in 1980 with 16 years of service. Allen Rodrigue, Hayward Guillot, Dicky Dupre, Murray Albarado, Edward Cavalier, and Tuco Rodrigue are pictured as well, but it is not known who is who. (Courtesy of Brenda Landry Templet and Norbert Templet.)

Four

Honoring Our Men

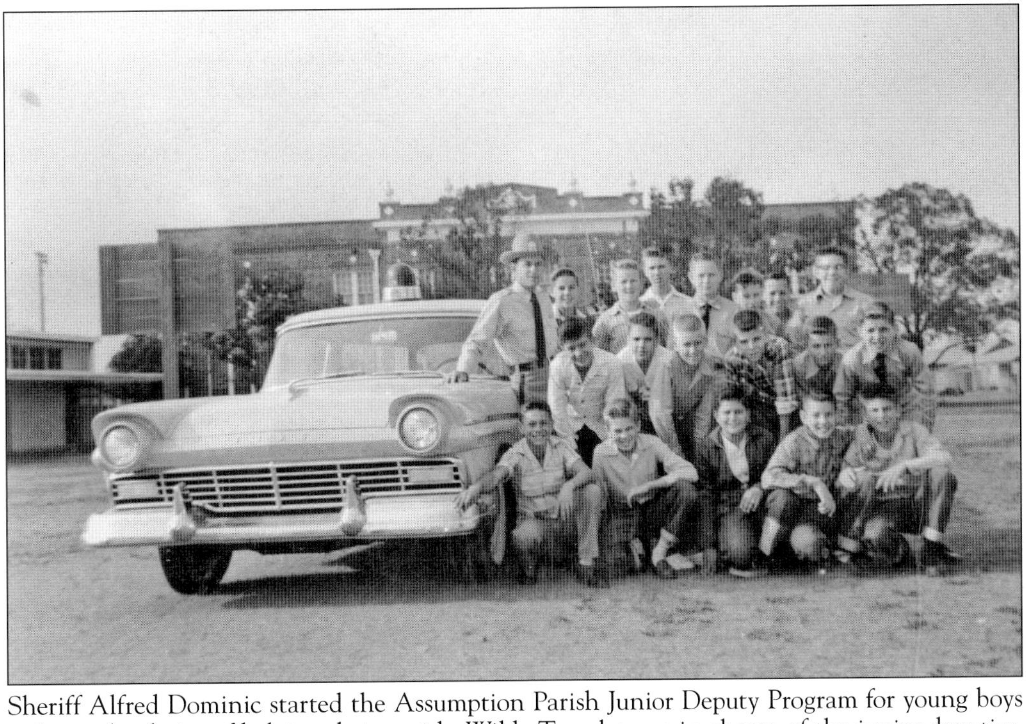

Sheriff Alfred Dominic started the Assumption Parish Junior Deputy Program for young boys to learn the duties of helping their parish. Wildy Templet was in charge of the junior deputies. He is standing on the side of the police car with his deputies in the 1950s at the courthouse in Napoleonville. (Courtesy of Wildy Templet and Hilda Templet.)

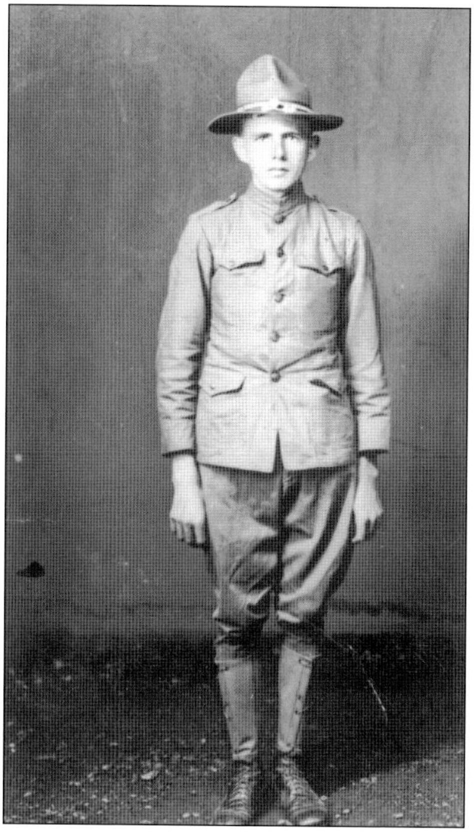

Noe Joseph Blanchard, born February 7, 1897, was inducted into the US Army on September 5, 1918, and served as a private in Company C, Development Battalion 1, at Camp Beauregard in Alexandria, Louisiana. He was honorably discharged on December 2, 1918. (Courtesy of T.J. Blanchard.)

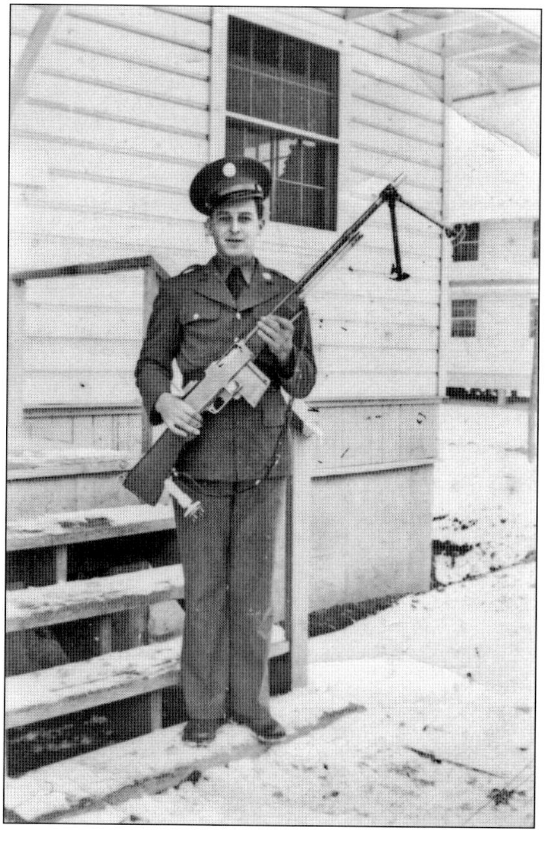

Ned Theriot is pictured at Fort Leonard Wood, Missouri, in 1941. He served as a technician 5th grade in the Army during World War II. Ned received the Bronze Star for combat at Luzon, Philippines, on January 25, 1945. He volunteered to go on the front line where the fighting was fierce and administer first aid. Ned helped evacuate wounded soldiers to safety and saved the lives of several of his comrades. (Courtesy of Nadine Theriot.)

Pictured in Honolulu, Hawaii, around 1942 are, from left to right, unidentified, Ned Theriot, and his brother-in-law LeRoy Matherne. They were stationed in the Pacific. LeRoy witnessed the bombing of Pearl Harbor on December 7, 1941, and was fortunate not to be injured when a bullet ricocheted off the pavement and landed in his shoe. It was several weeks before his family knew whether he had survived or not. (Courtesy of Nadine Theriot.)

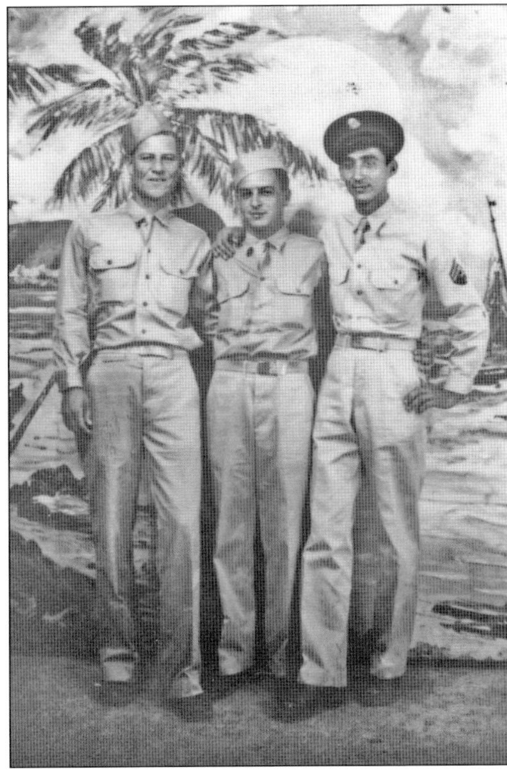

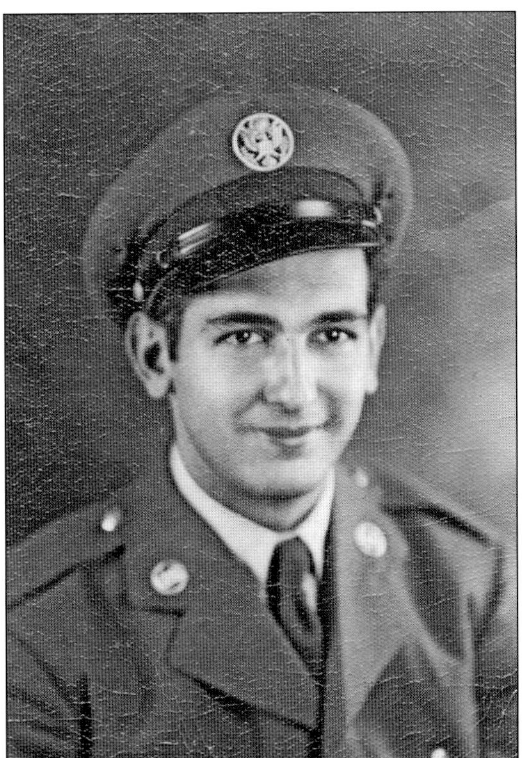

Albert Comeaux was drafted at the age of 19 during World War II. He is the son of Nicolas Comeaux and Lucy McCarthy. He married Mary Lee Margaret Giroir Comeaux. They have three daughters, Joanne Comeaux Chiappetta, Cathy Comeaux Walz, and Norma Comeaux Espinosa, and one son, David Comeaux. (Courtesy of Alice Alleman Cavalier.)

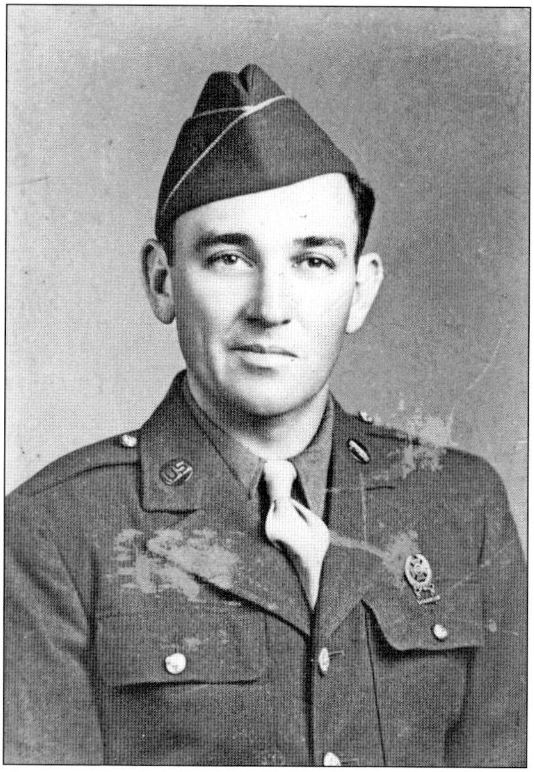

John McCarthy served in World War II. It is believed that he was 27 years old when this picture was taken. It is not known if he and his brother Harrison were at war together. (Courtesy of Alice Alleman Cavalier.)

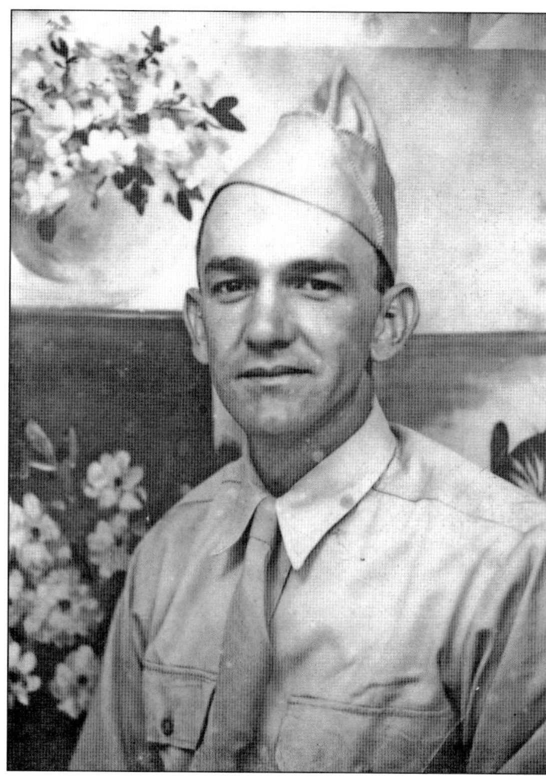

John McCarthy's brother Harrison was a World War II veteran. He was 24 years old when he had to go to war. It was hard to leave his wife with two children and one on the way. When his third child was born, he was released to take care of his family. (Courtesy of Alice Alleman Cavalier.)

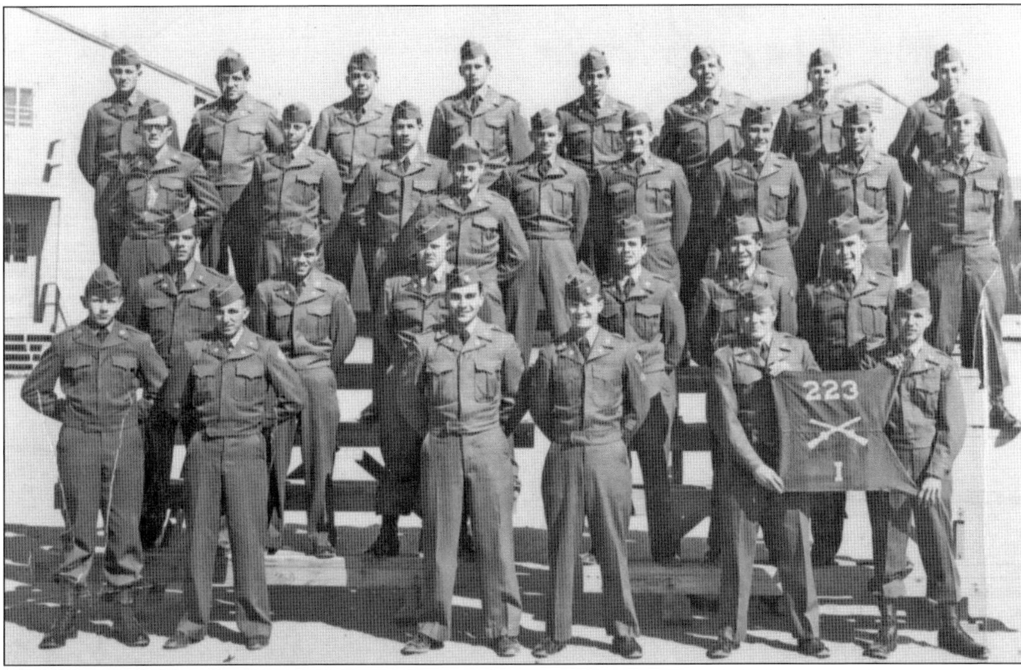

In this World War II photograph of the men of I Company, 223rd Infantry, only two men are identified. Alex Giroir is second from left in the first row, and Fred Daigle is fifth from left in the third row. It is unknown where the picture was taken. (Courtesy of Rebecca "Becky" Daigle.)

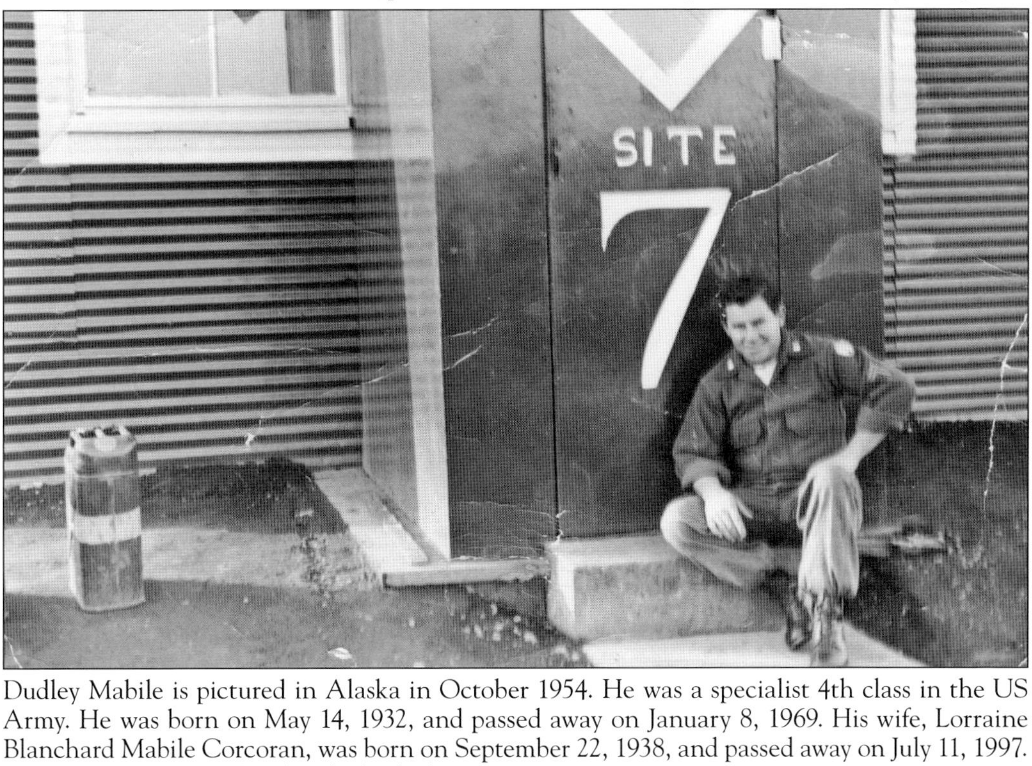

Dudley Mabile is pictured in Alaska in October 1954. He was a specialist 4th class in the US Army. He was born on May 14, 1932, and passed away on January 8, 1969. His wife, Lorraine Blanchard Mabile Corcoran, was born on September 22, 1938, and passed away on July 11, 1997. (Courtesy of Nancy Blanchard Charlet.)

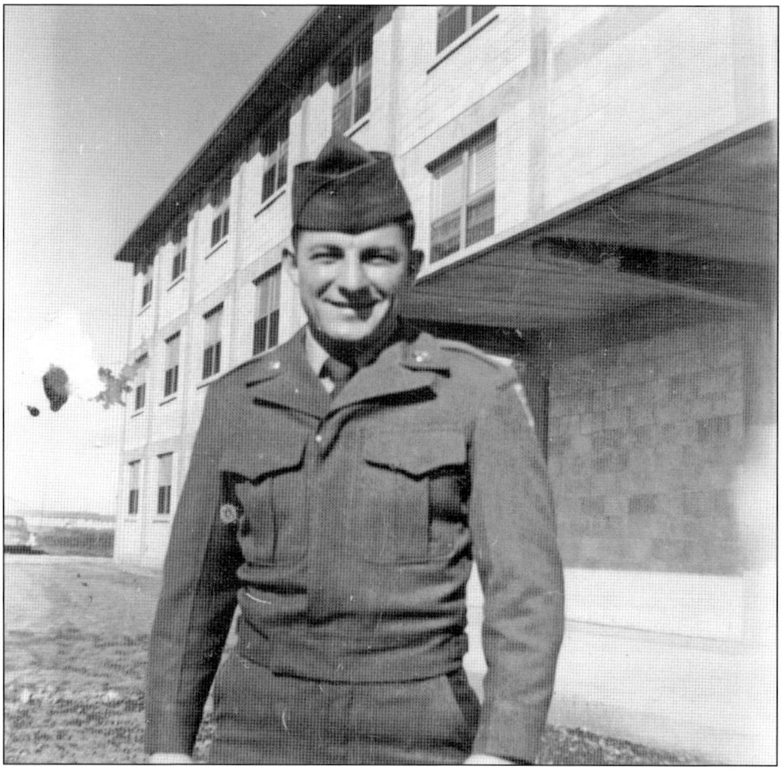

Oleus "Junius" Templet was drafted into the Army and served from 1953 to 1955. He is pictured in 1954 while based in Spokane, Washington. After serving his two years, he returned home. (Courtesy of Dorothy "Dot" Theriot Templet.)

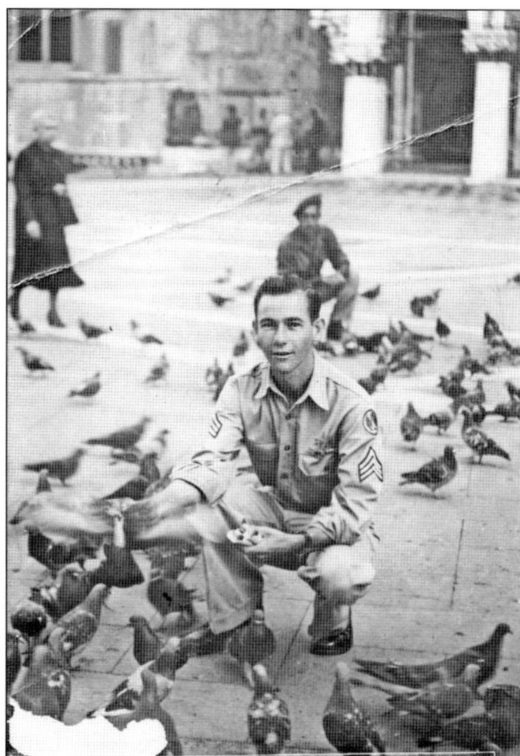

Gerald Guillot, the son of Bernadette Templet Guillot and Oibert Guillot, was drafted into the Army during World War II. He is pictured in the early 1940s feeding pigeons in Germany. (Courtesy of Lucille Theriot.)

Roger Phillip Landry served in the Army during the Korean War. It is not known if he had just returned or was leaving when this picture was taken. Roger was a retired oiler for J. Ray McDermott Offshore Division when he died at the age of 73. (Courtesy of Brenda Landry Templet and Norbert Templet.)

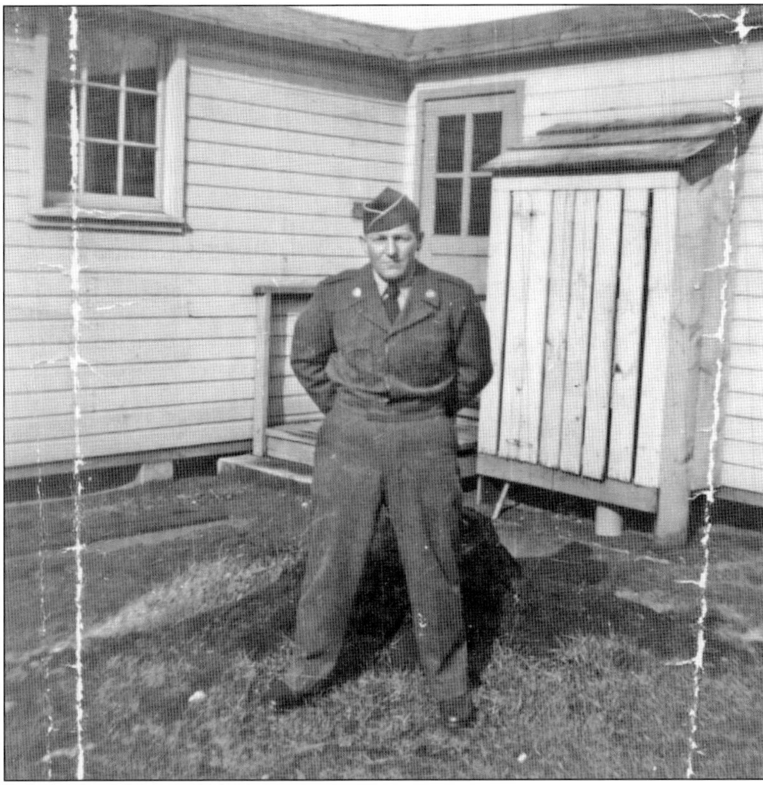

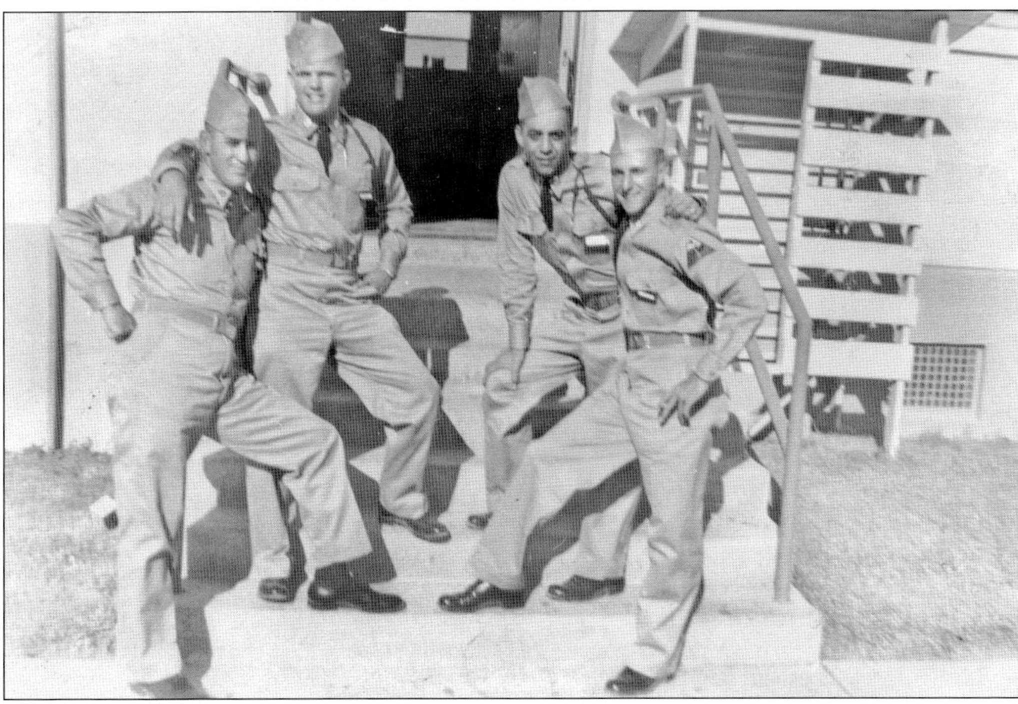

Playing around at the base are Rene "R.J." Landry (far right) and his buddies. This picture was taken in October 1956. (Courtesy of Dave Daigle and Tilsey Fryou Daigle.)

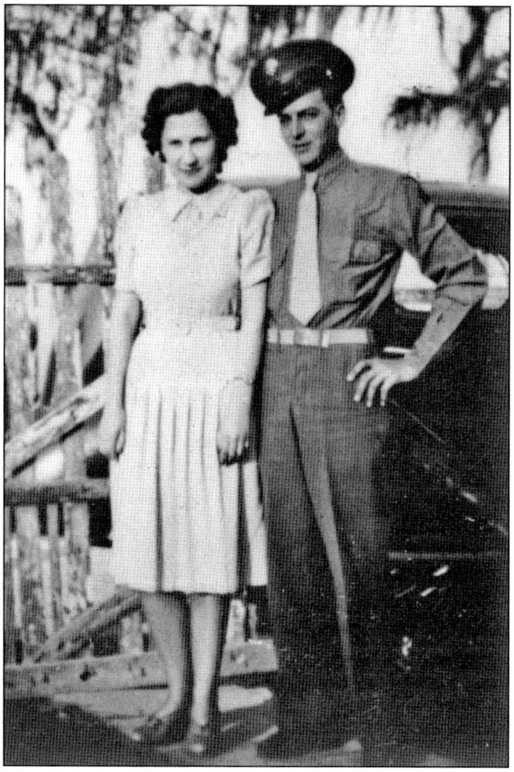

This picture was taken around 1942, before Ned Theriot was sent to the Pacific in World War II. Verniese Matherne Theriot and Ned Theriot are pictured at her parents' house down the bay. Verniese's parents were Paul Matherne and Christine Breaux Matherne. (Courtesy of Nadine Theriot.)

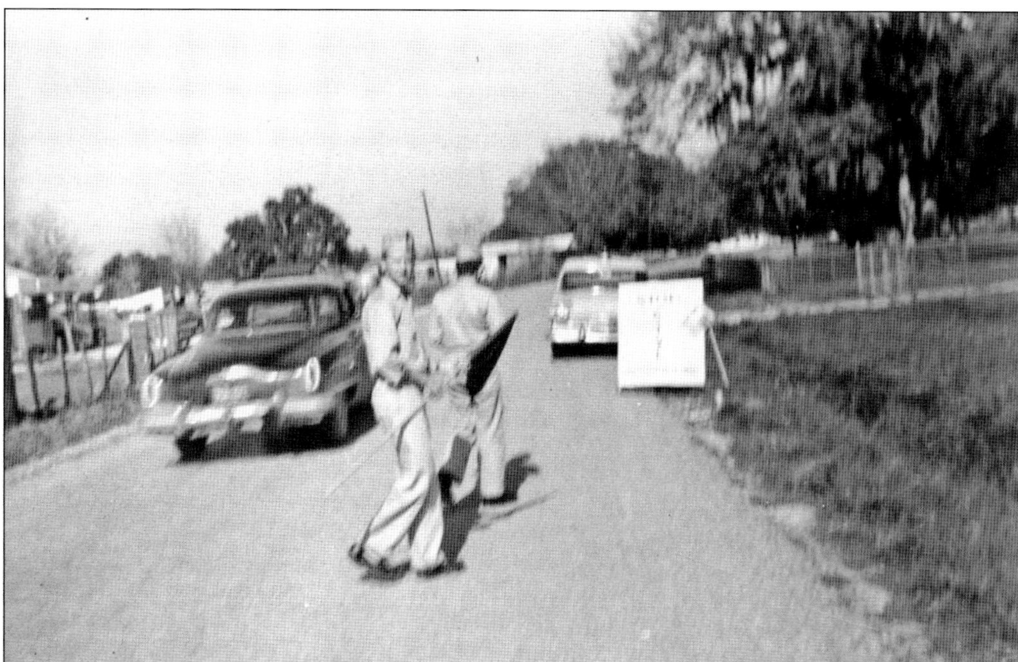

This picture was taken in front of the school. Based on the dirt roads and old cars, it must have been in the 1950s or earlier. The American Legion is having a can shake to collect money. (Courtesy of Wildy Templet and Hilda Templet.)

Five

Community Establishment and Remembrance

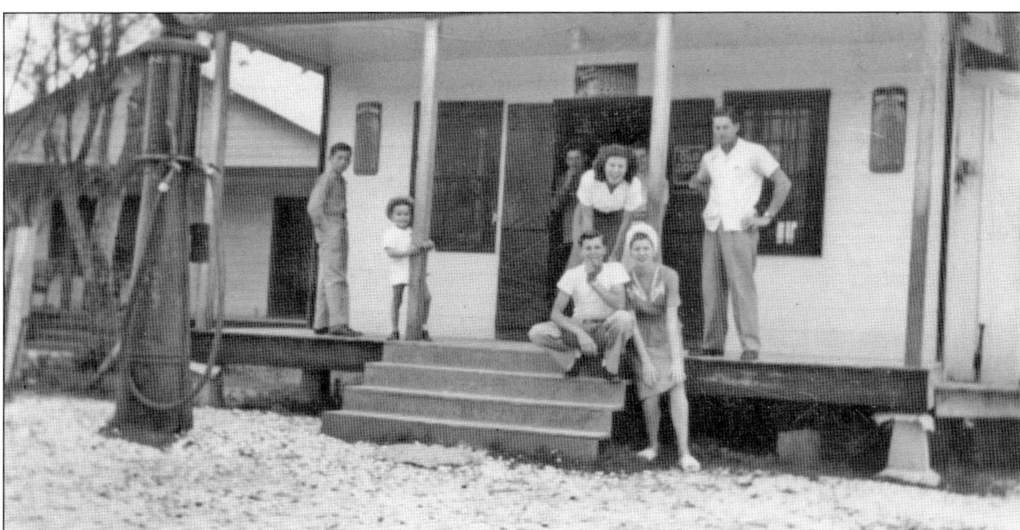

This is Dalbert Aucoin's store in upper Pierre Part. Some of his children are among those on the porch. Not everyone can be identified, but Euzatian Aucoin, Albert Aucoin, and Allie Aucoin Breaux are among the group. Dalbert was born on April 1, 1897. (Courtesy of T.J. Blanchard.)

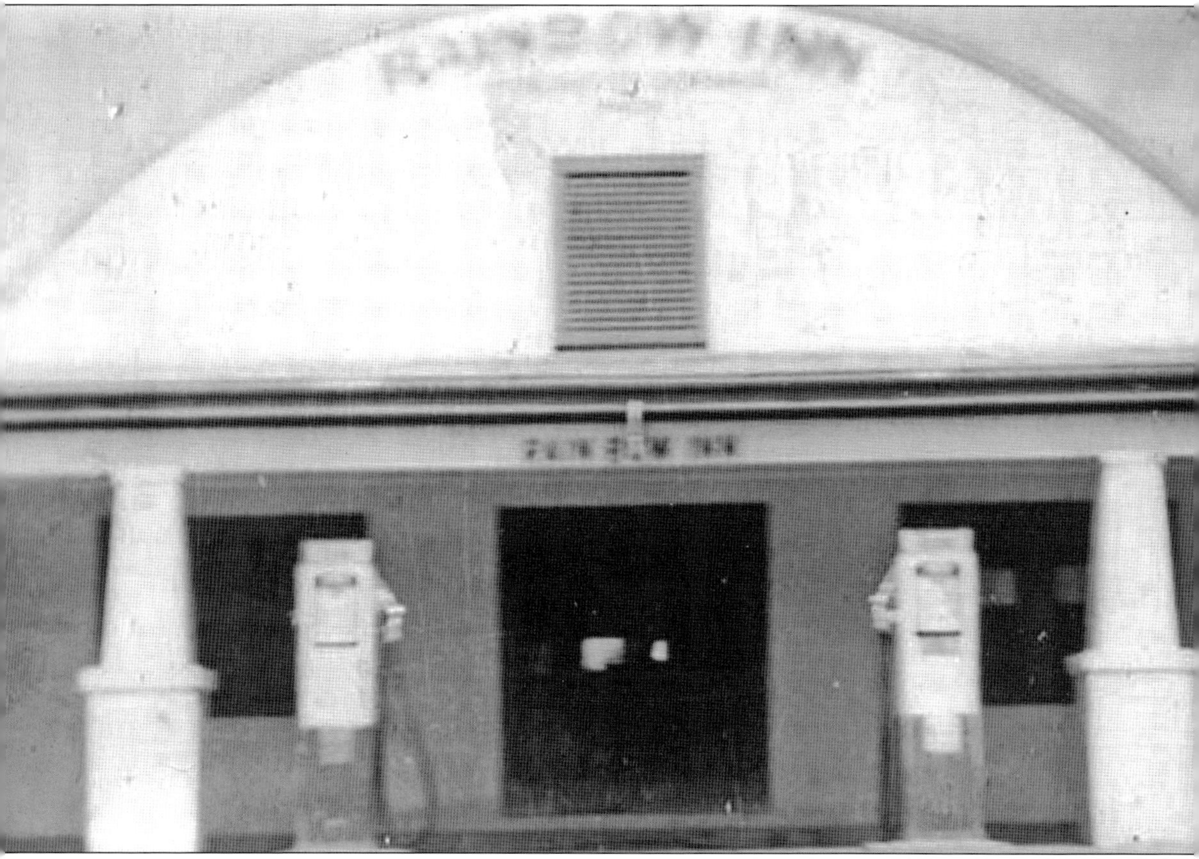

This is what the Rainbow Inn looked like when it was built in 1938. The top was round, and the inn had a covered front and gas pumps. The Rainbow Inn is one of the oldest landmarks that still stands today, although it is no longer open. (Courtesy of Nadine Theriot Theriot.)

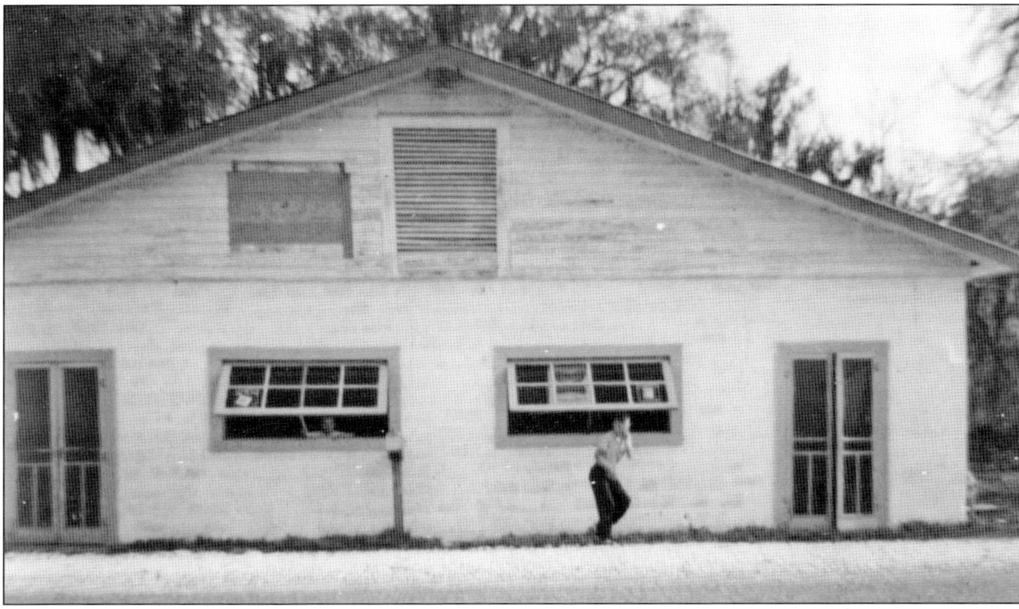

Live Oak Inn in Belle River was built by Elijah Miller and Calvin Lambert for a crab factory. Later, a Gros man added the blocks to the building, and Calvin turned it into a bar and dance hall. It was sold to Glofa Waste, who leased it to Andrew Metrejean. Then Glofa sold it to Randolph Cazes, who leased it to Rene Leonard Sr. Rene closed it, and a few years later, Curtis Landry leased it. This picture was taken in 1963. After Randolph and his wife, Myrtle, passed away, their son Llewellyn "Lew" Cazes had it torn down. (Courtesy of Gustave Joseph Gaudet and Sarah Leonard Gaudet.)

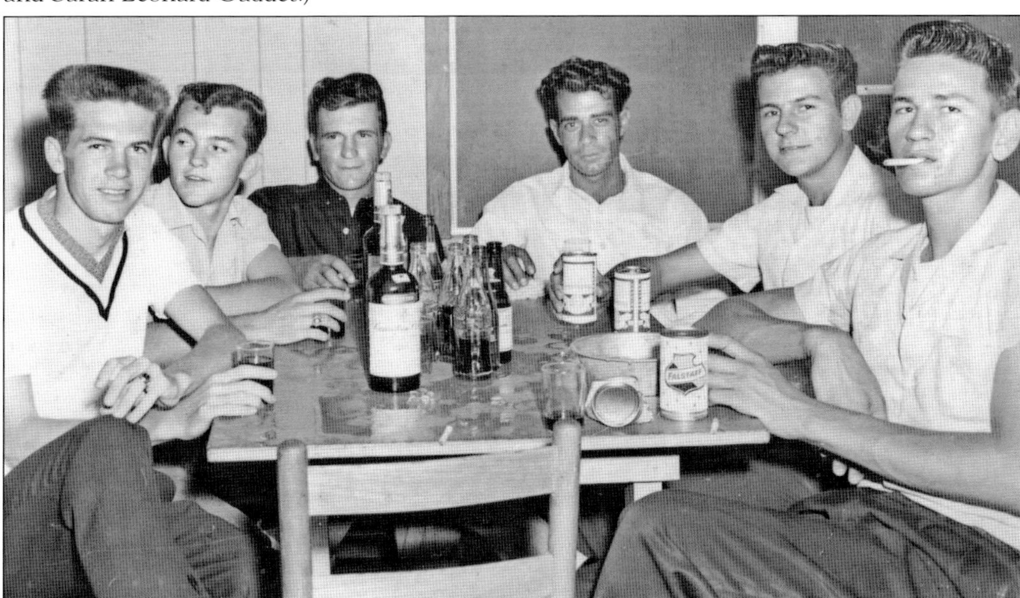

Valentine Inn is pictured in 1955. Sammy Landry built the place. It was a bar, dance hall, and a restaurant. Enjoying a drink with friends at the Valentine Inn was always a good time. From left to right are Harold Templet, unidentified, Jimmy Landry, Gus Joseph Gaudet Jr., John Breaux, and Ridley Aucoin. (Courtesy of Gustave Joseph Gaudet and Sarah Leonard Gaudet.)

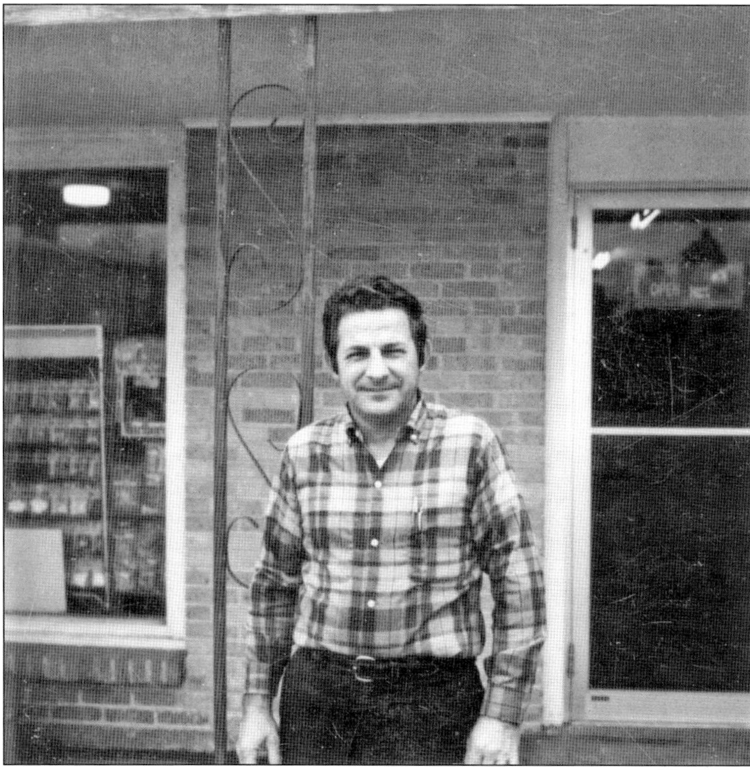

In 1955, Oleus Junius Templet Jr. and his brother Joe Templet opened Templet's Market and Grocery. Junius bought out his brother's share in 1976. Junius ran the store together with his wife, Dot, and their children, Chris, Vicki, Robert, Ellen, and Julie. (Courtesy of Dorothy "Dot" Theriot Templet.)

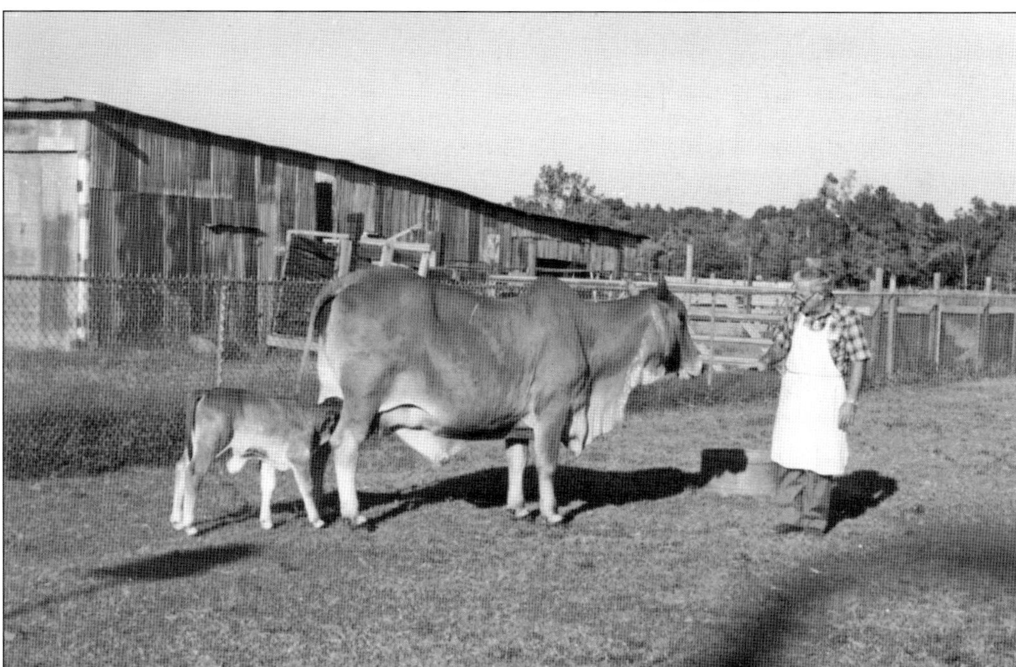

Oleus "Junius" Templet raised his cattle for his meat market. Templet is pictured in the back of his house with the cattle. He could always provide a good steak or some ground meat. His cattle and meat market were his life. (Courtesy of Dorothy "Dot" Theriot Templet.)

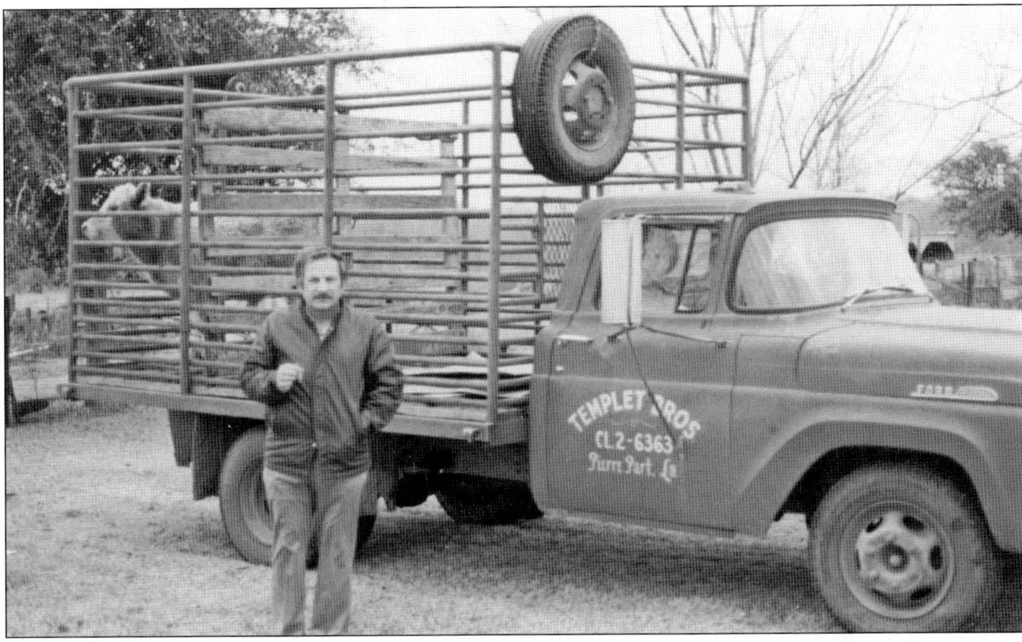

Customers could always get the freshest meat in town at Templet's Market and Grocery. Oleus "Junius" Templet stands in front of his cattle truck in the 1960s. He carried his own cattle to the processing plant before selling the meat at his meat market. (Courtesy of Dorothy "Dot" Theriot Templet.)

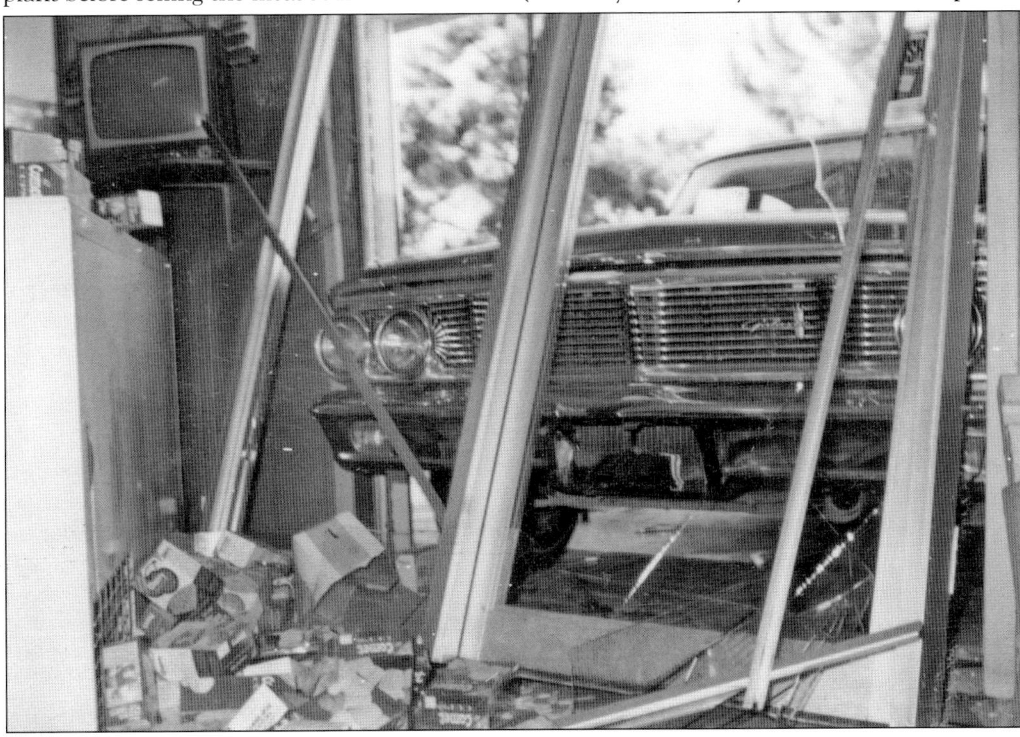

A car crashed through the door of Templet's Market and Grocery on August 4, 1970, taking the front door completely off the frame and surprising Oleus "Junius" Templet and his family. (Courtesy of Dorothy "Dot" Theriot Templet.)

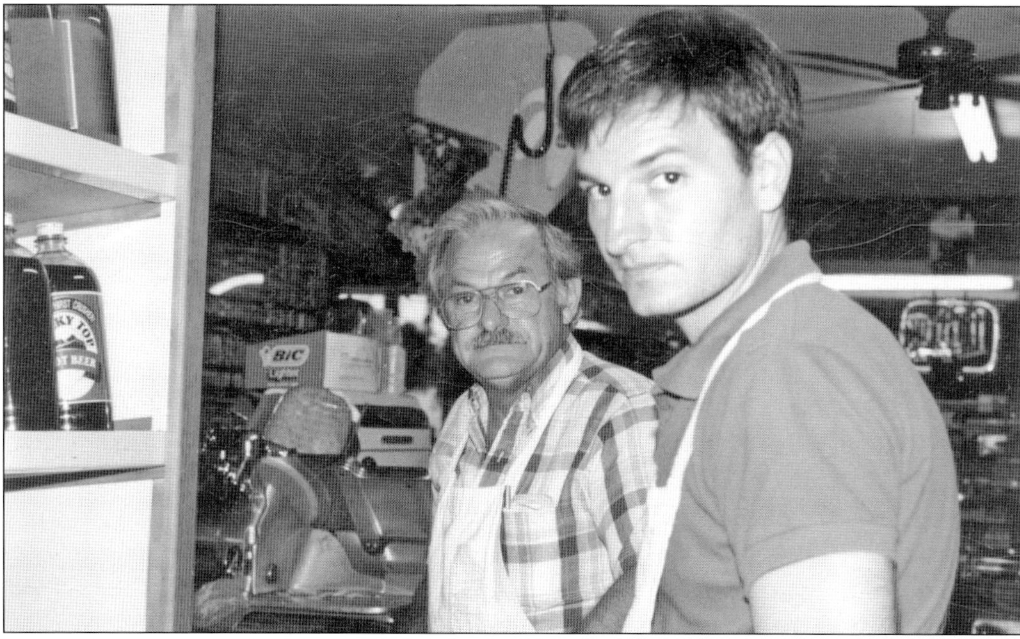

Pictured in 1990 are Oleus Junius Templet Jr. and his son Robert Templet. Robert worked many hours with his father. In 1996, Junius Jr. retired and sold the store to Robert. As of today, Robert still owns Templet's Market and Grocery with his wife, Lisa Crochet Templet, their daughters, Lindsey, Tracey, and Megan, and granddaughter Amelia. (Courtesy of Dorothy "Dot" Theriot Templet.)

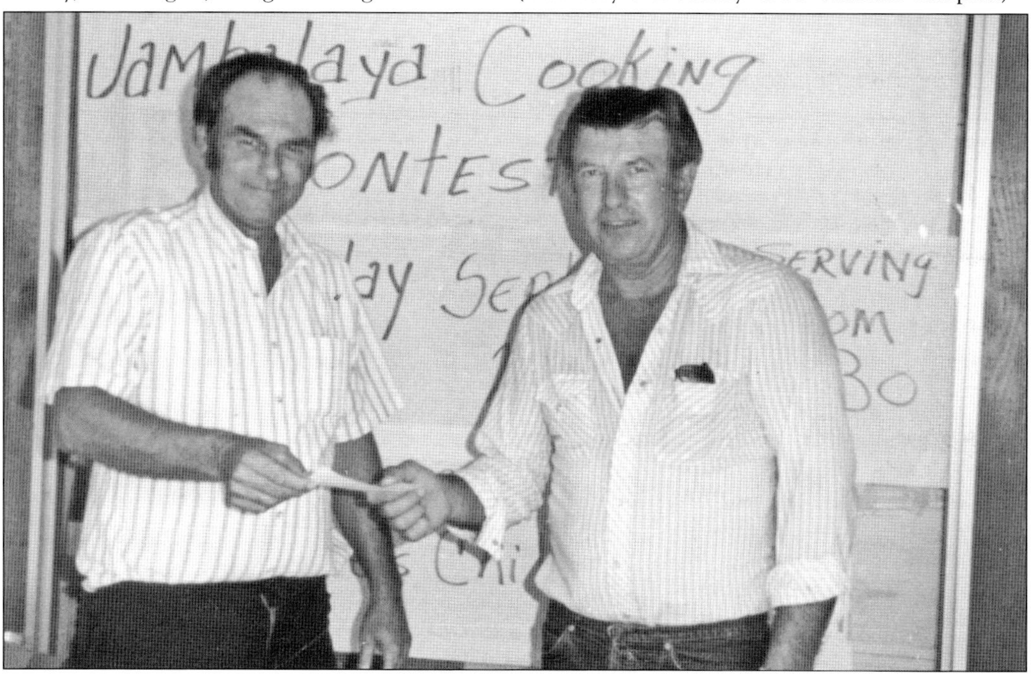

Belle River Groceries, owned by Jimmy Gaudet and Jane Landry Gaudet, sponsored a jambalaya cooking contest in 1986 to raise money for St. Jude Children's Hospital. They raised $597 that day. Jimmy (left) is pictured handing first-place winner Curtis Landry a check for $100. Curtis donated his prize to St. Jude Children's Hospital. (Courtesy of Jane Landry Gaudet.)

In the 1970s, Ed Lee Shell Beach Bar and Marina was the hot spot to be. On March 18, 1974, Haywood Hebert (left) and Jay Morales are enjoying a cold beer under the big oak trees. Jay and Haywood always hung out there with their friends. (Courtesy of Glenda Landry McGraw.)

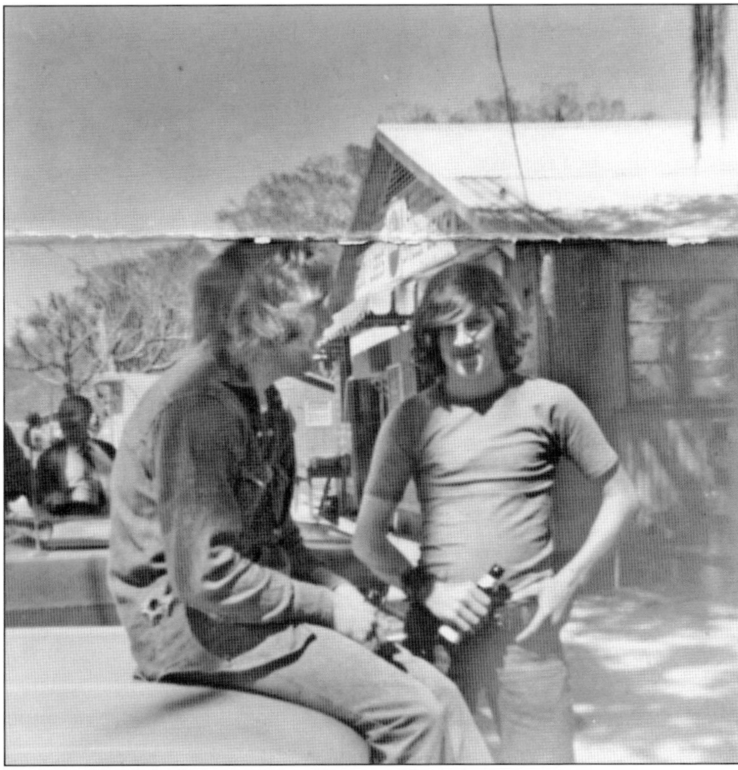

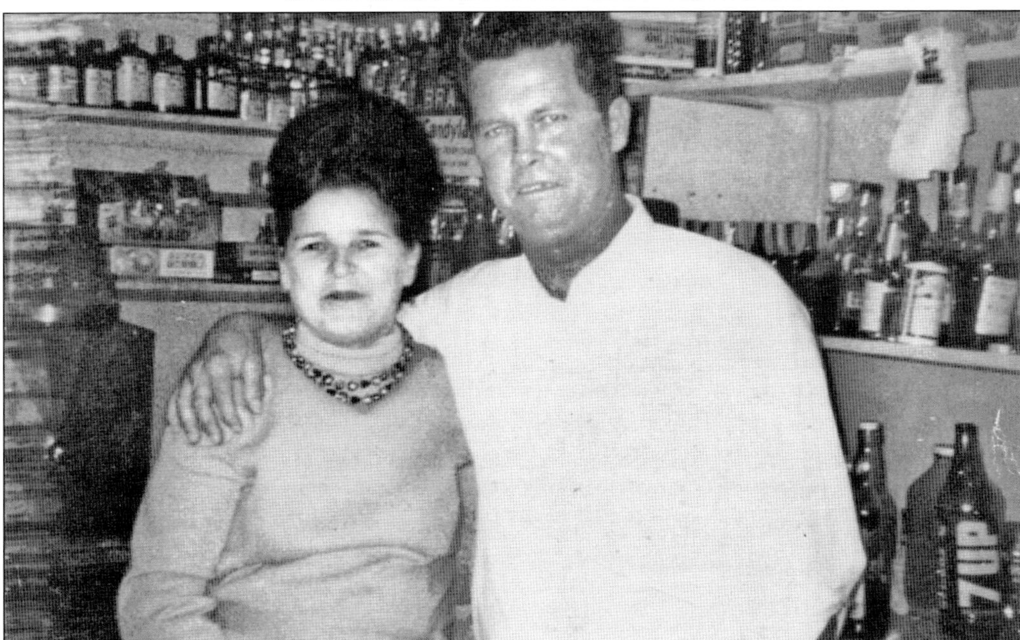

Pictured are Loretta Hebert and Wilbert Hebert. They were the owners of Lake View Inn, which everyone knew as "Mr. Wilbert's." They opened the bar in 1963 and later added a grocery store on the side. In 2010, Herman Cavalier took over the bar and called it T-Herm's. The bar was closed in 2013 and later torn down. (Courtesy of Tina Glynn Cavalier and Norman Cavalier.)

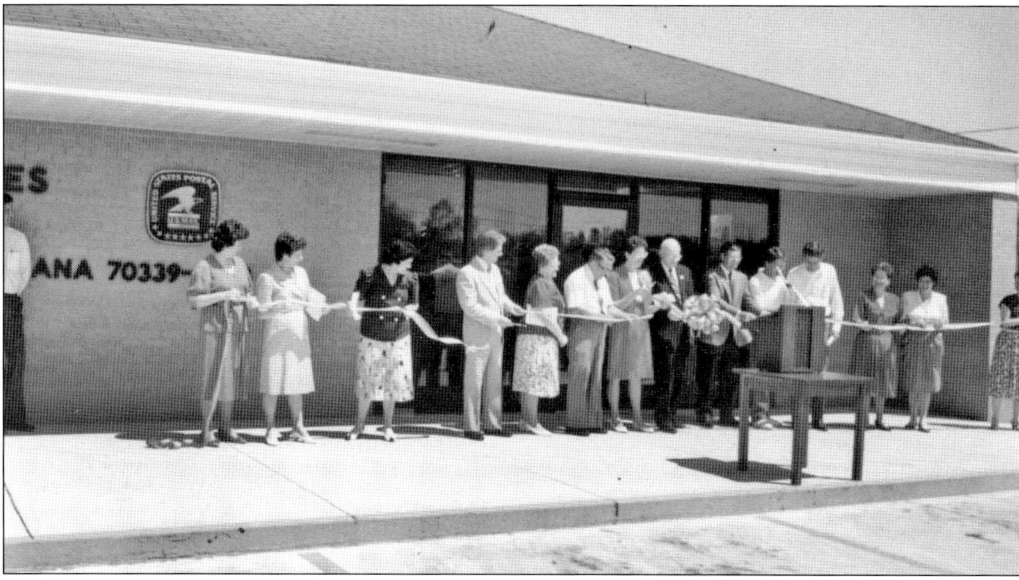

Postmaster Gonellie Domingue cuts the ribbon to open the new post office on April 16, 1989. From left to right are Gail Landry, Mary Jane Comeaux, Ann Giroir, Stanley Picou, Elda St. Germain, Honore St. Germain Jr., Gonellie Domingue, Ronnie Burke, Logi Guillot, Charlie Melancon, Tony Falterman, Connie Daigle, Jeanne Templet, and Kitty Blanchard. (Courtesy of Gonellie Domingue.)

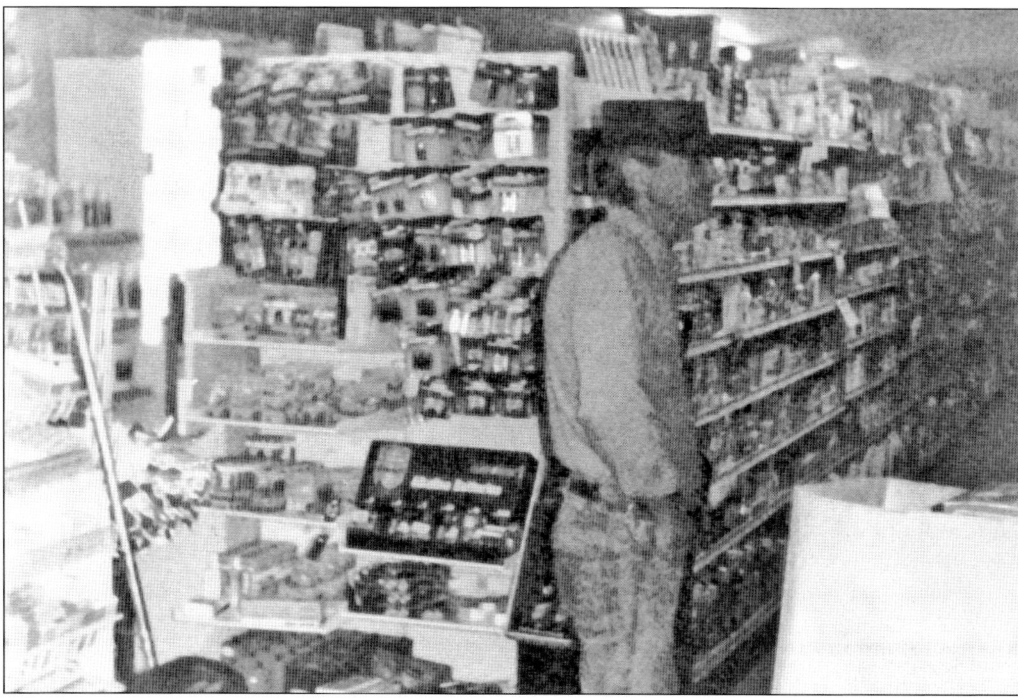

Pictured in Chedotal's Grocery, Wilbert "Duke" Metrejean is doing his shopping. Duke was a regular customer at Chedotal's. Lillian Chedotal and her staff were always willing to give him a helping hand. He looks like he is talking to someone and looking for something. (Courtesy of Lillian Mabile Chedotal.)

Many houses in Pierre Part flooded in 1973. Some only had a little water, but many people in the area lost everything they owned. Pictured at right is a house on North Bay Road, possibly Rita Metrejean's. Joseph "Joe" Daigle and Mary Ann "Marion" Gaudet Daigle had to move their furniture and belongings out of town to higher land. Pictured below is Joe and Marion's house on North Bay Road in 1973. (Both, courtesy of Gustave Joseph Gaudet and Sarah Leonard Gaudet.)

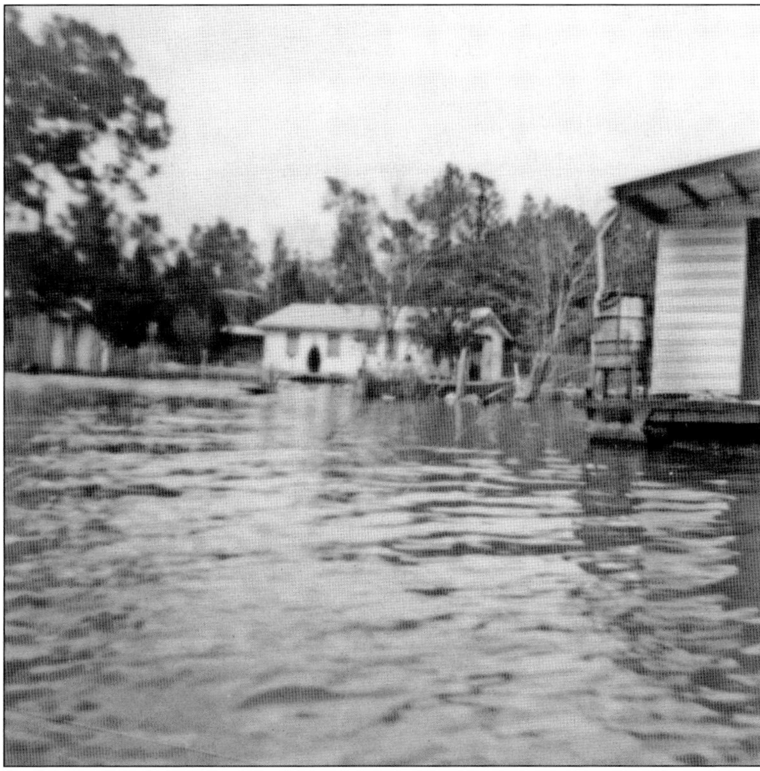

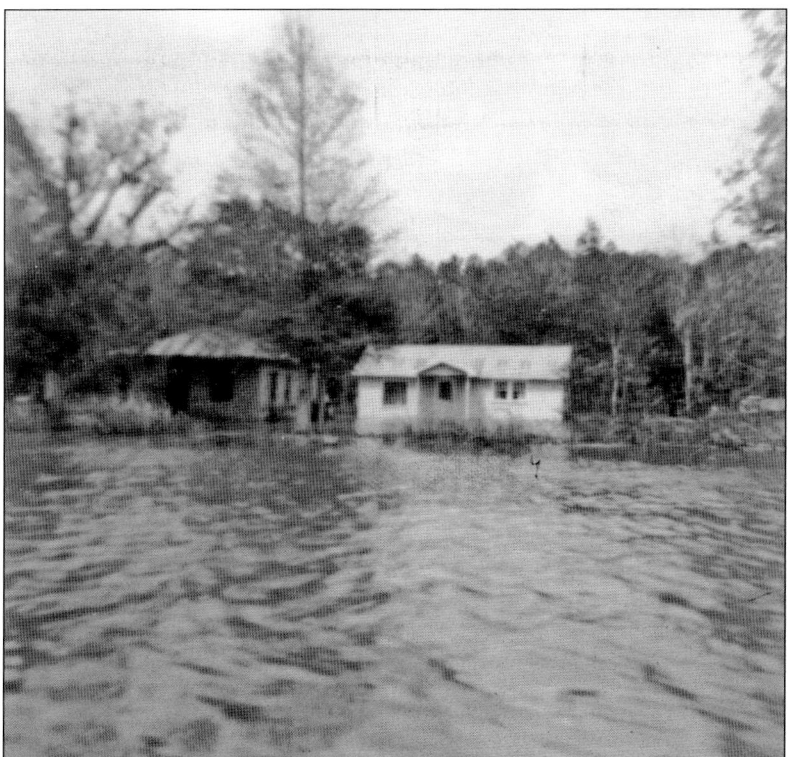

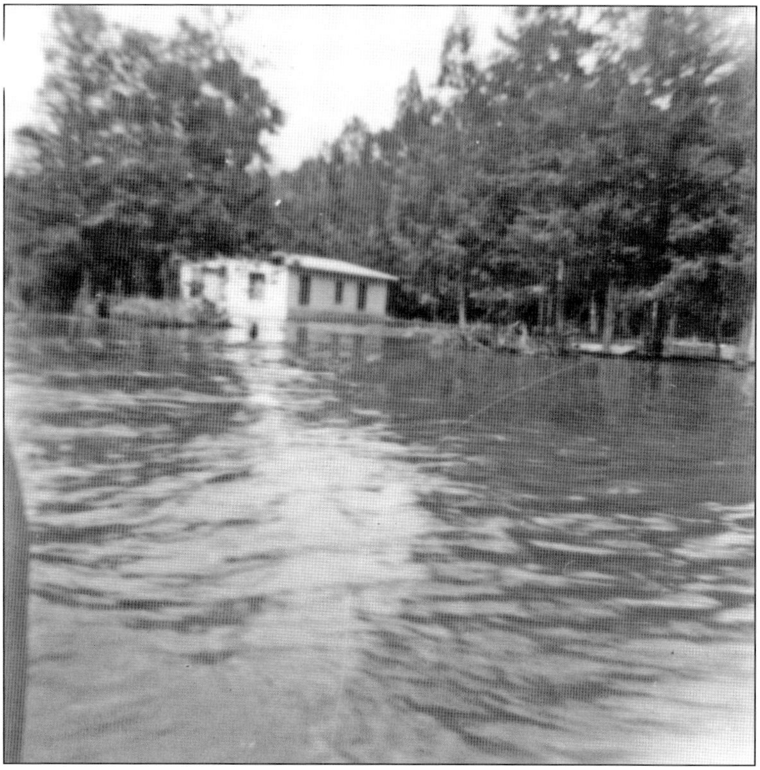

Water flooded many houses and businesses. It came from the swamp and the bay, spreading mud and slush everywhere. High water in 1973 put many feet of water in homes. Sand bags helped some, but not all. At left is the home of Nolan Richard and Noeline "Pokeen" Dupre Richard, and below is Lakeview Inn on South Bay Road. Lakeview Inn was owned and operated by Wilbert Hebert and his wife, Loretta Hebert. (Both, courtesy of Gustave Joseph Gaudet and Sarah Leonard Gaudet.)

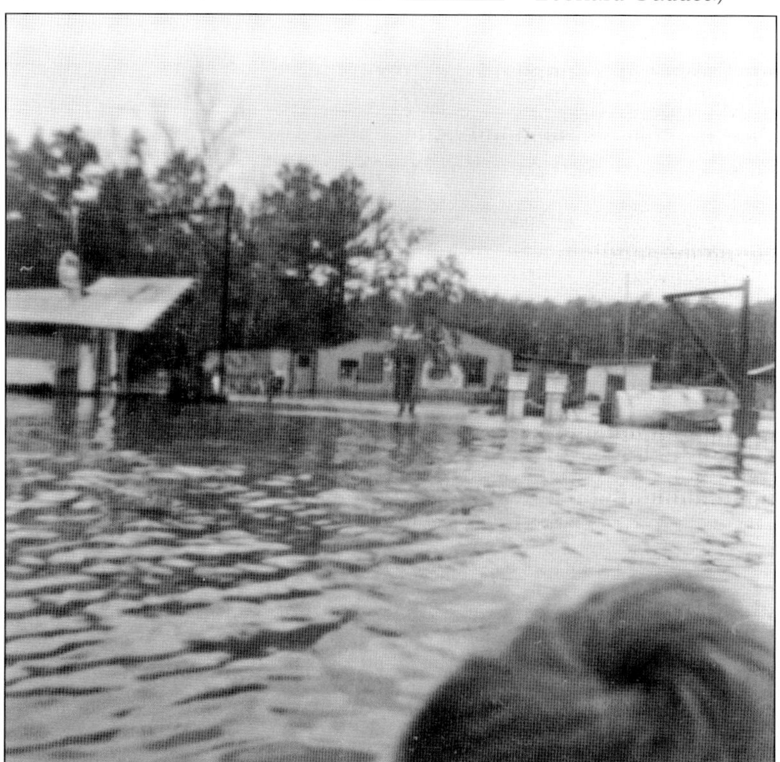

Pictured is a mail vehicle in water. March 1973 brought flooding and danger to everyone in and around this little town. With high water just about everywhere, it was hard to deliver the mail. (Courtesy of Gonellie Domingue.)

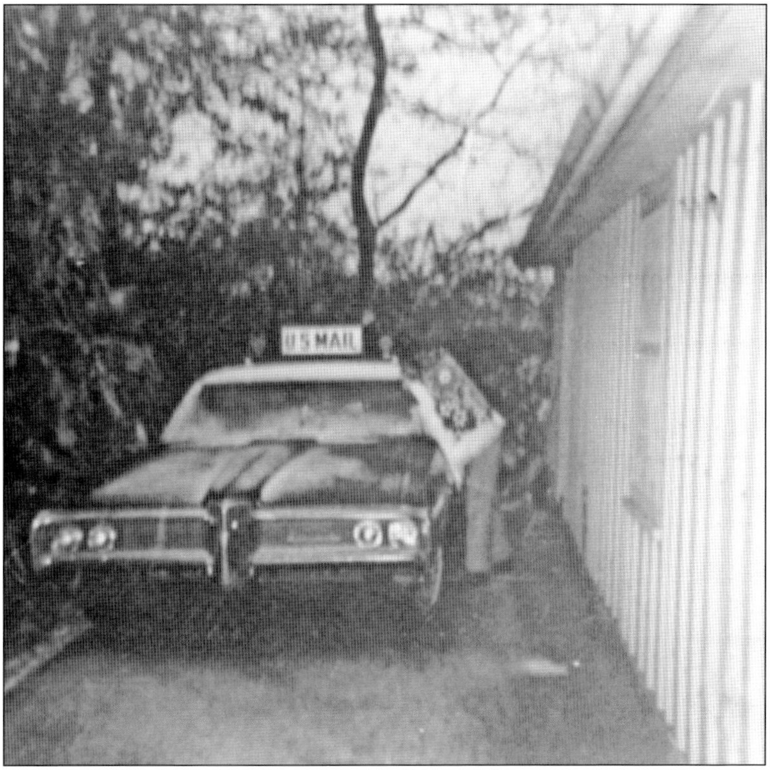

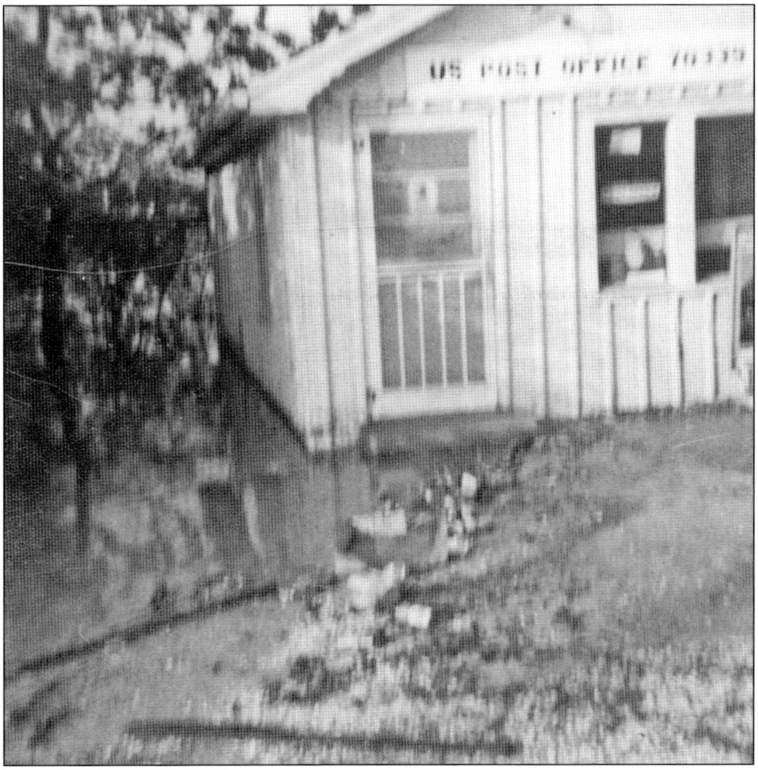

The first Pierre Part Post Office opened on June 1, 1967, at the bayou across from Chedotal's Grocery. Lucy Casteigne was the postmaster, while Gonellie Domingue served as clerk. It was the only post office where people could get their mail by boat. In 1973, rising floodwater surrounded the building, and the post office had to be moved to higher ground. A mobile building was put next to Richard's Pharmacy to serve as the post office. (Courtesy of Gonellie Domingue.)

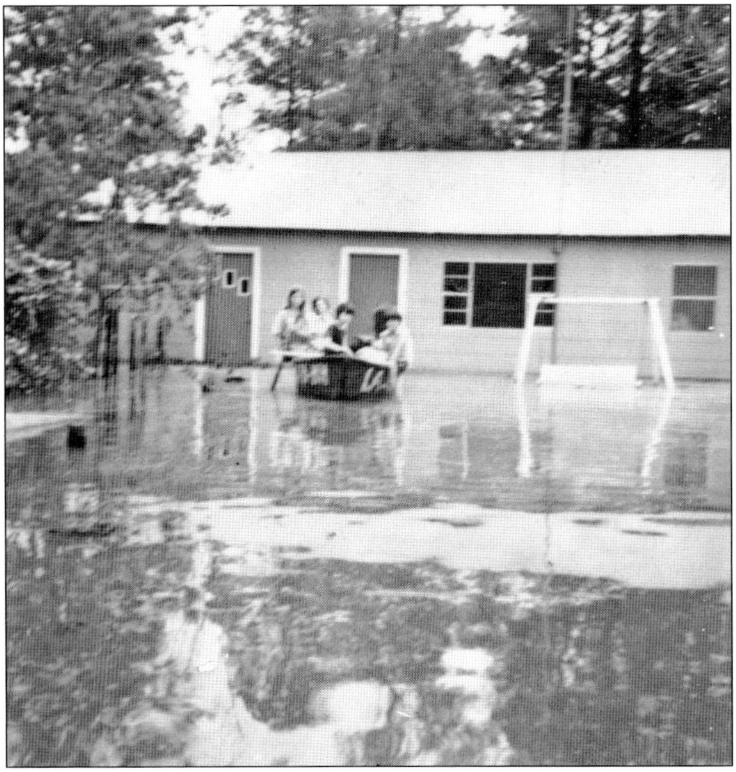

The 1973 flood caused Ulysse Landry and Leabee Hebert Landry to move their family to higher ground. Leabee and her children had to use a boat to get some things they needed out of the house. Pictured in the boat are, from left to right, Brenda Landry Templet, Leabee, Peter, Thomas, and Carol; their other daughter, Patrica Landry Cavalier, did not go; she stayed on the road. (Courtesy of Brenda Landry Templet and Norbert Templet.)

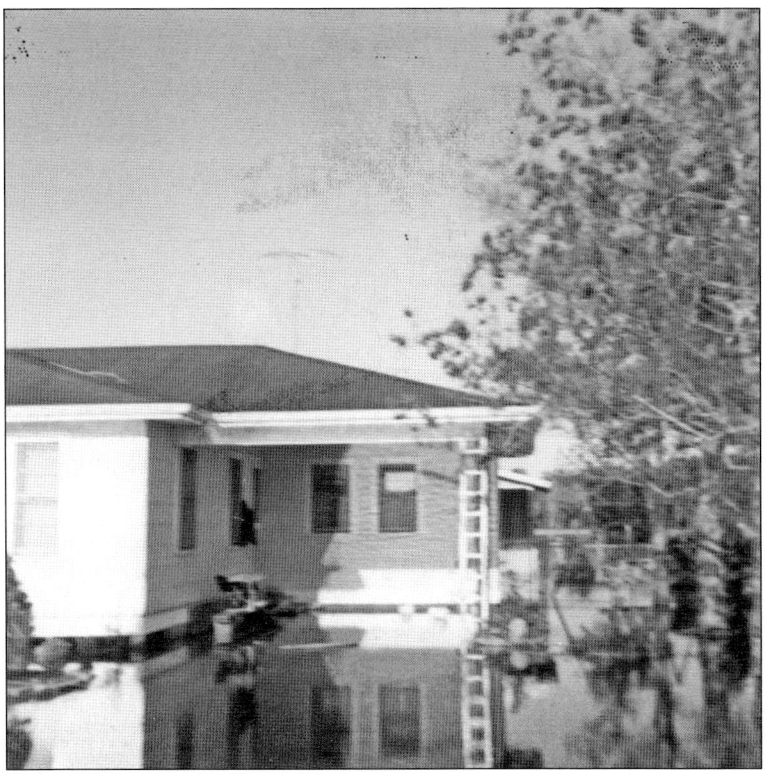

In 1973, high water was everywhere. Many people had to leave their home for higher ground. Oleus "Junius" Templet and Dorothy "Dot" Templet were lucky to only have a little water. Their house is pictured here. (Courtesy of Dorothy "Dot" Theriot Templet.)

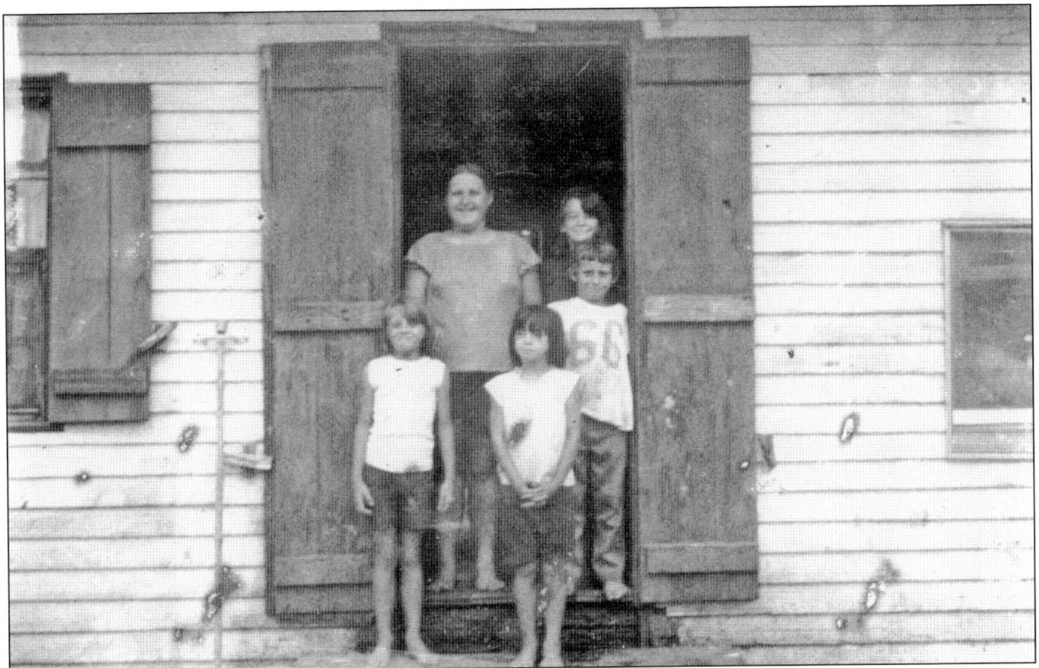

Flooding in 1975 kept many families worried. The Gros family, among many, lived in a low-lying area. The children had to stay indoors because there was no land to play on. At the doorway are, from left to right, (first row) Gertrude Gros Sanchez and Paula Gros; (second row) Carol Gros Charlet and Michael Gros; (third row) Kathleen Gros. (Courtesy of Carol Gros Charlet.)

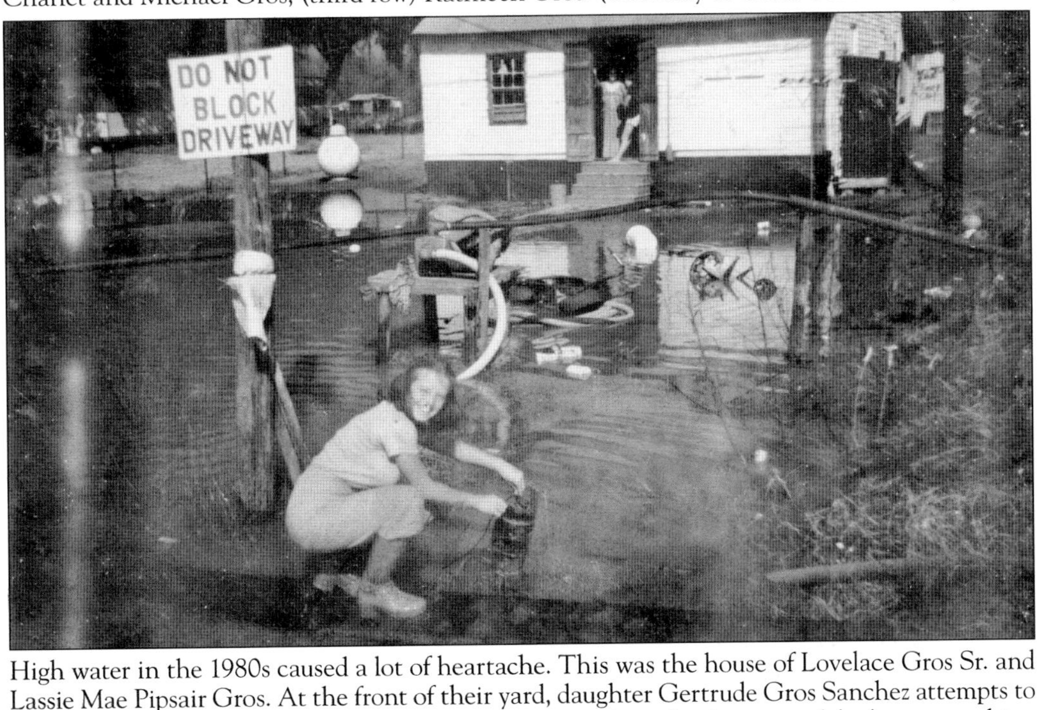

High water in the 1980s caused a lot of heartache. This was the house of Lovelace Gros Sr. and Lassie Mae Pipsair Gros. At the front of their yard, daughter Gertrude Gros Sanchez attempts to fix the broken water pipe. Her mother, Lassie Mae, stands in the doorway of the house watching her. This picture was taken on January 8, 1980. (Courtesy of Carol Gros Charlet.)

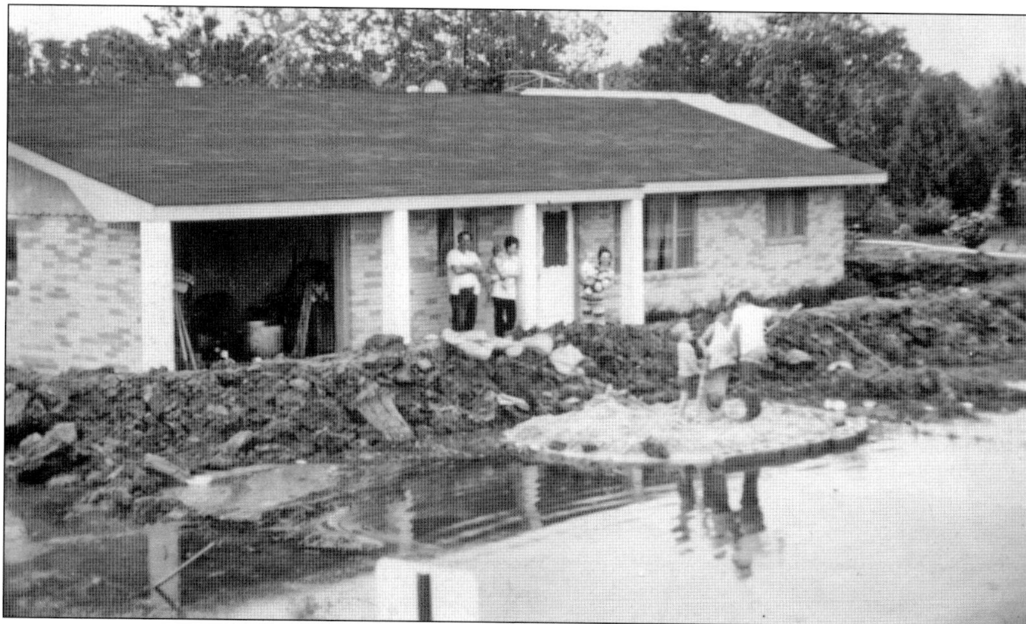

The floods of 1973 were devastating. Many homes had water in them. Jimmy Gaudet and Jane Landry Gaudet were one of the many families that were able to make a levee of sand bags and dirt around their house to keep the water out. It was not an easy task; the water had to be watched day and night. Pumps were even used to help keep the water out. From left to right, Jimmy, Jane, Chett, Mrs. Charles LeBlanc, and her son are watching Jeff, Carl, and Darrell playing in the sand. (Courtesy of Jane Landry Gaudet.)

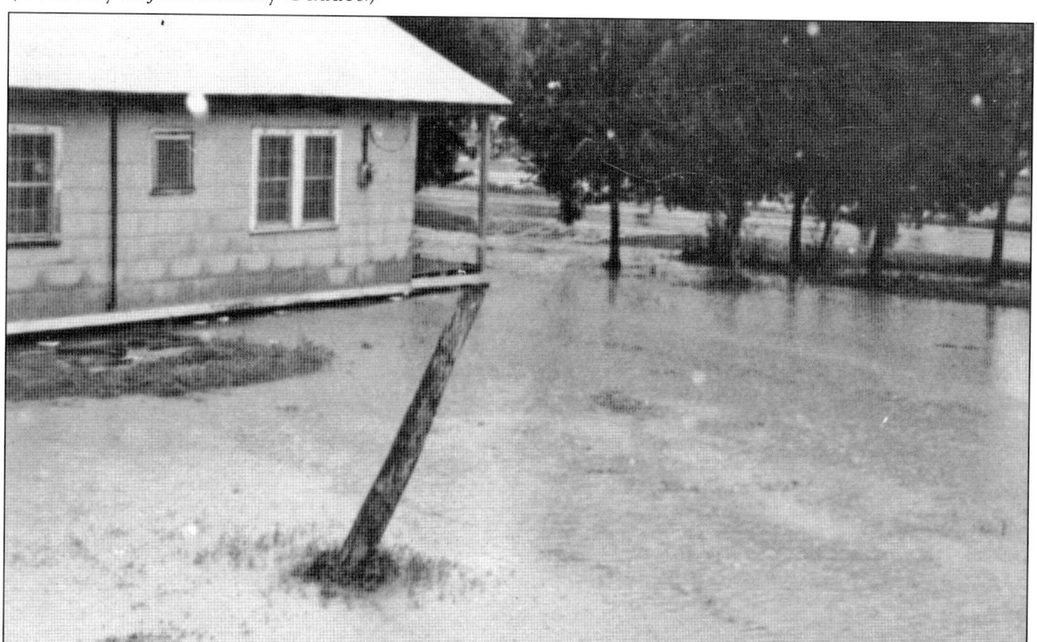

Noe Joseph Blanchard and Noeline St. Germain Blanchard's house is pictured during a flood in 1983. It is unknown if this flood was caused by rain or by high water from a hurricane. The Blanchards lived in upper Pierre Part. (Courtesy of T.J. Blanchard.)

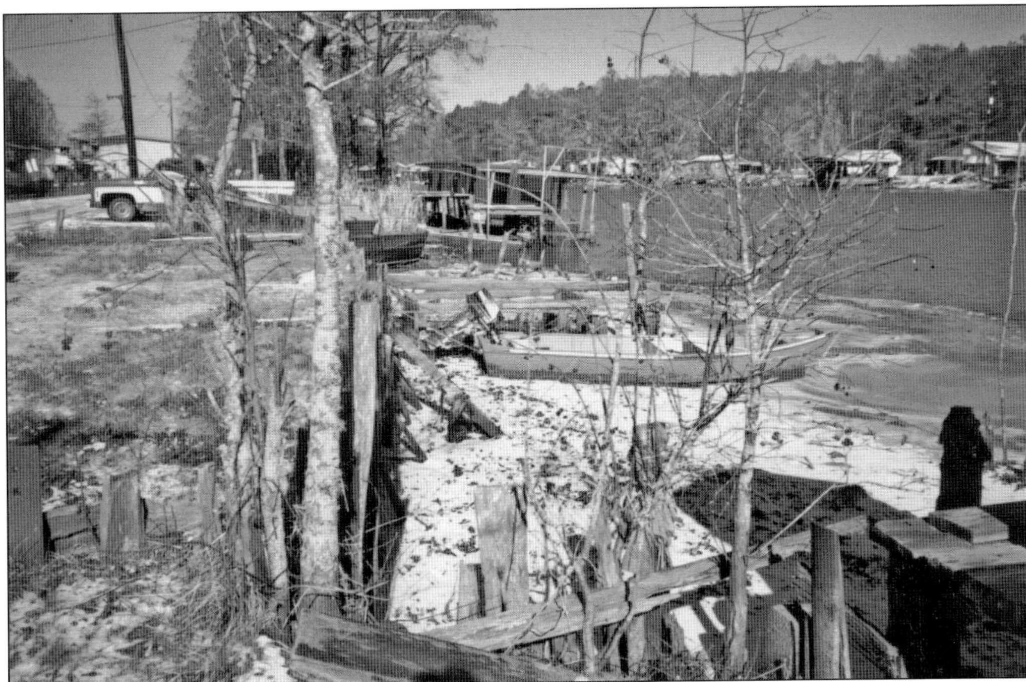

Freezing weather in December 1989 brought ice everywhere, and boats were frozen on the edge of the bay. The bay had just a little open water in the middle, but the rest was all frozen. This picture was taken at the bayou across from Ulysse Landry's house down the bay. (Courtesy of Brenda Landry Templet.)

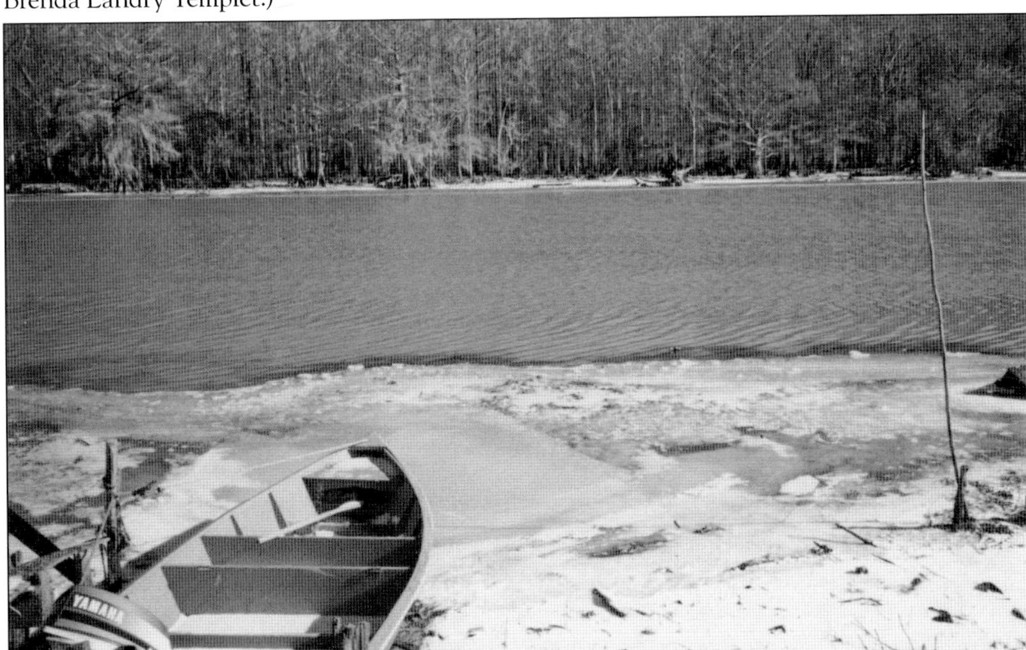

With freezing temperatures all week, the ice kept boats frozen in place and very hard to move. The temperature had lots of people in their homes. Ice was fun but also dangerous for children and adults. There were many trees and power lines down that week. (Courtesy of Brenda Landry Templet.)

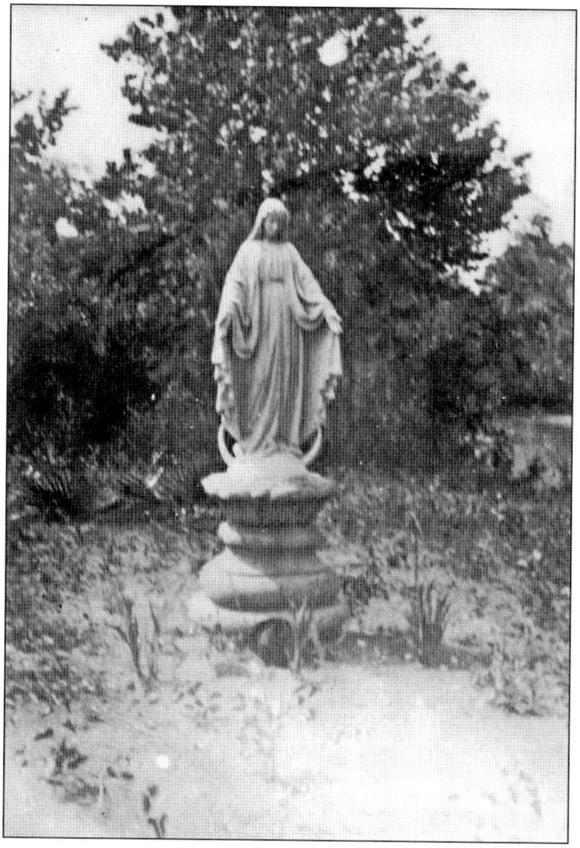

The old Mary statue on the Island of the Blessed Virgin Mary was covered by high water at the time this picture was taken. This statue was eventually destroyed and replaced with another one, and the island has been totally redone. (Courtesy of Nadine Theriot Theriot.)

In December 1982, the Pierre Part Christmas Parade rolled from P.J. Blanchard's IGA to the Pierre Part Store. The Boy Scouts and Cub Scouts are pictured in front of the Rainbow Inn. The boys marched proudly down the parade route with some holding flags and signs for their troops. (Courtesy of Tina Glynn Cavalier and Norman Cavalier.)

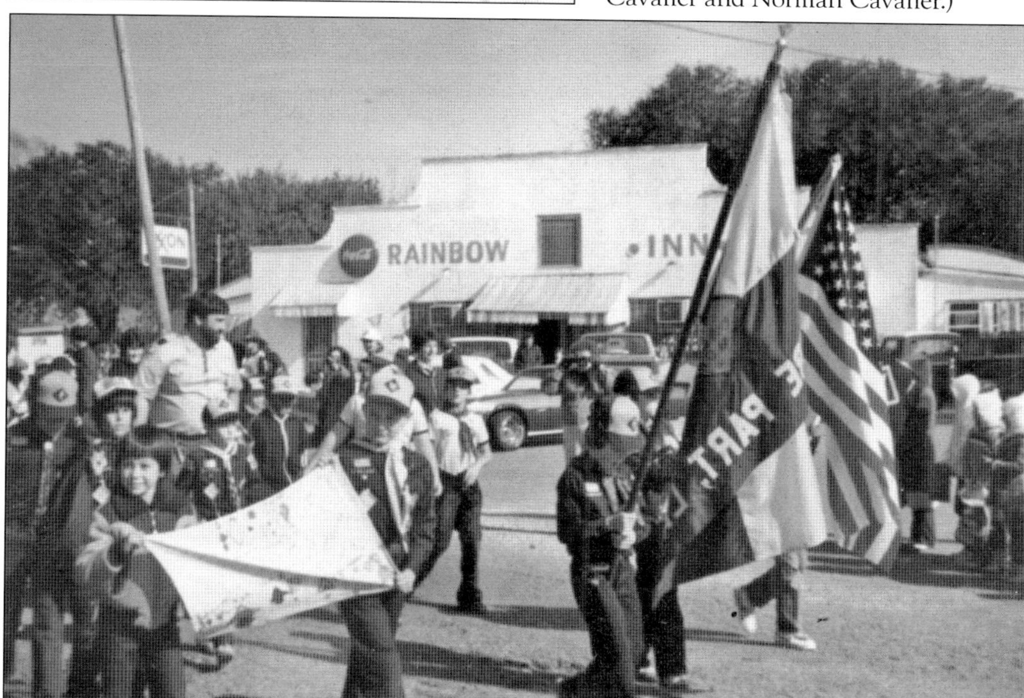

Being Crawfish Jubilee Queen was a huge deal. Emma Nell Sedotal Luneau was crowned queen at the age of 20 in 1971. She is pictured with her crown and roses. This was the first pageant that was held for the jubilee. (Courtesy of Emma Nell Sedotal Luneau.)

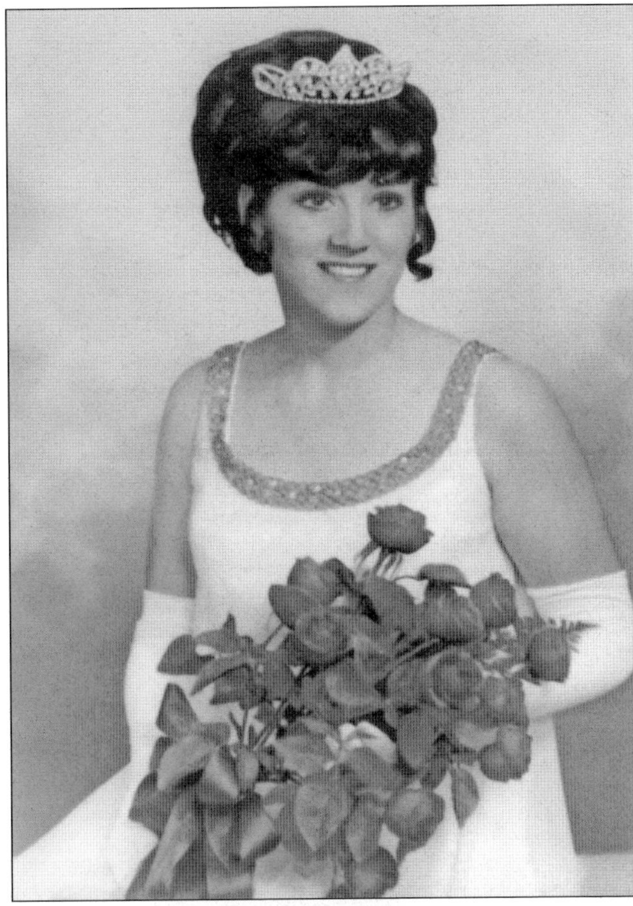

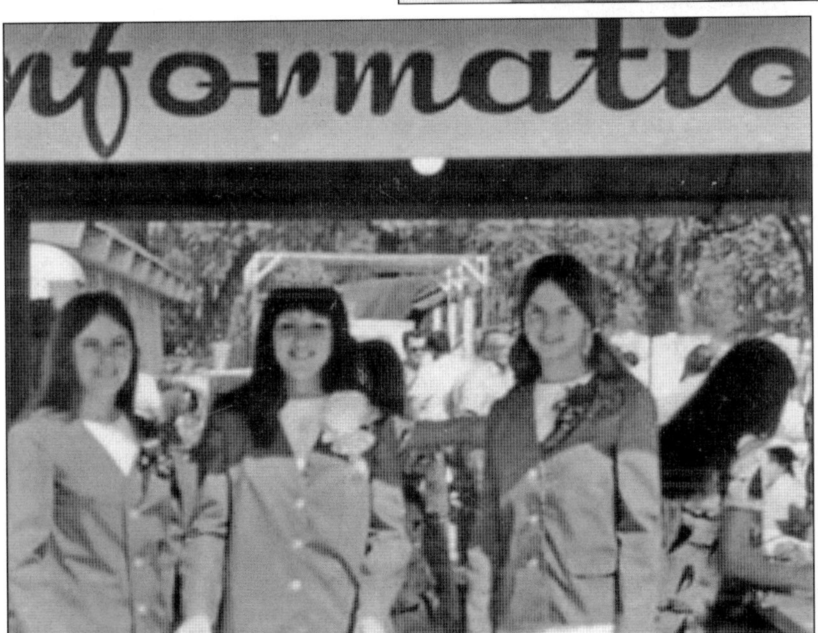

The 1971 Crawfish Jubilee Queen and her court are pictured here. From left to right are Susan Richard Alleman Landry, first maid; Emma Nell Sedotal Luneau, queen; and Janice Hebert Farmer, second maid. (Courtesy of Emma Nell Sedotal Luneau.)

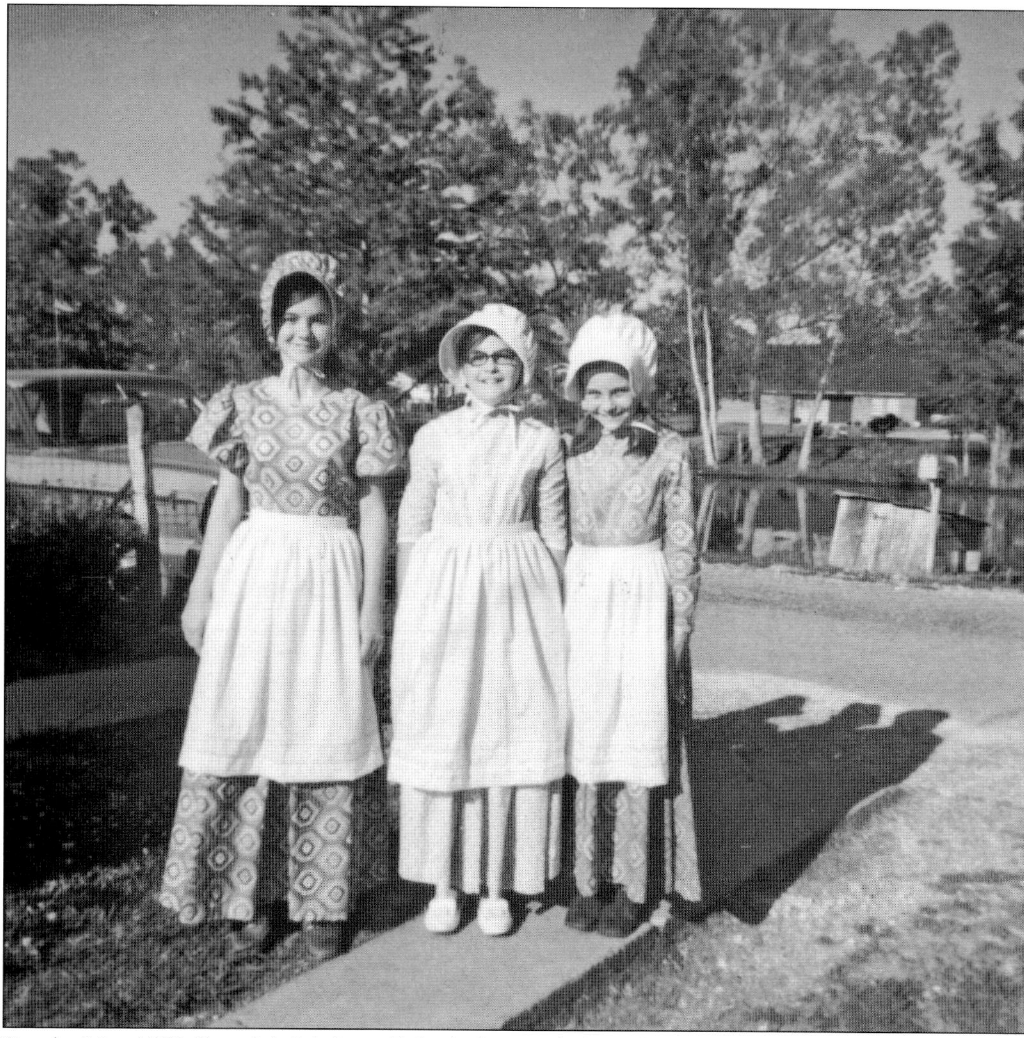

For the May 1970 Crawfish Jubilee, all the ladies made long dresses for themselves and their girls. From left to right are Rita Mabile Barras, 13; Arlene Mabile Blanchard, 11; and Jenifer Mabile Brouillette, 10. (Courtesy of Leonard Mabile and Regina Dupuis Mabile.)

Six

Simple Times

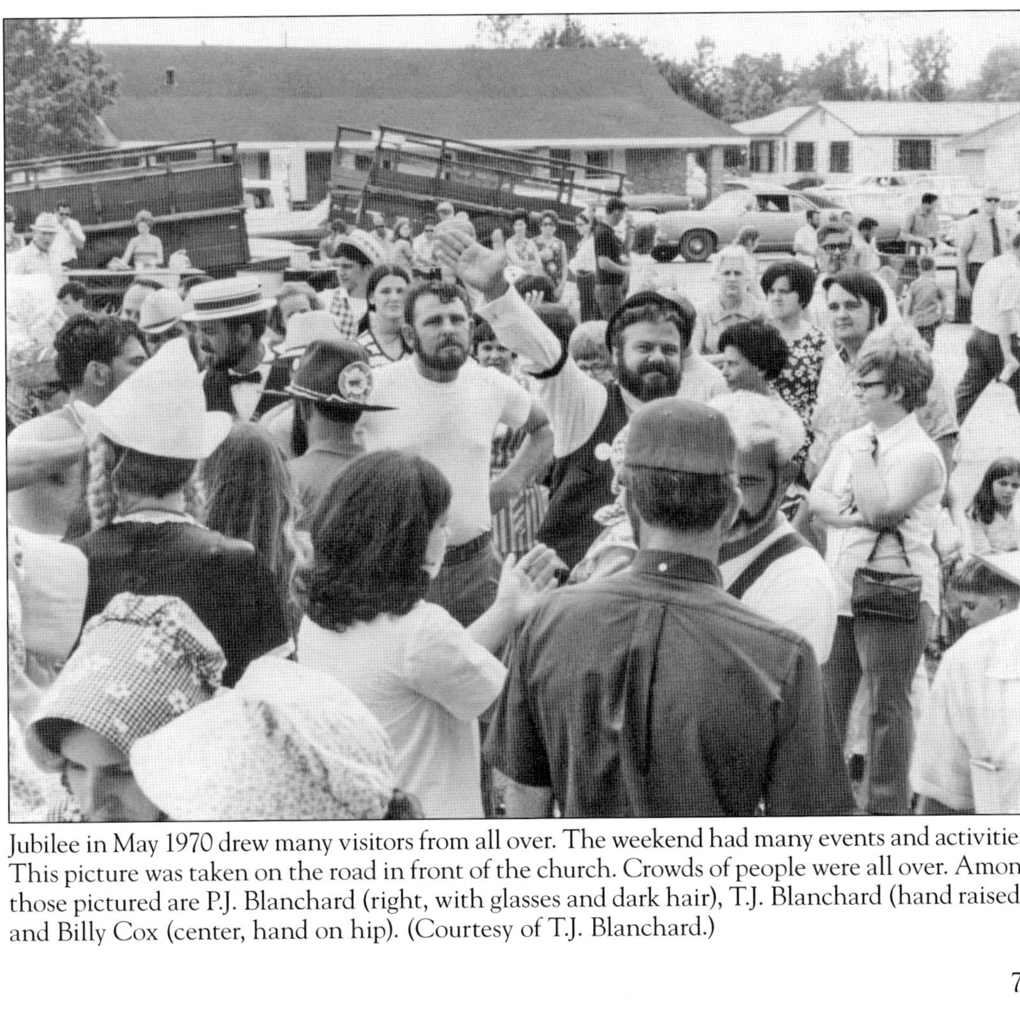

Jubilee in May 1970 drew many visitors from all over. The weekend had many events and activities. This picture was taken on the road in front of the church. Crowds of people were all over. Among those pictured are P.J. Blanchard (right, with glasses and dark hair), T.J. Blanchard (hand raised), and Billy Cox (center, hand on hip). (Courtesy of T.J. Blanchard.)

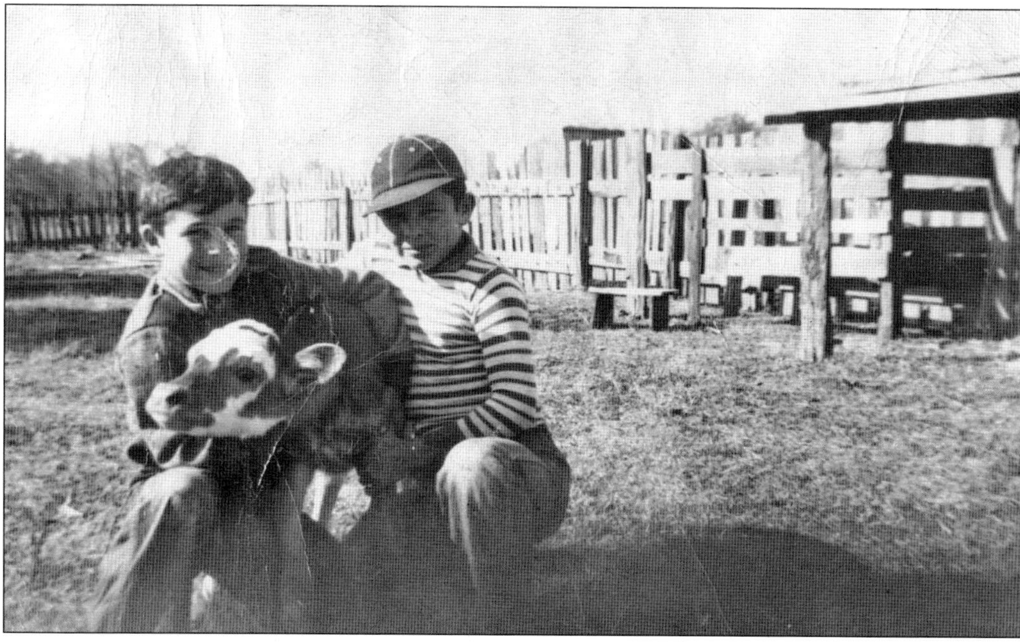

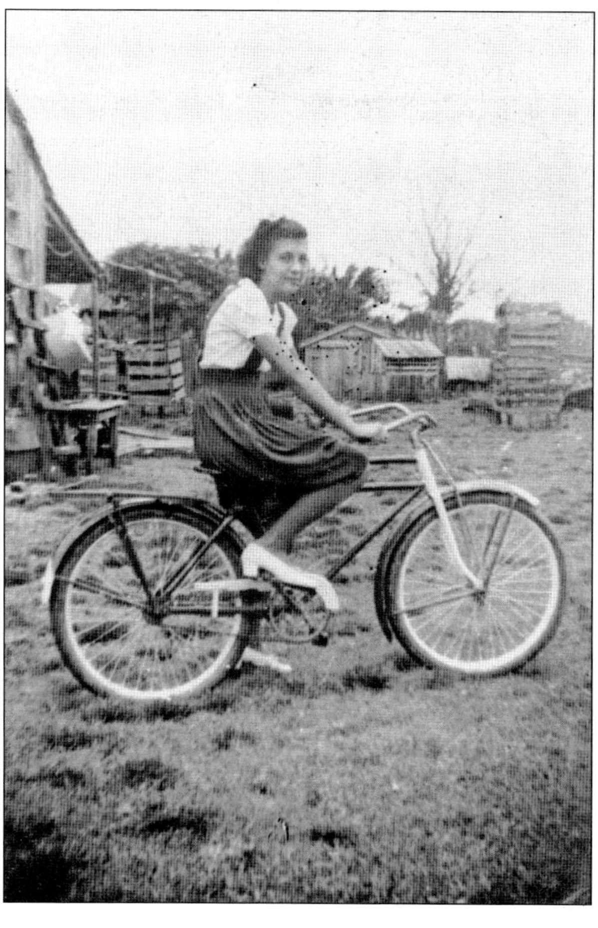

Earl Breaux (left) and Jeffery Breaux hold a baby calf at the home of their grandparents Marie Morales Breaux Hebert and Herbert Breaux in upper Pierre Part. The brothers liked to help and play with the animals. They had chickens, cows, and pigs. (Courtesy of Jackie Breaux Sanchez.)

Beatrice Blanchard Tullier rides her bike in the backyard of her parents, Noe Blanchard and Noelie St. Germain Blanchard. She was 14 years old at the time. She was born on January 17, 1929. Beatrice married Gerald Tullier on January 17, 1954. They had four children. (Courtesy of T.J. Blanchard.)

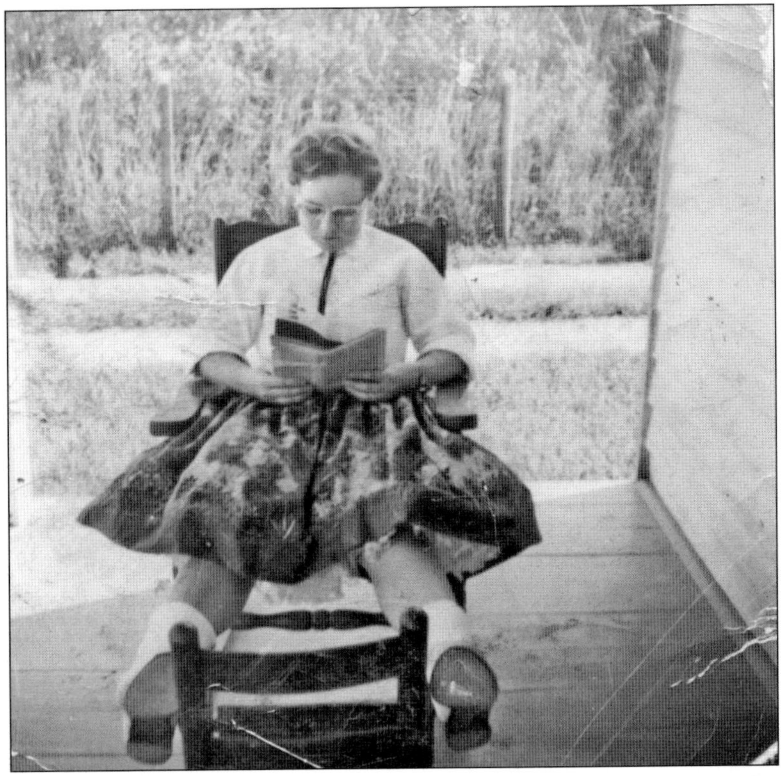

It is a Saturday evening, and 17-year-old Lucille Theriot is all dressed up with her cang-cang skirt, bobby socks, and white shoes ready to go dancing. She sits and reads at home while she waits on her date, A.J. Theriot, in 1958. Her parents were Phillip Theriot and Therese Guillot Theriot. (Courtesy of Lucille Theriot.)

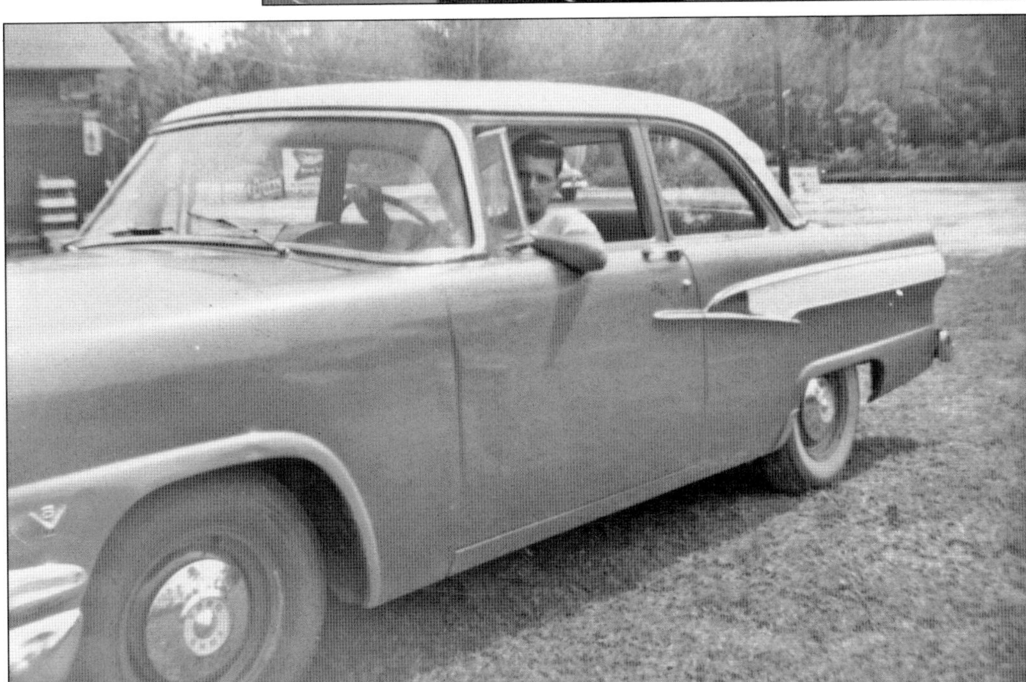

Floyd Cavalier is pictured in his 1956 Ford. Floyd loved to go places in his nice car. He is in Mississippi in this picture. Born on July 1, 1935, he is 21 years old here, waiting for his girl to get ready so they can go riding around town. (Courtesy of Alice Alleman Cavalier.)

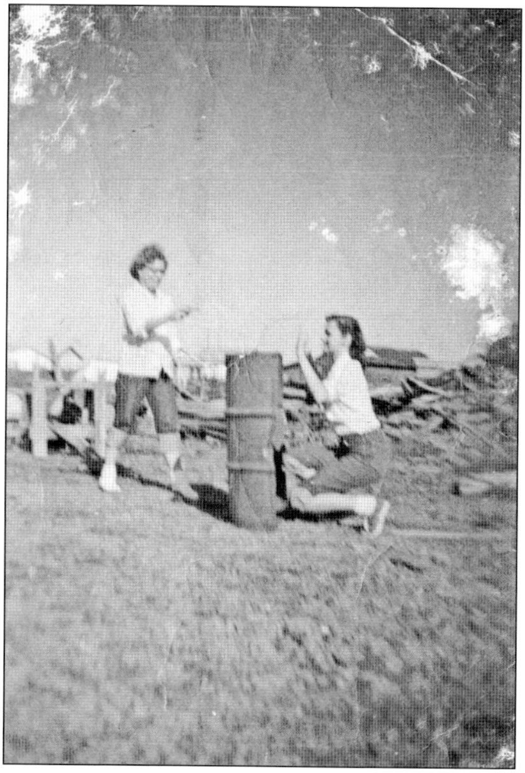

Even as teens, youngsters enjoyed themselves playing outside. With very few toys, they had to do a lot of pretending. Lucille Theriot (left), 16, and LeAnna Theriot Dugas, 17, are playing cowboys. Lucille and LeAnna are cousins and lived near each other. (Courtesy of Lucille Theriot.)

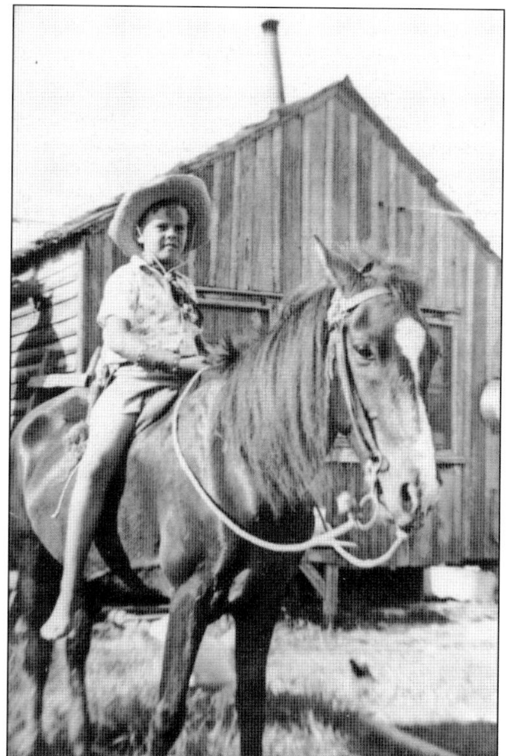

T.J. Blanchard started riding horses when he was five years old. He is pictured at six with his trusty steed Dick in the backyard of his parents, Noe and Noelie St. Germain Blanchard. They had large fields to ride horses in. (Courtesy of T.J. Blanchard.)

Easter in the early 1970s was lots of fun. Everyone gathered to celebrate together. From left to right are (first row) Sullivan Gaudet and Leona Richard Domingue; (second row) JoAnn Gaudet Leal and Phillip "P.J." Richard. (Courtesy of Gustave Joseph Gaudet and Sarah Leonard Gaudet.)

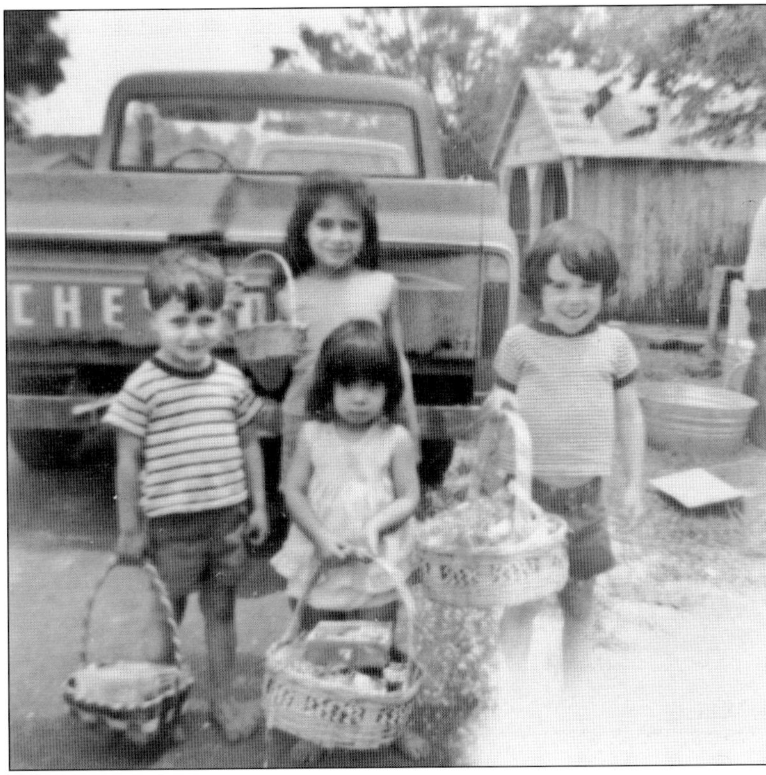

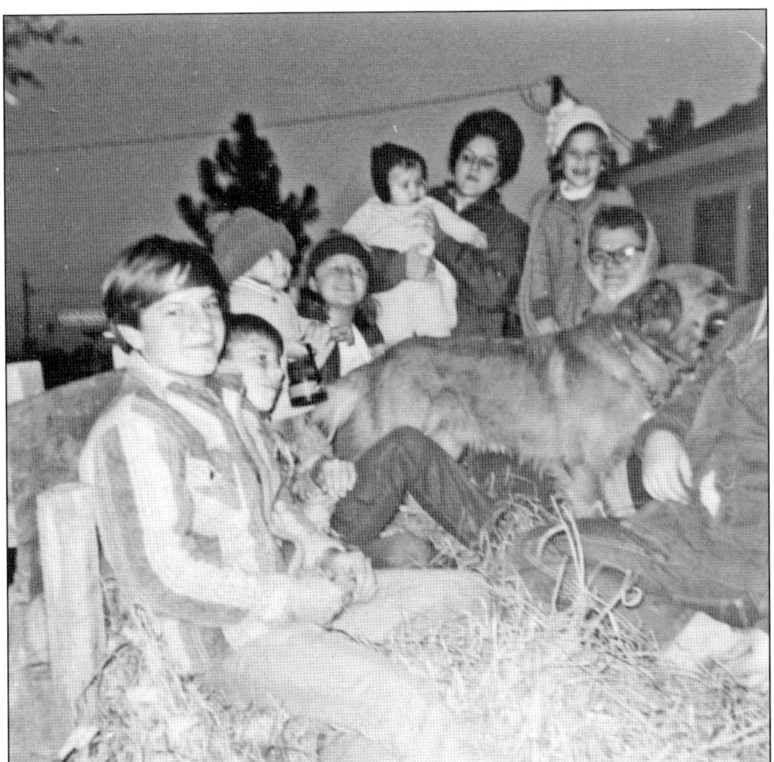

Many loved a good family hayride. It was no different in the Theriot family. At Christmastime in 1970, Leonie Theriot Jr. and Elise Breaux Theriot take their family on a hayride. All bundled up, they are gathered together on the back of the wagon filed with hay. (Courtesy of Dorothy "Dot" Theriot Templet.)

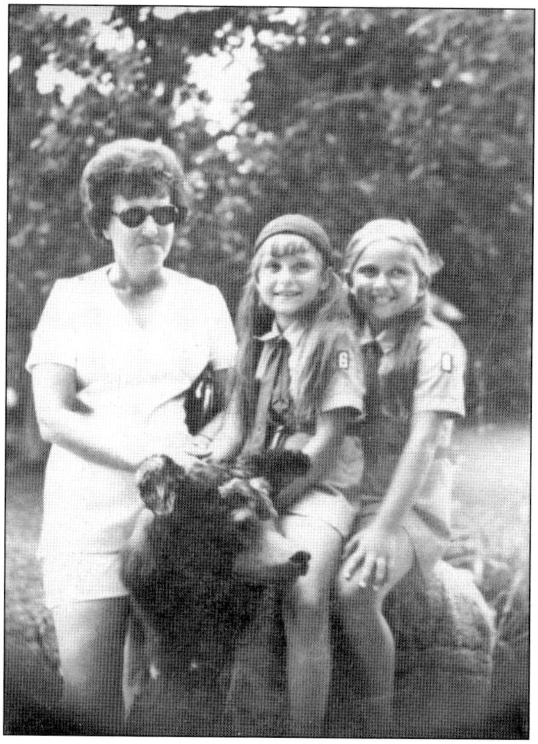

A Girl Scout outing visits the Audubon Zoo and Aquarium in New Orleans. They enjoyed themselves in the playground. From left to right are Alice Alleman Cavalier and her daughters Loretta Cavalier Domingue and Lillian "Missy" Cavalier Lang. Lillian was named after her grandmother. (Courtesy of Alice Alleman Cavalier.)

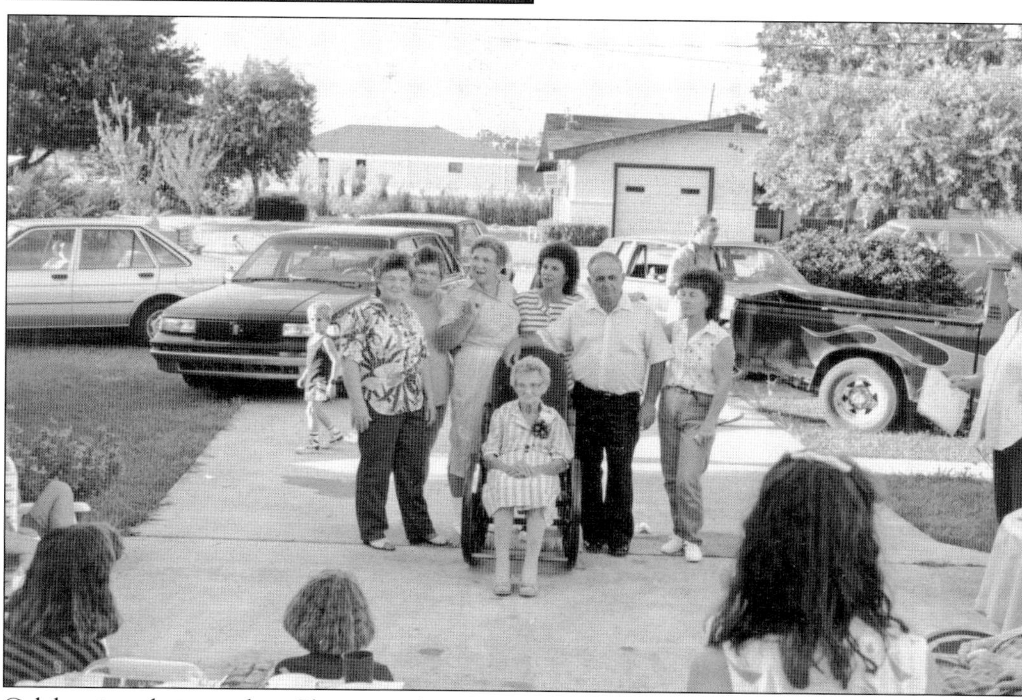

Celebrating their mother Clemence Aucoin Cavalier Domingue's birthday are, from left to right, Elsie Cavalier, Thelma Cavalier Morales, Lillian Cavalier Gros Leonard, Lucy Cavalier Daigle, Armond Cavalier, and Inez Cavalier Leonard. Other children of Clemence not pictured are Clement Cavalier, Floyd Cavalier, and Lloyd Cavalier. (Courtesy of Elsie Cavalier Cavalier.)

A party to celebrate Rebecca "Becky" Daigle's birthday was attended by lots of family and friends. Among those pictured are Becky, Jeffery Carlin, Gregory Dupre, Barbara Landry Sutton, Janice Landry Gaudet, Glenda Metrejean, Rodney Metrejean, Bradley Richard, Jennifer, Pam, Randy Carline, Tilsey, Doreen, Veronica, Bobby, Kathleen Dupre Hebert, Georgina, and Geneve. (Courtesy of Joseph "Joe" Daigle and Mary Ann "Marion" Gaudet Daigle.)

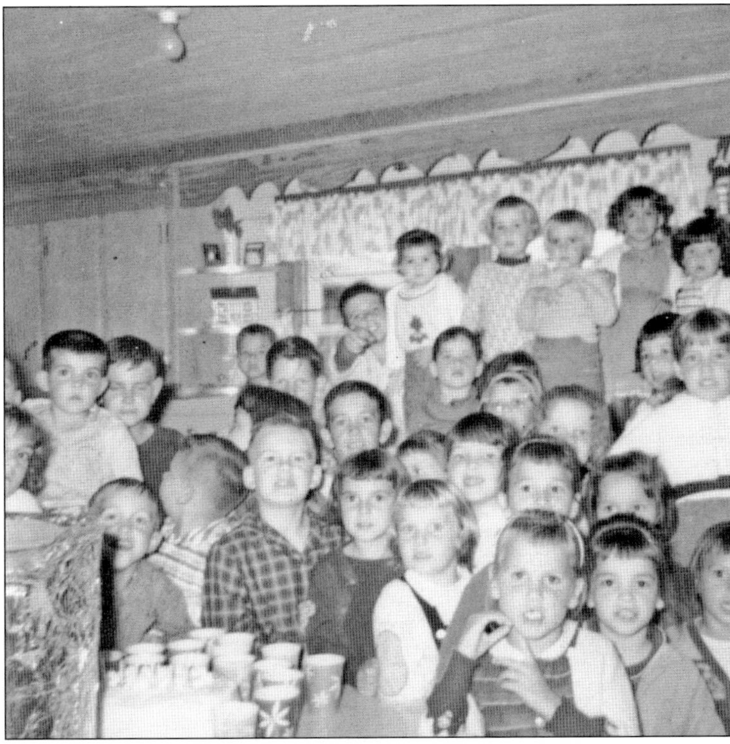

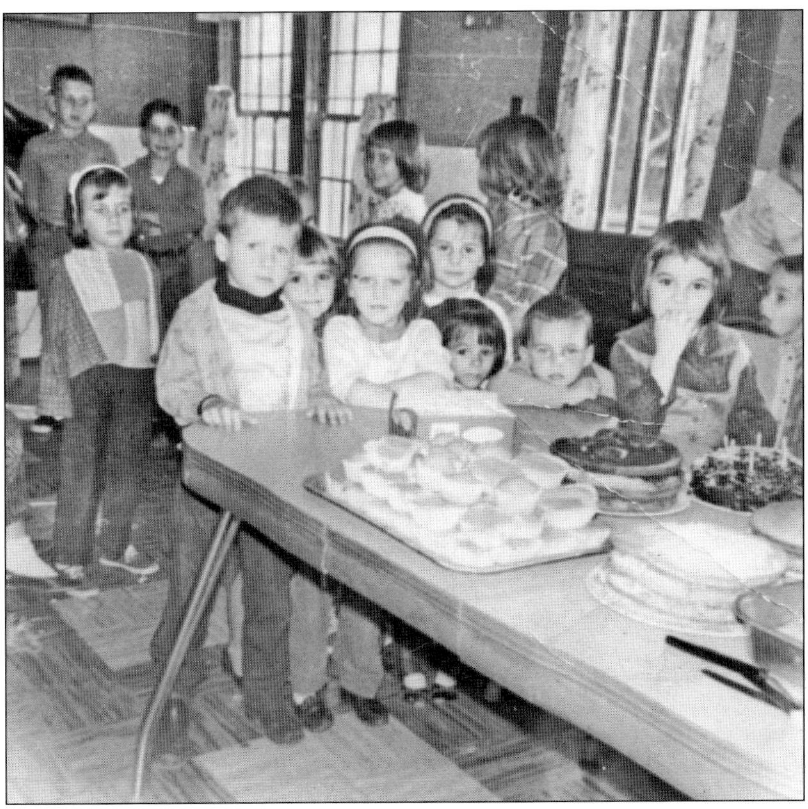

A birthday party at the Mabile house includes, from left to right, (in back) two unidentified, Nelson Mabile, and Karen Mabile; (around the table) Carl Mabile, Arlene Mabile Blanchard, Sheila Mabile Cavalier, Christine Mabile Leonard, Cindy Mabile Grandin, possibly Raleigh St. Germain Jr., and Rita Mabile Barras. (Courtesy of Leonard Mabile and Regina Dupuis Mabile.)

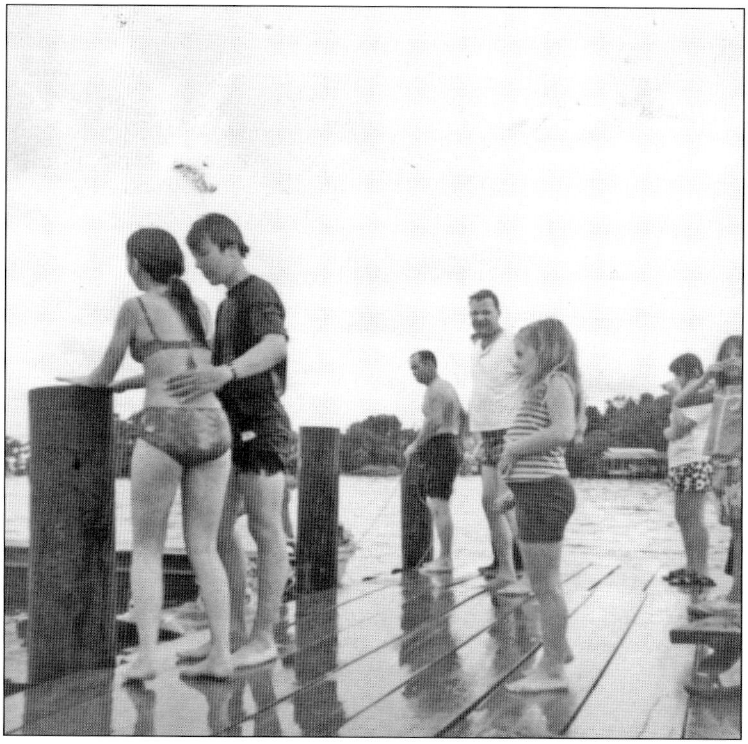

Summertime was always fun at Ed Lee's wharf on beautiful Lake Verret, with a camp across the street from the wharf. From left to right are Cheryl Bosarge, Tommy Corley, Lloyd Landry, and Ferrel Bosarge; the others are unidentified. (Courtesy of Glenda Landry McGraw.)

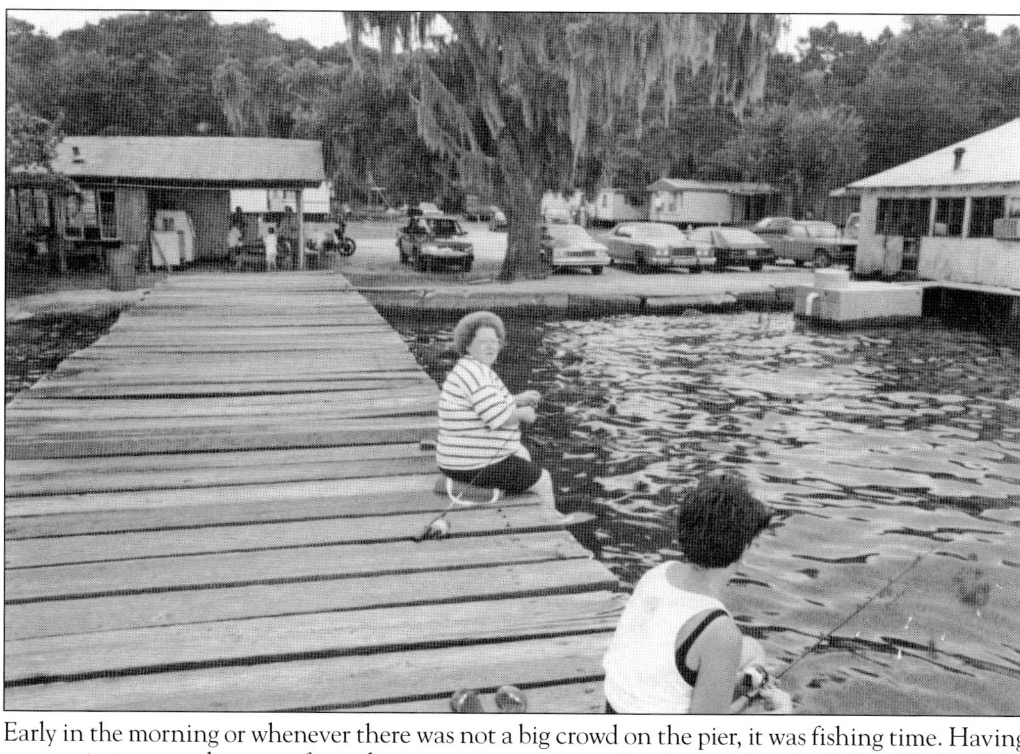

Early in the morning or whenever there was not a big crowd on the pier, it was fishing time. Having a camp just across the street from the pier was convenient for the Landrys, including Birdie (left) and her daughter Wendy Landry Thibodeaux. (Courtesy of Glenda Landry McGraw.)

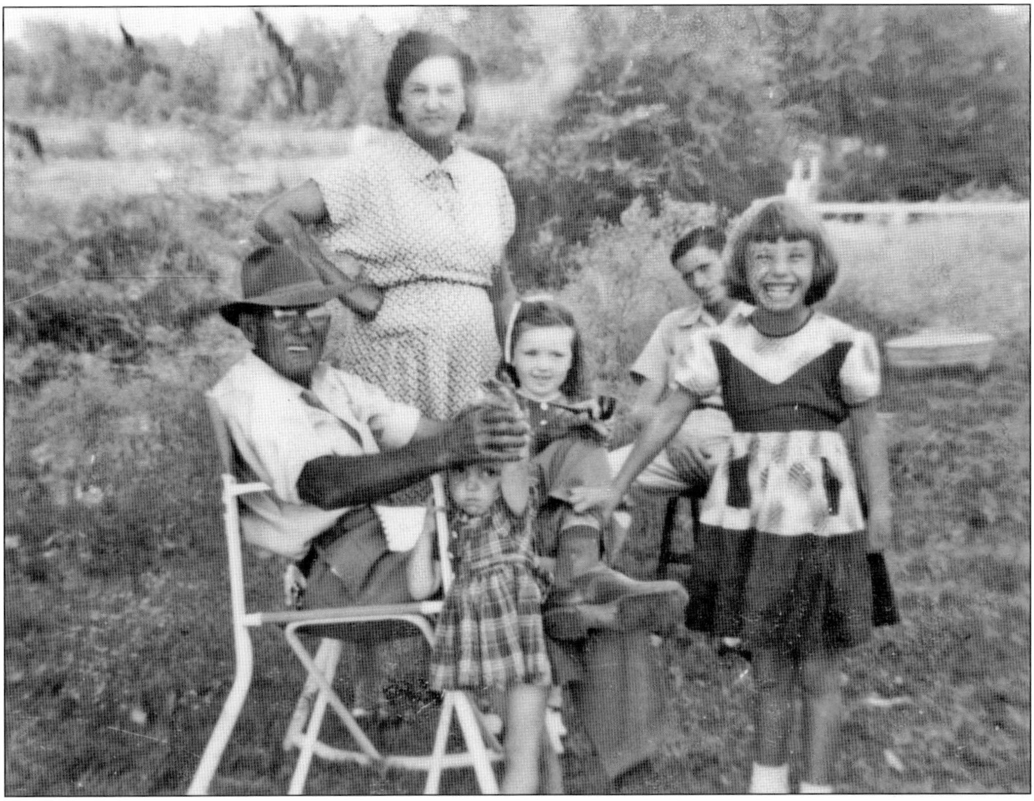

A visit to Vacherie was always a nice time. From left to right are (sitting) Daily Alleman holding three-year-old Barbara Cavalier Domingue by the hand, Irma Jean Mathern, Brenda Cavalier Domingue Cavalier, Lillian McCarthy Alleman, and Irvin "Red" Mathern. (Courtesy of Alice Alleman Cavalier.)

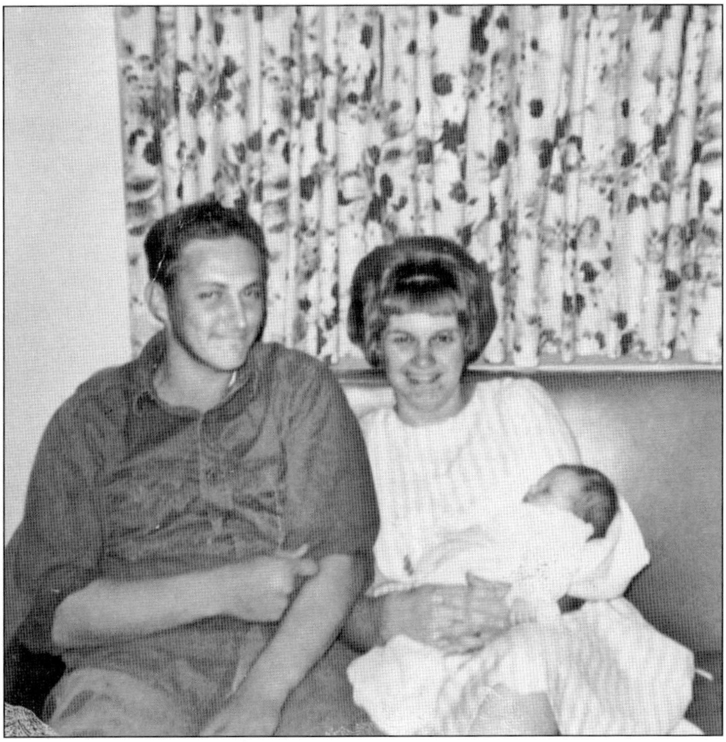

Charles Crochet and Geraldine Carline Crochet and their daughter Tonya Crochet Olivier are pictured in December 1966. They look very happy with their new baby. (Courtesy of Tonya Crochet Olivier.)

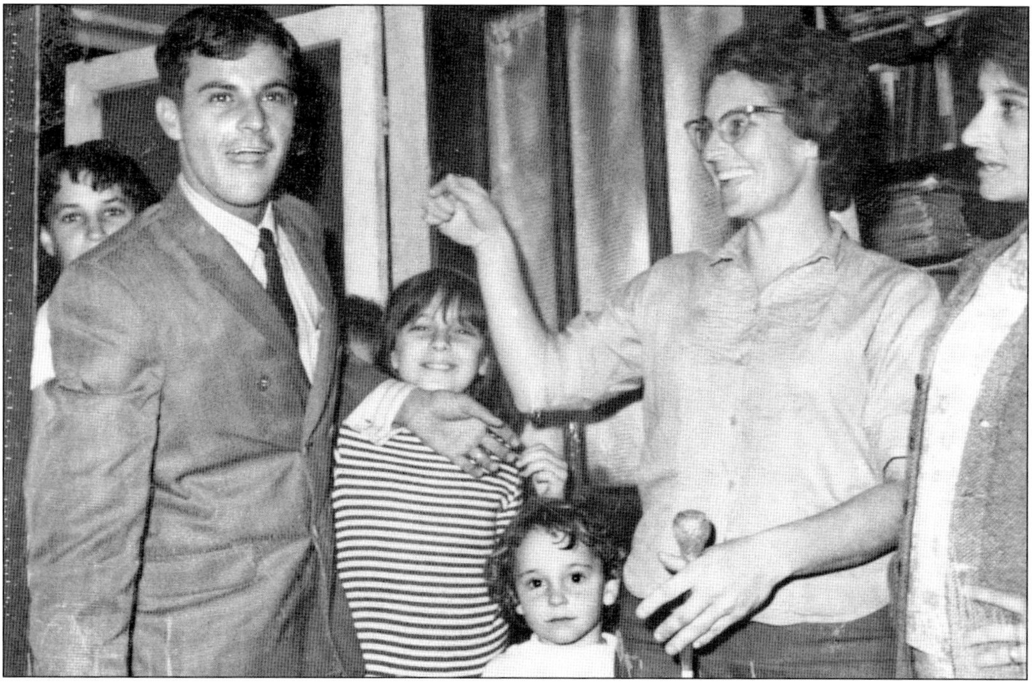

At a family get together, everyone is happy to see each other. Those faces bring back fond memories of happy times. From left to right are unidentified, Earl Crochet, Susan Landry Blanchard Coupel, Donna Guillot, Maude Crochet Landry, and Annabelle Crochet. (Courtesy of Tonya Crochet Olivier.)

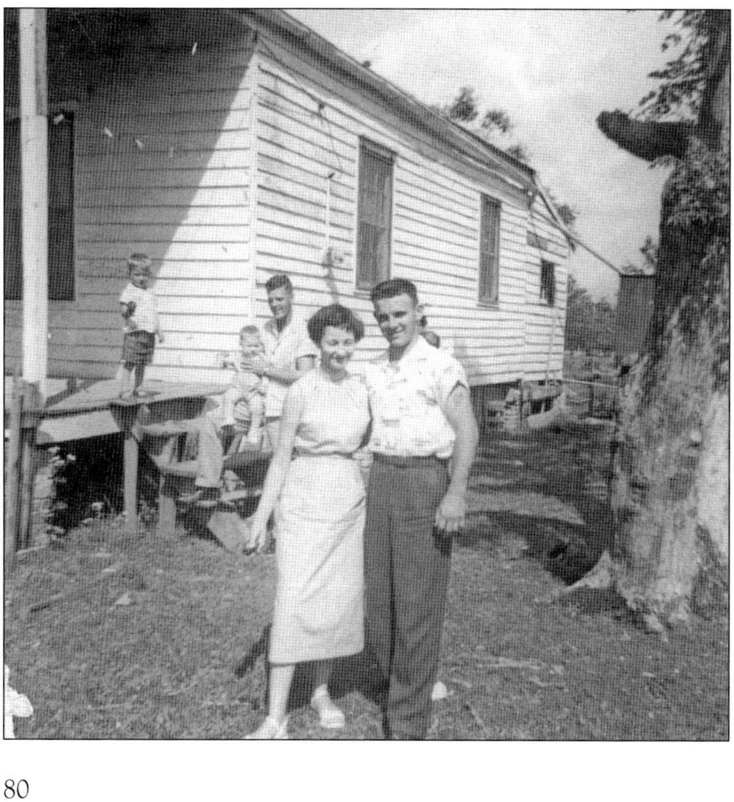

Cecile Guillot Mabile and Carroll Mabile are standing in their front yard, while E.J. Blanchard sits on the steps holding his youngest son. E.J.'s oldest son, Kirby Blanchard, stands on the front porch. This picture was taken in the late 1950s. (Courtesy of Cecile Guillot Mabile.)

Martille J. Alleman and Antoinette Rivere Alleman are pictured at their Pierre Part home in 1942. They were the parents of Daily Alleman. Martille was born on March 15, 1877, and passed away on February 13, 1942. Antoinette was born January on 11, 1879, and passed away on September 8, 1963. (Courtesy of Alice Alleman Cavalier.)

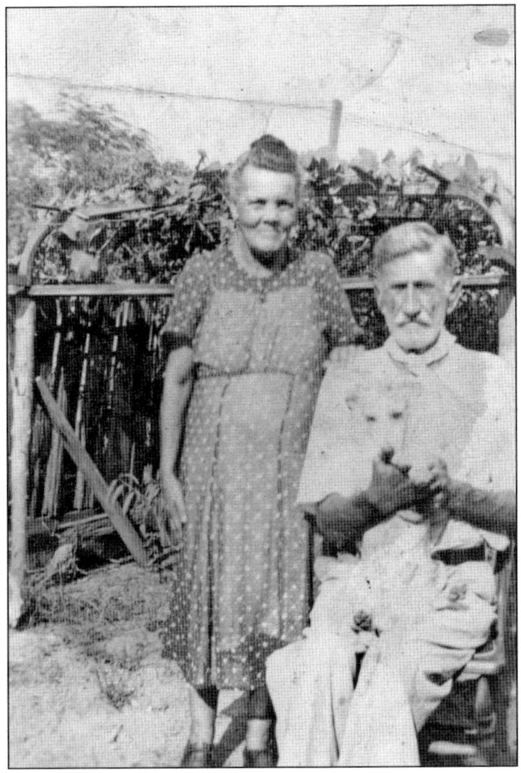

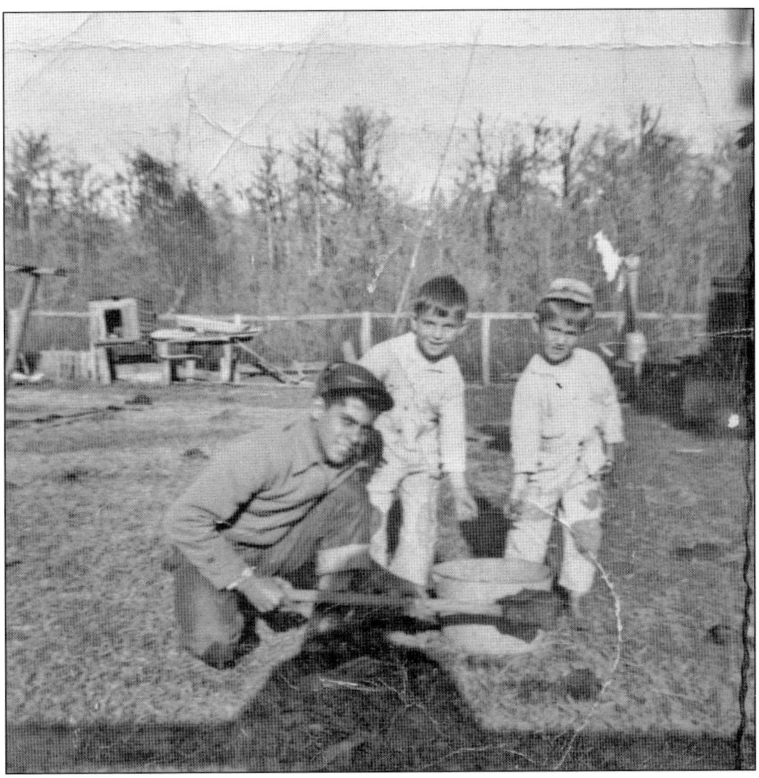

At an early age, children had daily chores. One of Shelby Gaudet's chores was to pick up the cow manure out in the yard. Here, Shelby shovels manure while Elwood Metrejean (center) and Lanson Metrejean help hold the tub. (Courtesy of Joseph "Joe" Daigle and Mary Ann "Marion" Gaudet Daigle.)

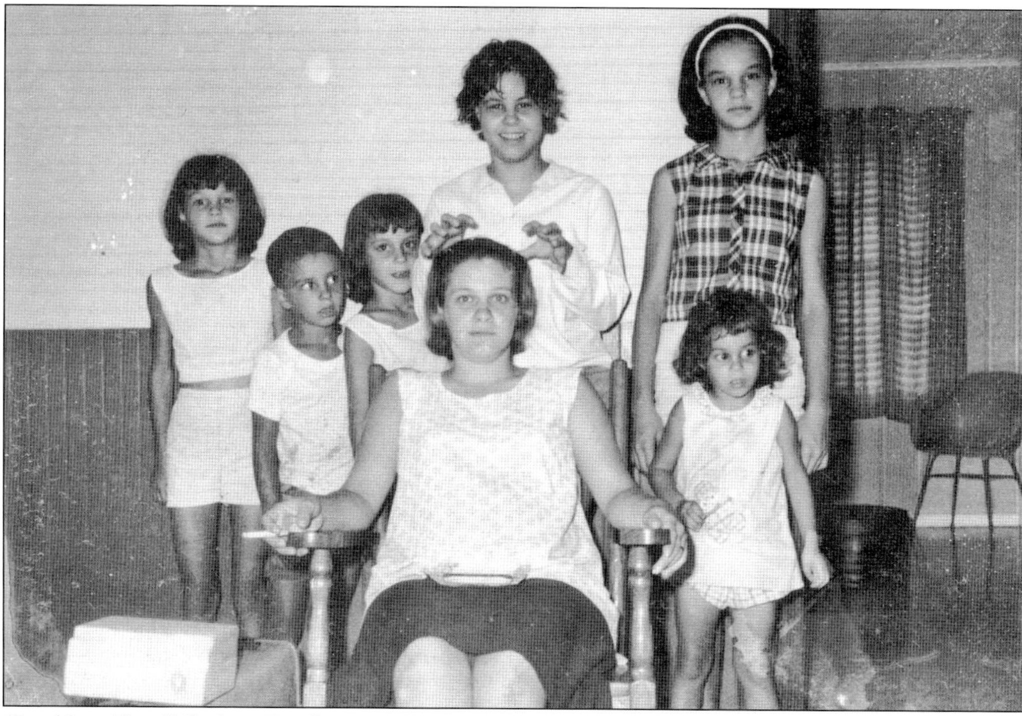

Geraldine "Jean" Carline Crochet is pregnant, so she is relaxing with her feet up. She is pictured with her sister-in-law's children (from left to right), Pam Templet Alleman, Timmy Templet, Kim Templet Sanchez, Susan Templet Dugas, Myra Templet Blank Blanchard, and Lena Templet Alleman. Susan is fixing to scare her or mess with her hair. (Courtesy of Tonya Crochet Olivier.)

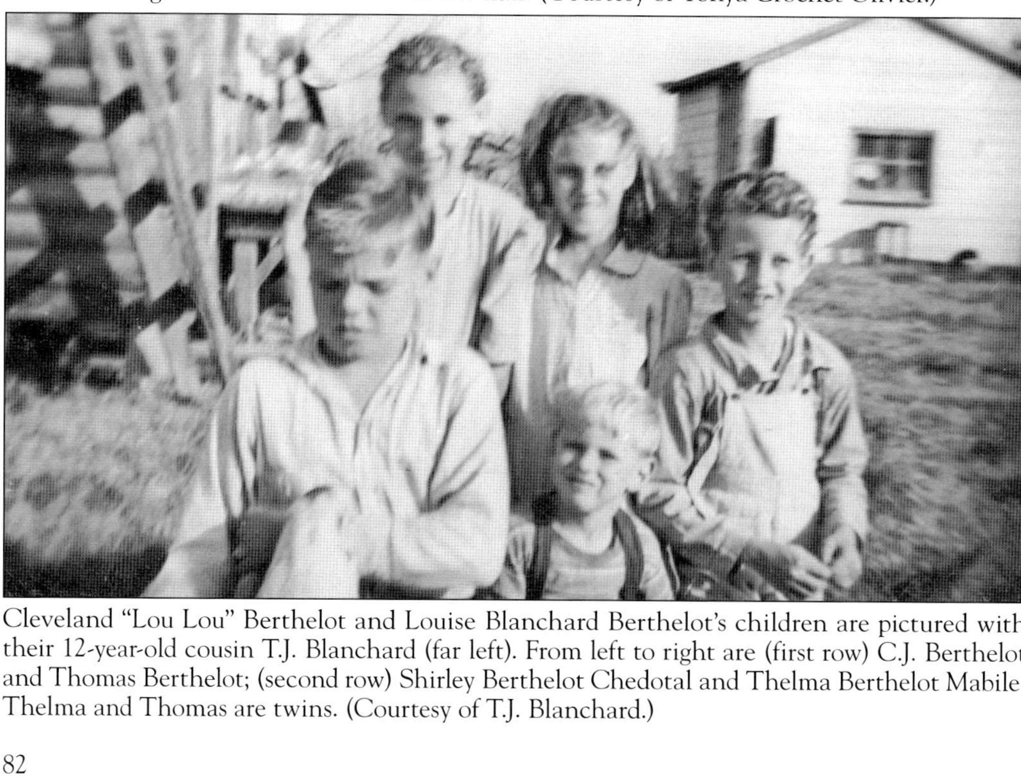

Cleveland "Lou Lou" Berthelot and Louise Blanchard Berthelot's children are pictured with their 12-year-old cousin T.J. Blanchard (far left). From left to right are (first row) C.J. Berthelot and Thomas Berthelot; (second row) Shirley Berthelot Chedotal and Thelma Berthelot Mabile. Thelma and Thomas are twins. (Courtesy of T.J. Blanchard.)

Therese Guillot Theriot enjoys the outdoors with 10-month-old Cecile Guillot Mabile. Cecile loved her aunt Therese and enjoyed being lifted up in the air and then back down. (Courtesy of Brenda Landry Templet and Norbert Templet.)

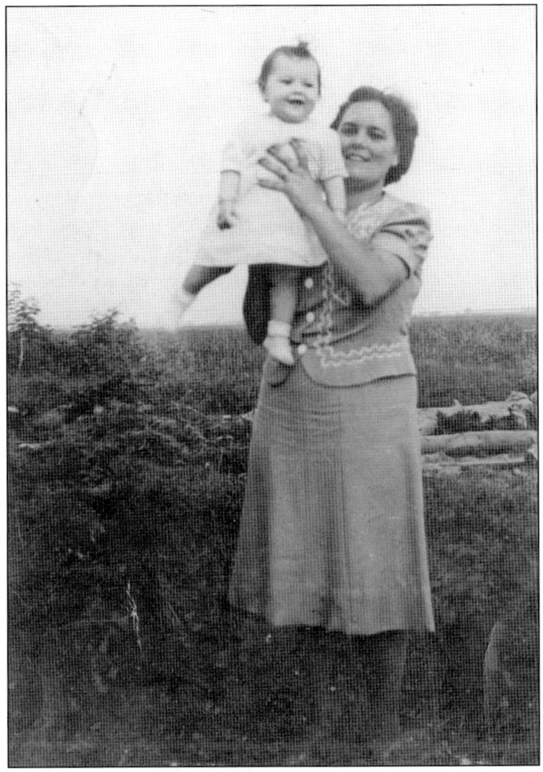

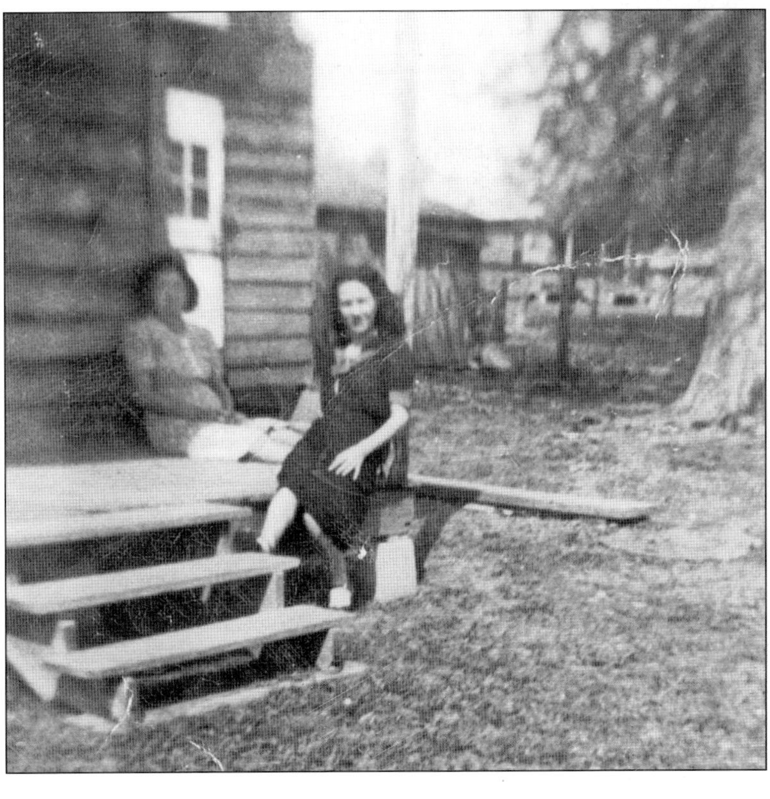

The little house across from the school and graveyard has many fond memories. Lillian McCarthy Alleman sits on the front porch with her daughter Gladys Alleman Mathern. When all the work is done, the front porch is the place to be. Everyone loved to sit on their porch. (Courtesy of Alice Alleman Cavalier.)

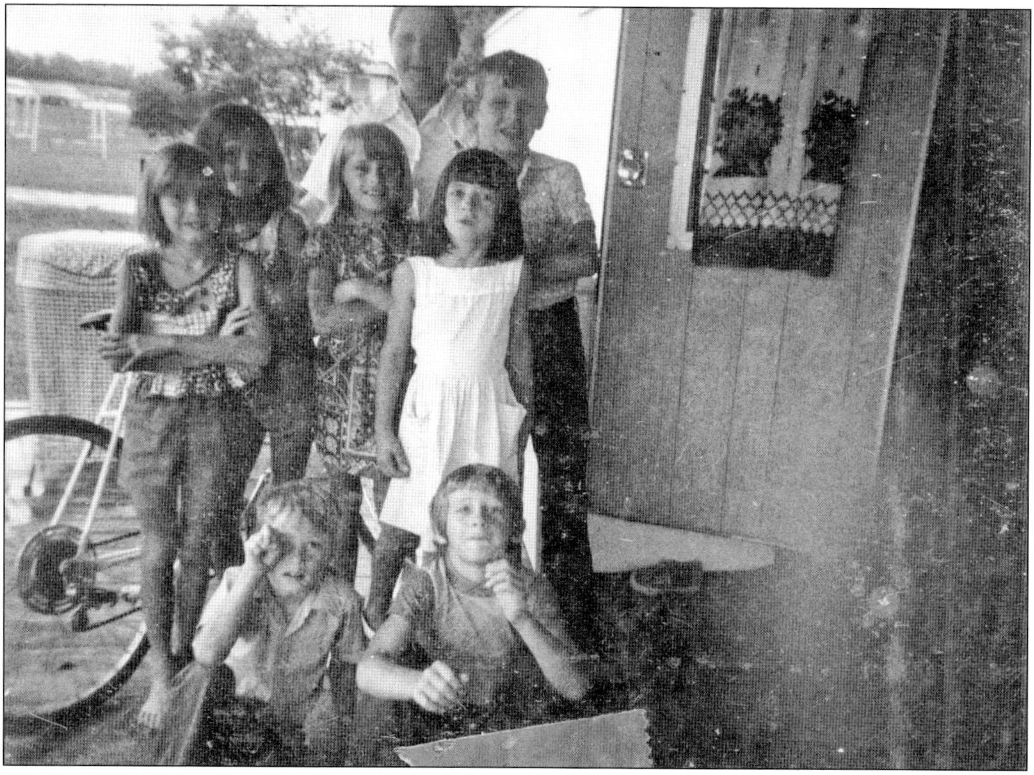

The Blanchard and Gros children are, from left to right, (first row) Carl Blanchard and Michael Gros; (second row) Carla Blanchard Dartez and Paula Gros in a white dress; (third row) Charlotte Blanchard Ratcliff, Gertrude Gros Sanchez, and Lovelace Gros Jr.; (fourth row) Carol Gros Charlet. (Courtesy of Carol Gros Charlet.)

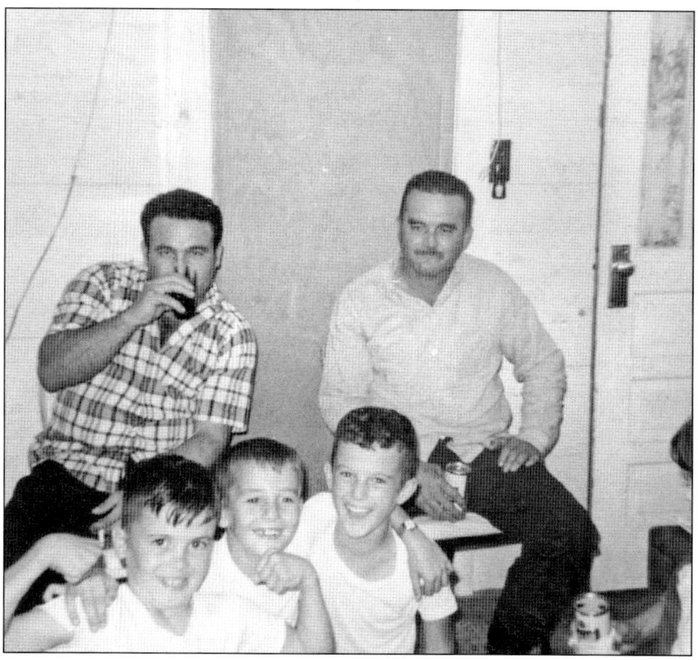

Marie Morales Breaux Hebert loved it when her family would get together at her house down the bay. From left to right are (first row) Bogette, Wayne, and Woody Breaux; (second row) Earl and Galbert Breaux. Bogette, Wayne, and Woody loved to play together, and Earl and Galbert enjoyed watching the boys horse around. (Courtesy of Jackie Breaux Sanchez.)

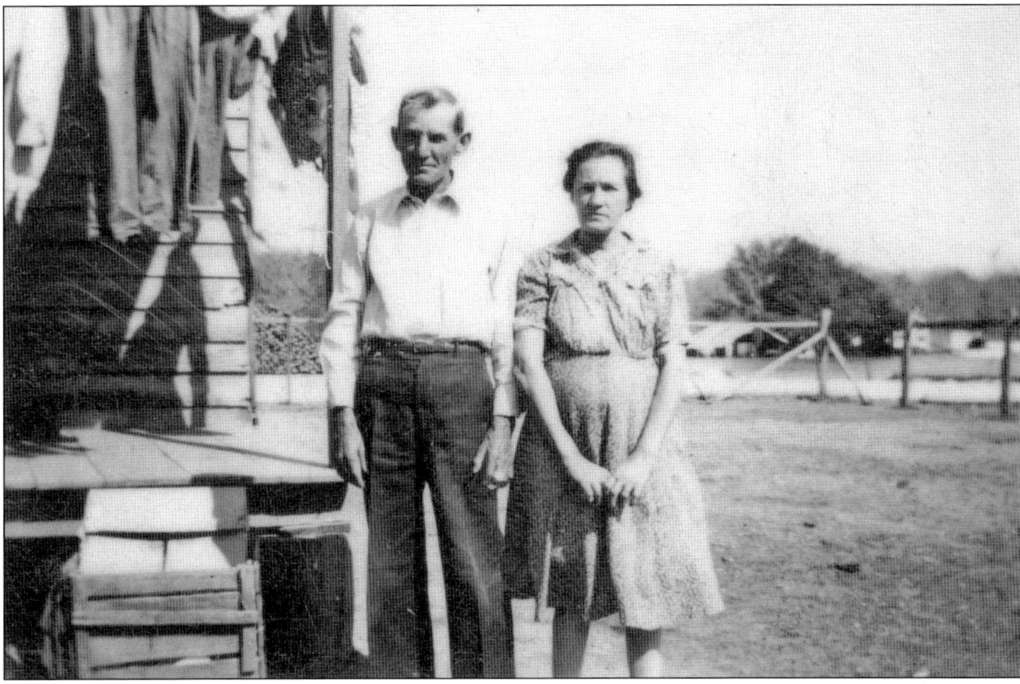

Clay Templet and his wife, Egladie Hebert Templet, had 10 children. In 1940, Clay and Egladie were in a tornado that took the lives of many of their friends and family. Egladie had all the bones in her arm crushed. With no doctors around, she had to stay like that. Clay had many cuts and scrapes. (Courtesy of Frank Templet.)

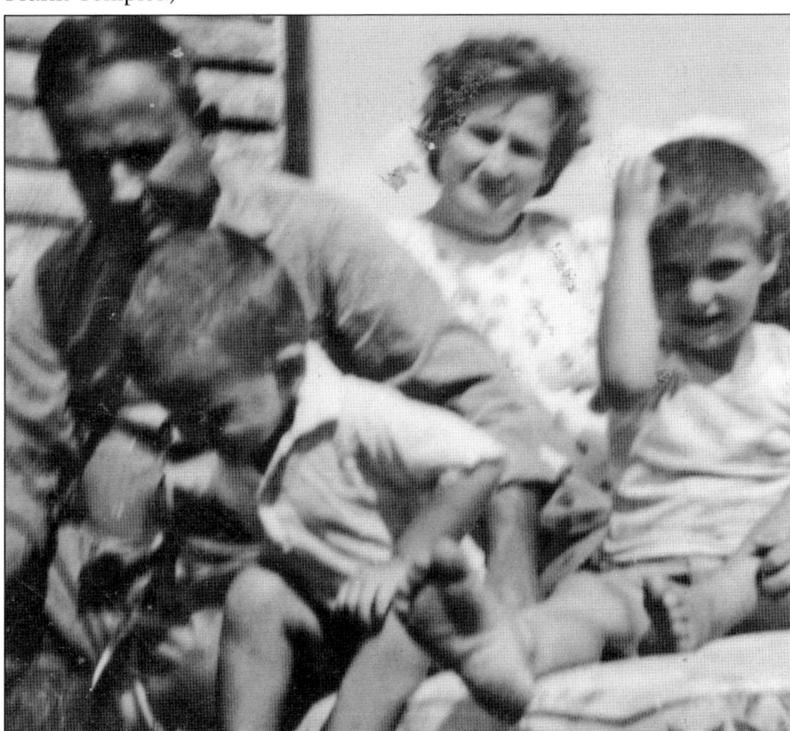

Armand Cavalier Sr. and Angelle Hebert Cavalier are pictured with their two youngest boys at the time, Armand "June" Cavalier Jr. (left) and Randy Cavalier (right). It is hard to see, but June has put a cigar in his mouth, does not like it, and is trying to spit it out. (Courtesy of Judy Cavalier Breaux.)

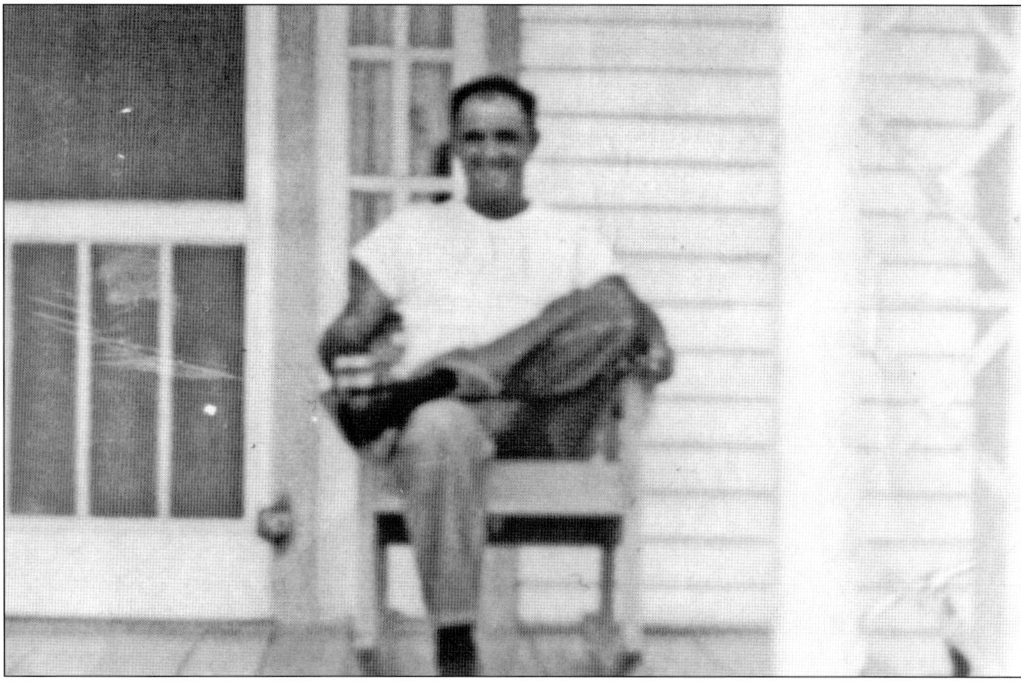

Alphonse Daigle enjoys the rocker on his front porch. Every day he would sit in his rocker and watch the cars go by. He was born on September 12, 1922, and passed away on October 25, 1976, at the young age of 54. He married Gertie Domingue Daigle and they had three children. Gertie had a daughter before she married Alphonse, who he also raised. (Courtesy of Dave Daigle and Tilsey Fryou Daigle.)

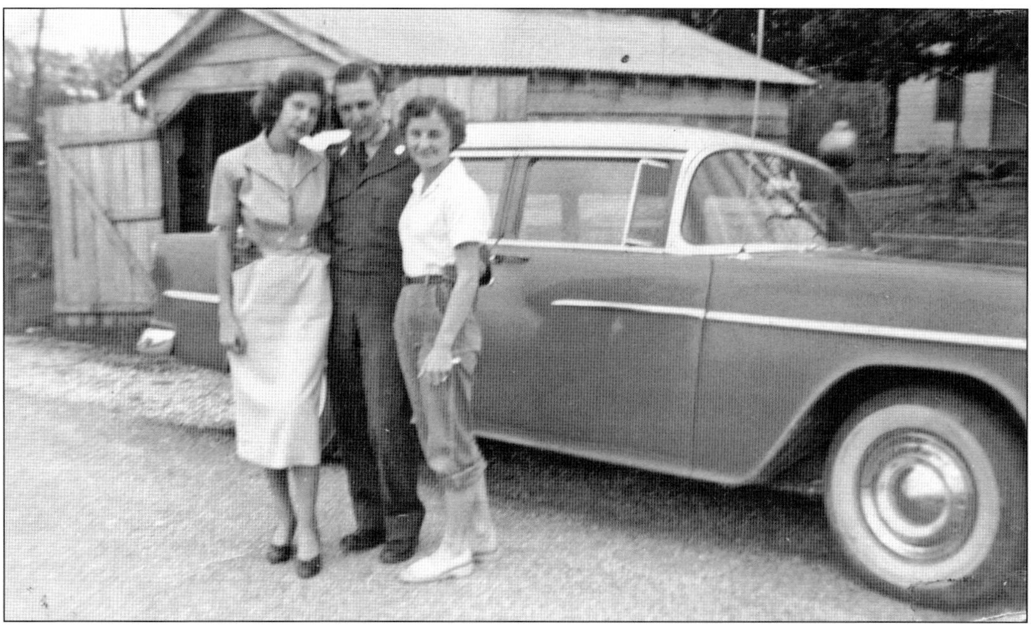

Rene "R.J." Landry has just returned from Korea and is pictured with his wife, Betty Verette Landry (left), and cousin Effie Landry (right). They are standing in the road in front of the house. (Courtesy of Dave Daigle and Tilsey Fryou Daigle.)

Lillian Mabile Chedotal (left) and her brother Russel Mabile (right) are pictured in the yard of Gervais Mabile. On the left is the kitchen of their house. The house was turned into a grocery store on North Bay Road. (Courtesy of Lillian Mabile Chedotal.)

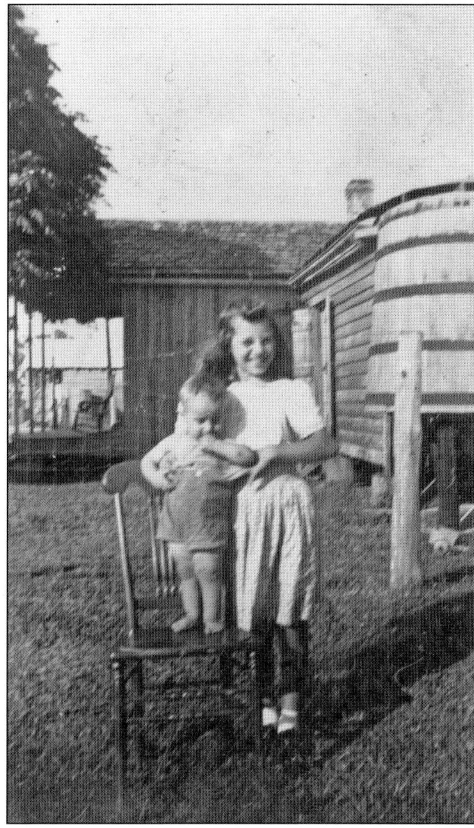

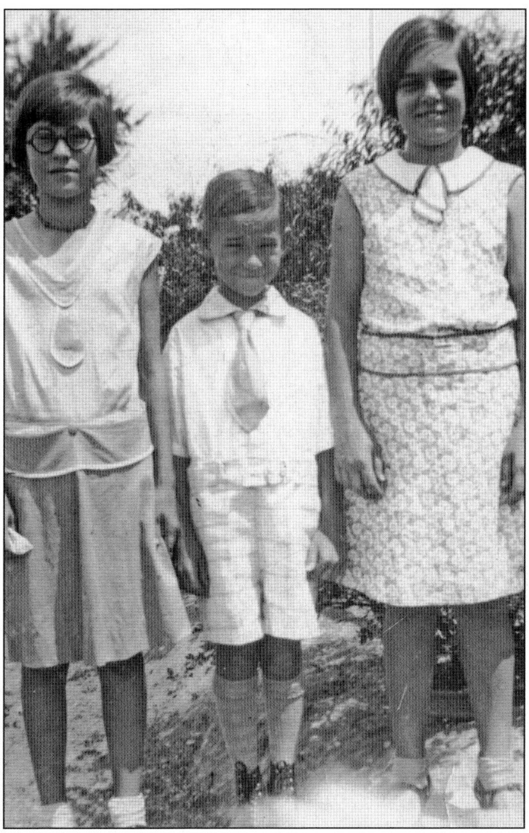

Pictured from left to right are Rosa Guillot Blanchard, Gerald Guillot, and Therese Guillot. This picture had to be taken in the mid-1920s. They are the children of Oilbert Guillot and Bernadette Templet Guillot. They are all dressed up for some occasion. (Courtesy of Brenda Landry Templet and Nobert Templet.)

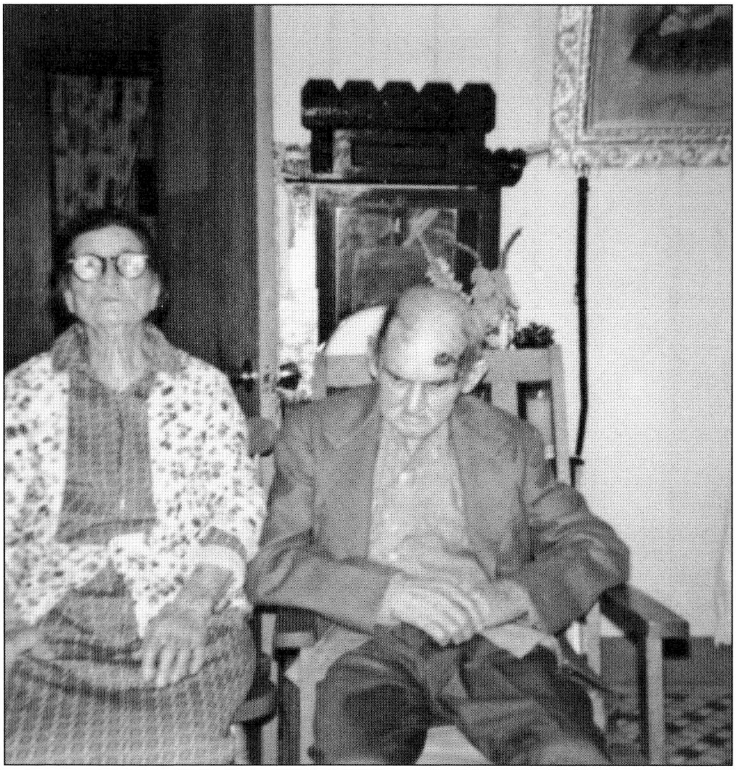

Lorena "Gram Nana" Landry Templet is pictured with Bernard Templet. He loved his rocking chair. They were very poor but they were some of the best people in the world. She was born in 1891 and died on March 4, 1988, at the age of 97. (Courtesy of Brenda Landry Templet and Nobert Templet.)

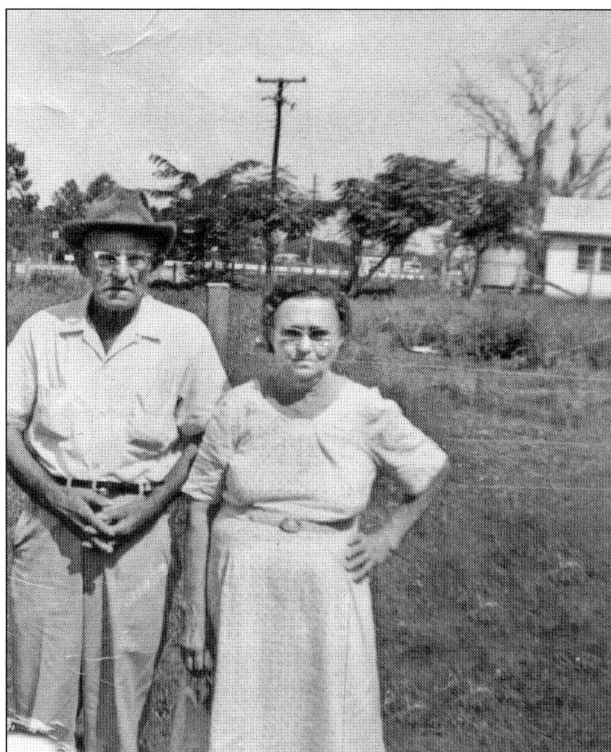

Richard Mabile and Altha Theriot Mabile had six children. Richard was born on February 14, 1896, and died on May 9, 1962, at the age of 66. Altha was born on March 21, 1900, and died on October 27, 1993, at the age of 93. They are seen here standing in their yard. (Courtesy of Leonard Mabile and Regina Dupuis Mabile.)

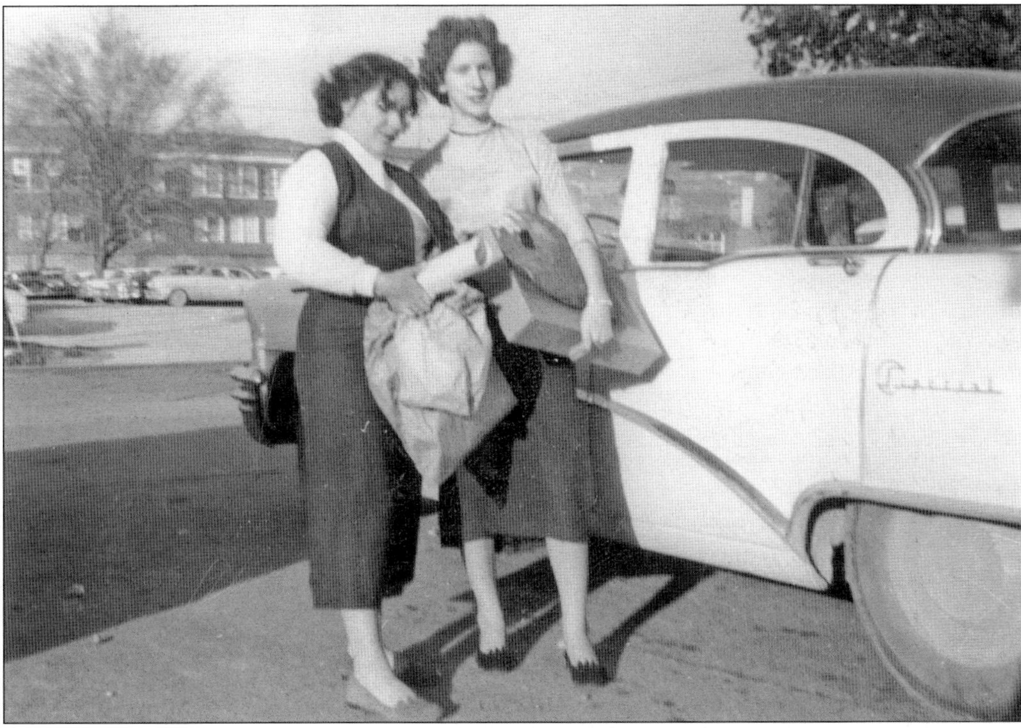

This picture was taken in Baton Rouge on a shopping trip. Lula Mae (left) and Betty Verette Landry were best friends. Lula Mae brought Betty shopping all day long in Baton Rouge. It is not known if Betty was married or not at the time. (Courtesy of Dave Daigle and Tilsey Fryou Daigle.)

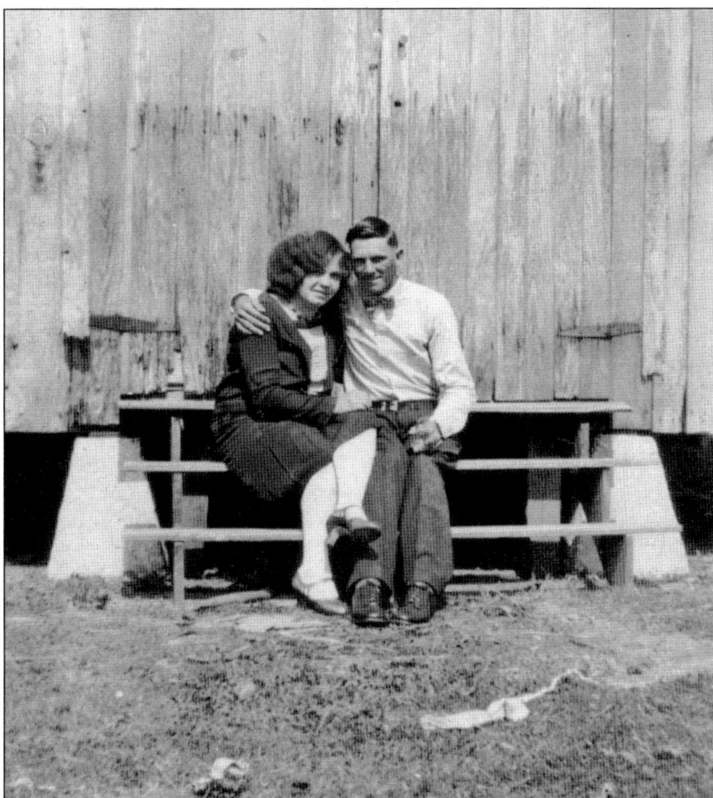

Rudolph Theriot was born on January 6, 1909, and passed away on March 16, 1989. His parents were Alcee Zephirin Theriot and Lucia Maria Templet Theriot. Rudolph's wife, Nolia Giroir Theriot, was born in 1901 and passed away in 1978. They had two children. (Courtesy of Lucille Theriot.)

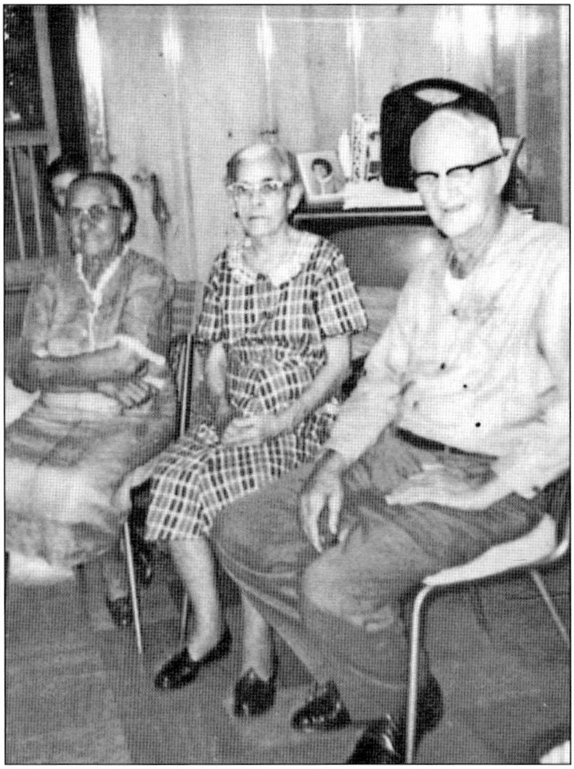

It is not known what the occasion was for this picture. From left to right are Evelyn Theriot Simoneaux (poking her head out), Georgiana Crochet Theriot, Bernadette Templet Guillot, and Leonie Theriot Sr. Georgiana and Leonie are husband and wife and Evelyn's grandparents. (Courtesy of Lucille Theriot.)

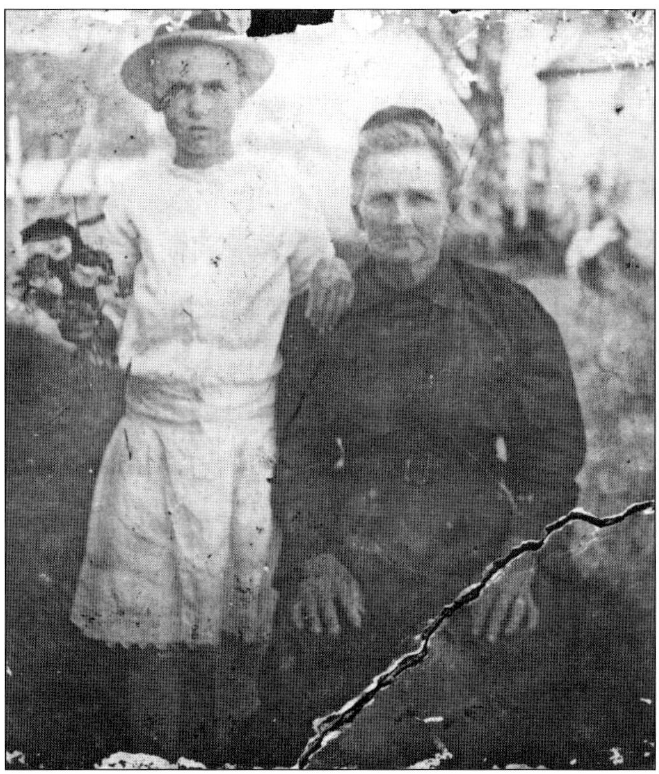

Adele Hebert Cavalier is pictured with her mother, Ozila "Gram Toot" Berthelot Hebert. Gram Toot was a midwife who delivered many babies in Pierre Part and Bayou Pigeon. When it was time for a baby to come into the world, people would go by Gram Toot's house and pick her up and take her to their house. (Courtesy of Frank Templet.)

Anthony "Tony" Rogacki (left) and brother-in-law Lloyd Matherne Sr. are pictured in front of Paul and Christine Breaux Matherne's home down the bay on furlough. Tony was a native of Buffalo, New York, and was stationed in New Orleans during World War II. It was there that he met May Matherne, sister of Lloyd Matherne, and they married a few months later. Lloyd also served in the Army and was stationed in France. (Courtesy of Nadine Theriot.)

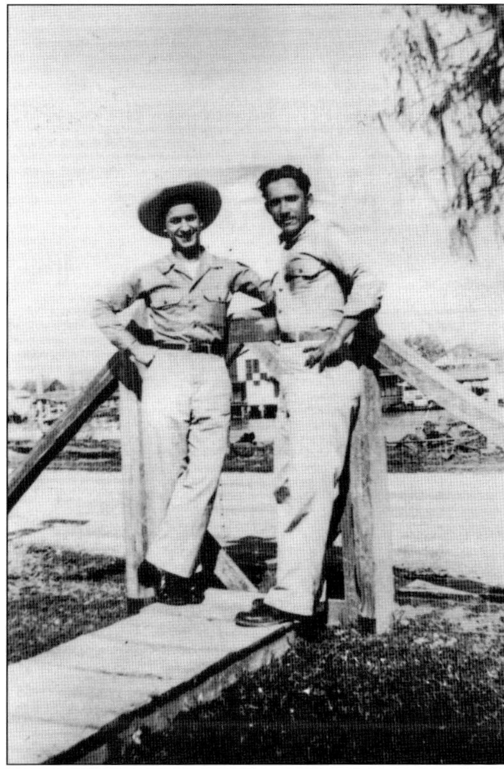

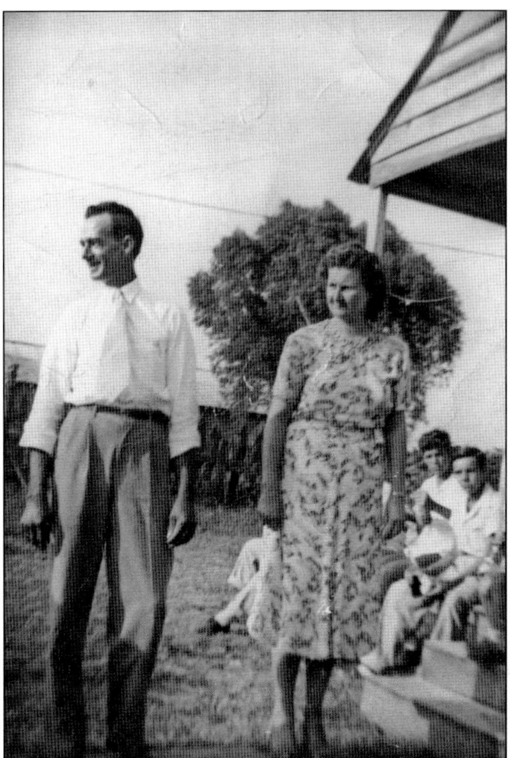

Reno and Faustina Blanchard Crochet are pictured on their porch with some boys. They are in their Sunday best. Reno was born on January 14, 1912, and passed away on April 18, 2007. Faustina was born on May 30, 1919, and passed away on January 7, 1994. (Courtesy of T.J. Blanchard.)

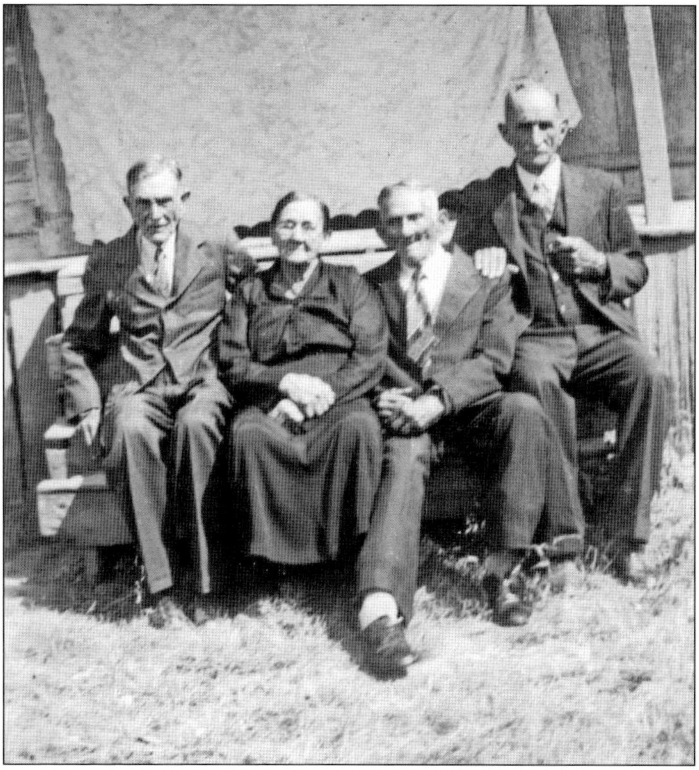

From left to right are siblings Jean Baptist, Aimee, Edvidge, and Lusignan Blanchard. Their parents are Timothe Arsene Blanchard and Adeline Henneritette Crochet Blanchard. This picture was taken in the early 20th century. (Courtesy of T.J. Blanchard.)

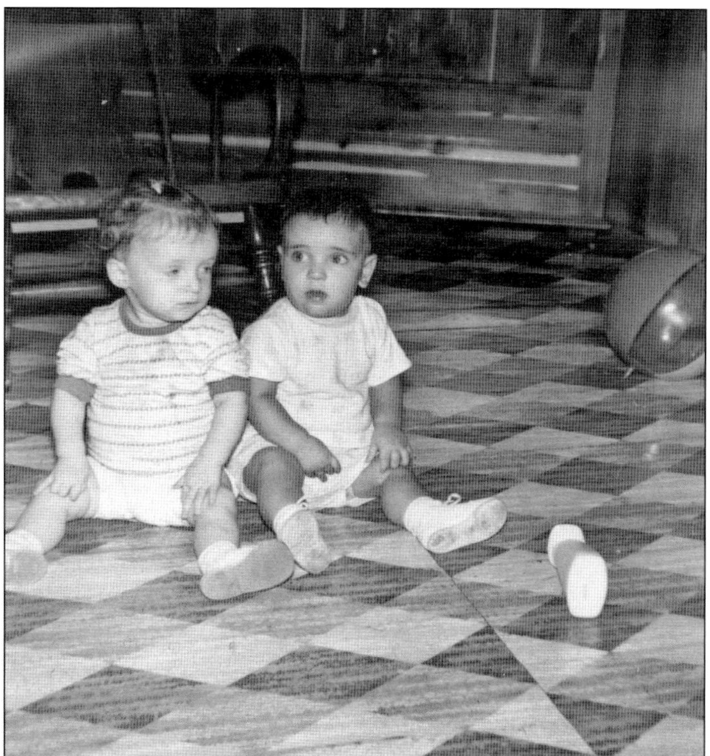

In 1960, at the age of one, Carol Gros Charlet and Donald Pipsair sit on the floor for a picture. They are at the house of Carol's grandparents Joseph and Nobie Pipsair Leonard in Belle River. (Courtesy of Carol Gros Charlet.)

Palmire Gaudet Breaux and Desire Breaux Jr. had two daughters. Palmire is pictured with her daughters, Christine Breaux Matherne (left) and Alida Breaux Blanchard (right), in the early 1900s. Christine married Paul Matherne, and Alida married Philip Blanchard Sr. (Courtesy of Nadine Theriot.)

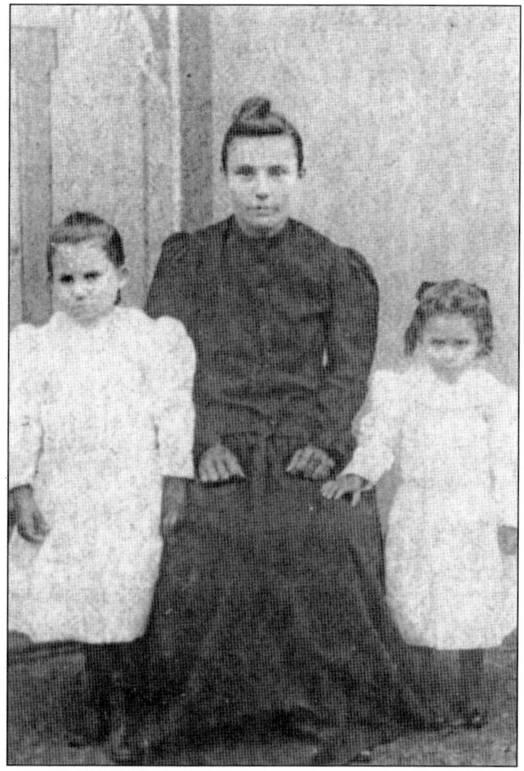

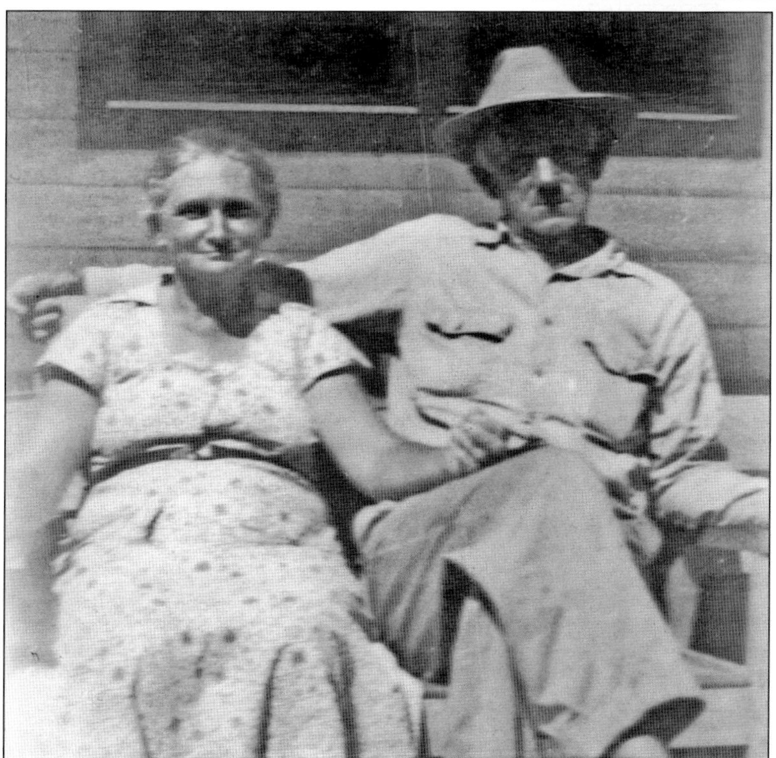

Olivia Aucoin Leonard and Lawerence Leonard sit on the front porch. Olivia was born on November 30, 1900, and died on February 3, 2000, at the age of 99. Lawerence was born in 1894 and died in 1960 at the age of 66. They had five children. (Courtesy of Odile Crochet Landry.)

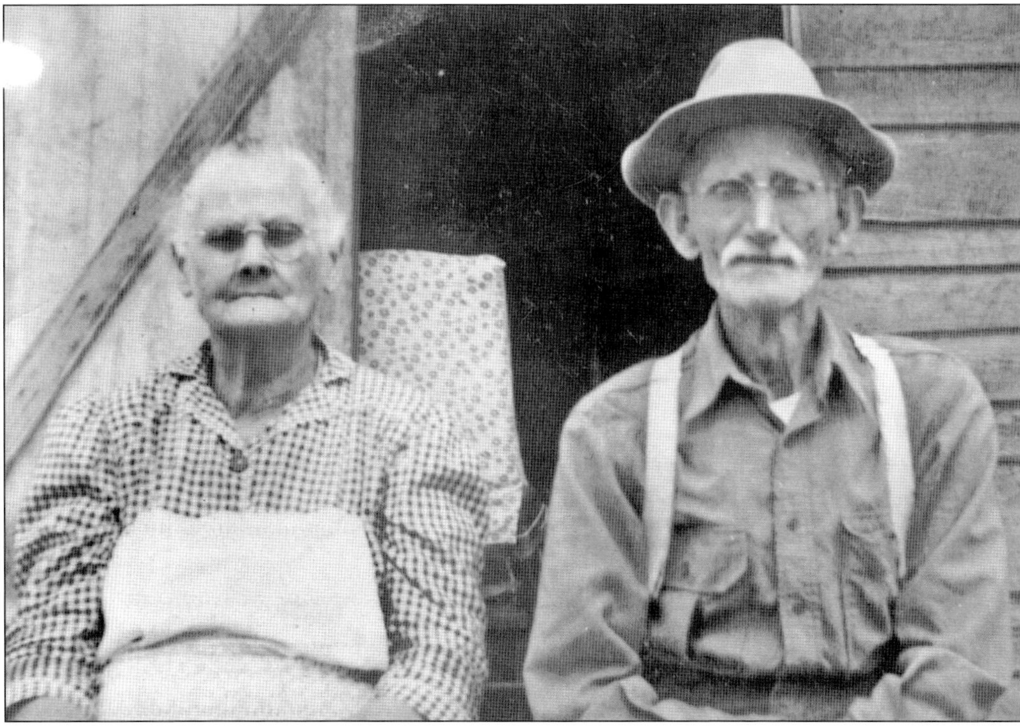

Marie Hebert Aucoin and Seraphin Sylvane Aucoin are pictured outside their house in Tee Bayou. Marie was born in 1880 and died in 1978 at 98. Sylvane was born in 1879 and died in 1957 at 78. Seraphin did not like his name, so he changed it to Sylvane. (Courtesy of Odile Crochet Landry.)

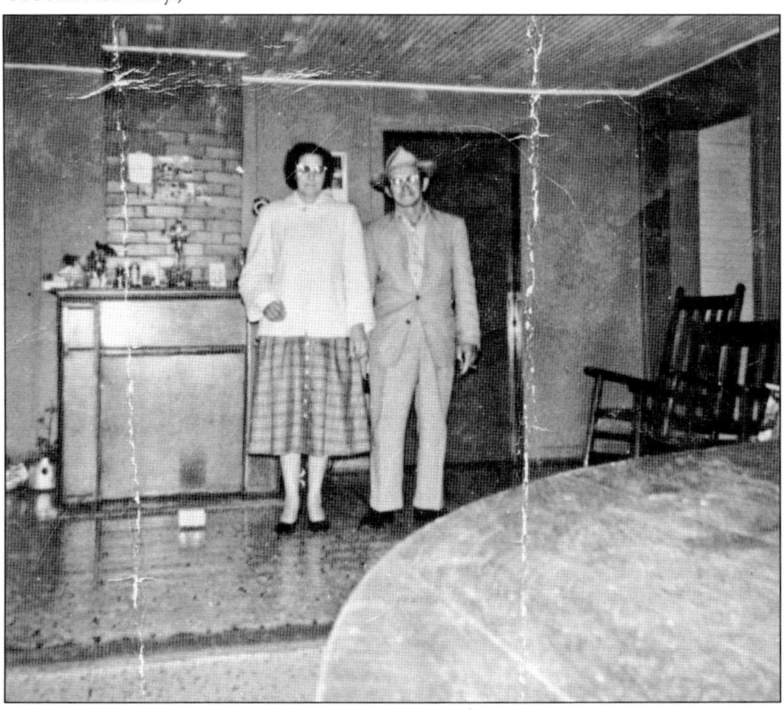

Wilfred Blanchard and Elise Hue Blanchard pose for a photograph in their house. Wilfred was born on August 2, 1905, and died in January 1973. Elise was born on October 17, 1909, and died in June 1982. (Courtesy of Odile Crochet Landry.)

Noe Joseph Blanchard and his wife, Noeline St. Germain Blanchard, have their picture taken on Christmas Day 1964. Noe is enjoying his cup of coffee. He was the son of a farmer and made his living farming his own land. Their children are Floyd Blanchard, T.J. Blanchard, and Bernice Blanchard Tullier. (Courtesy of T.J. Blanchard.)

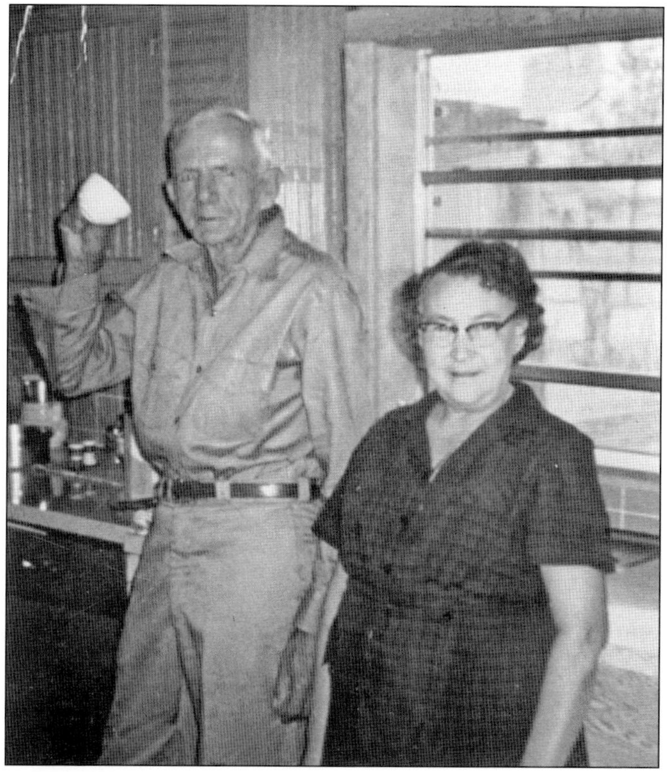

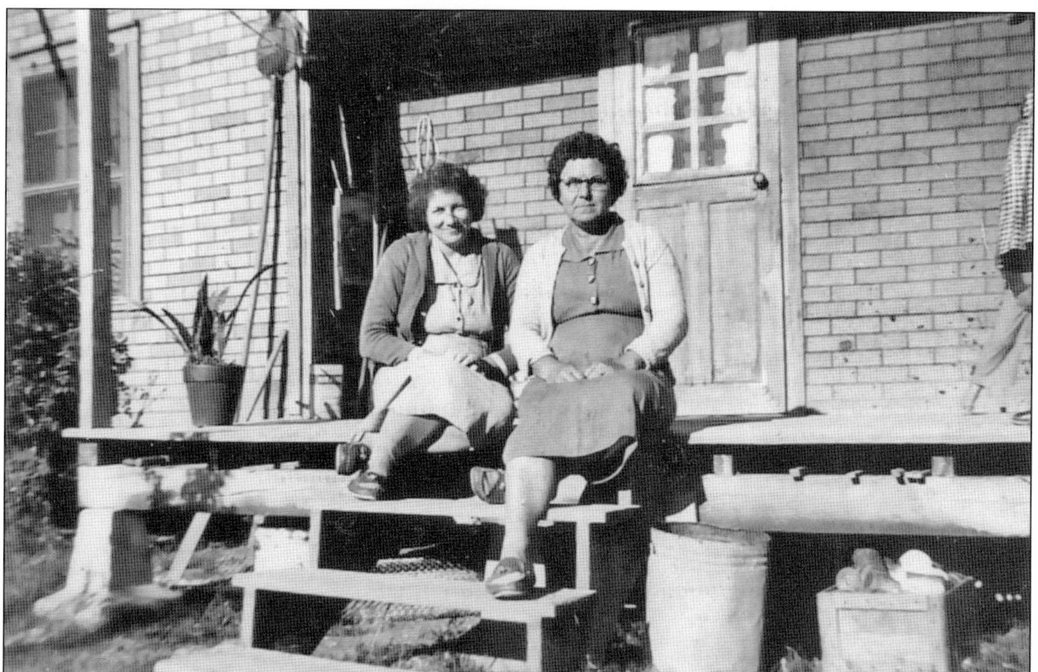

People used to love to sit on their porches and visit with their family and friends after their work was done. Back then, the women always wore dresses. Estelle Hue Landry (left) and Alta Eshine Cavalier have a good time visiting on the porch in the 1950s. (Courtesy of Jane Landry Gaudet.)

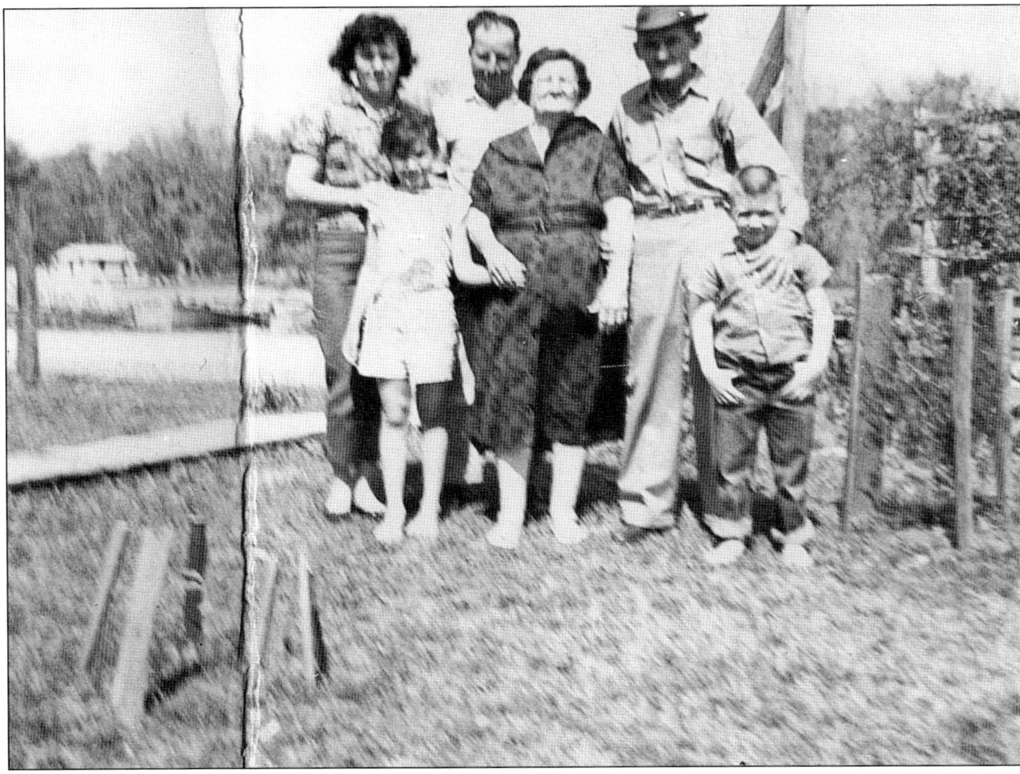

From left to right are two unidentified, Minus Templet, his parents Lorraina Landry Templet and Bernard Templet, and Norbert Templet. This picture was taken in the early 1960s down the bay. The children back then did not like to wear shoes. (Courtesy of Brenda Landry Templet and Norbert Templet.)

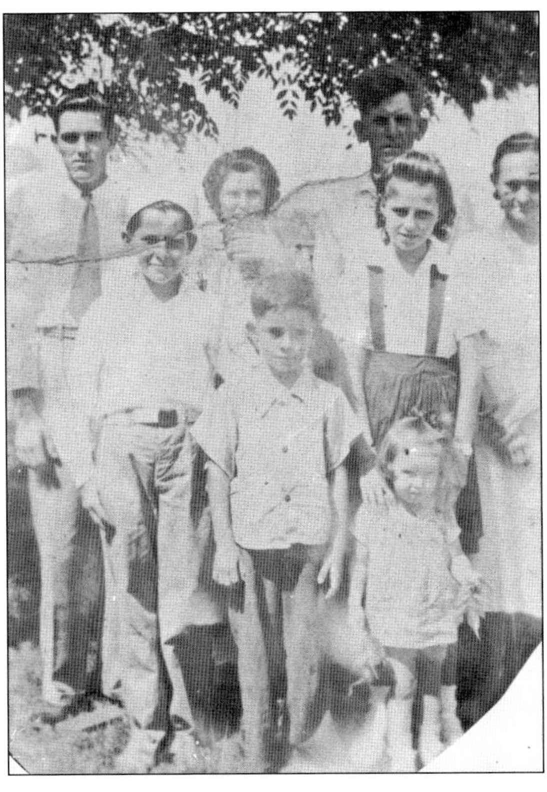

From left to right are (first row) Sally Blanchard Breaux and Carroll Mabile; (second row) Dudley Mabile, Leanna Mabile, and Altha Theriot Mabile; (third row) Edwin Mabile, Leonita Mabile Blanchard holding baby Nancy Blanchard Charlet, and Richard Mabile. (Courtesy of Cecile Guillot Mabile.)

Alfred Rodrigue (left) and Frank Fournerette are all suited up for a picture in the late 1920s. They both lived and raised their families in Pierre Part. (Courtesy of Wildy Templet and Hilda Templet.)

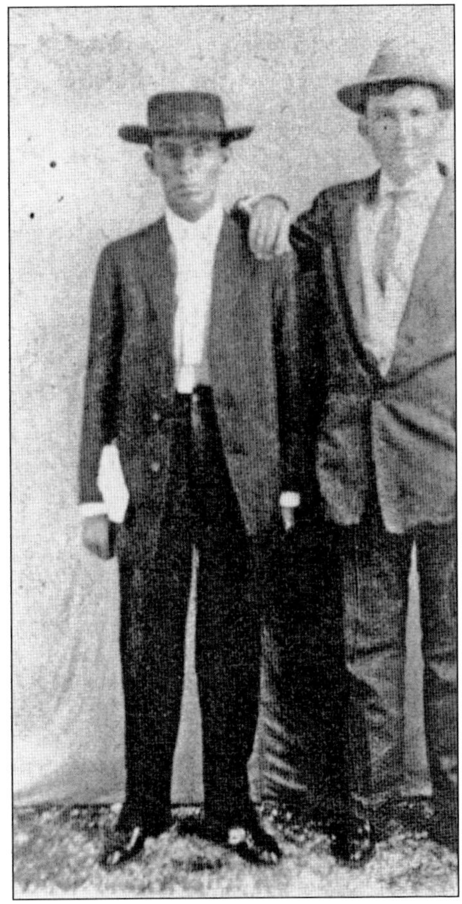

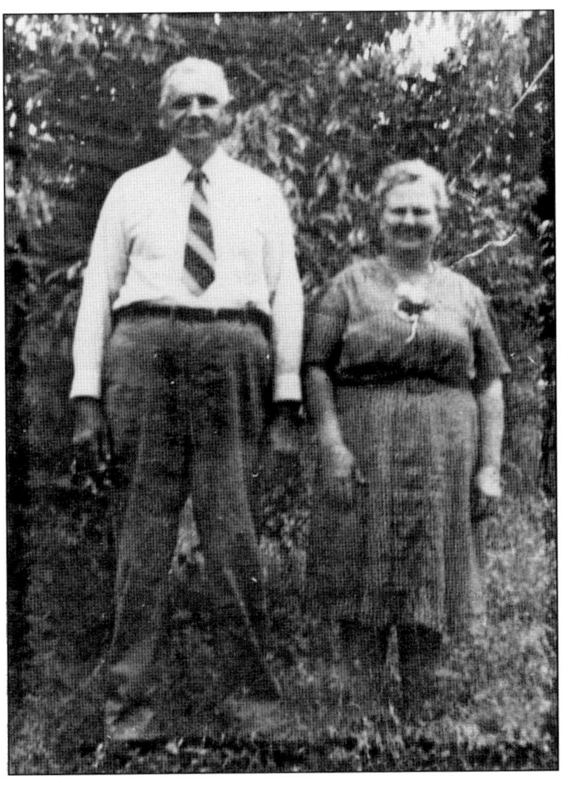

Simon Blanchard was born on October 28, 1883, and his wife, Cecile Simoneaux Blanchard, was born in 1885. Simon's parents were Nicholas Blanchard and Olphida Rodrigue Blanchard. (Courtesy of Cecile Guillot Mabile.)

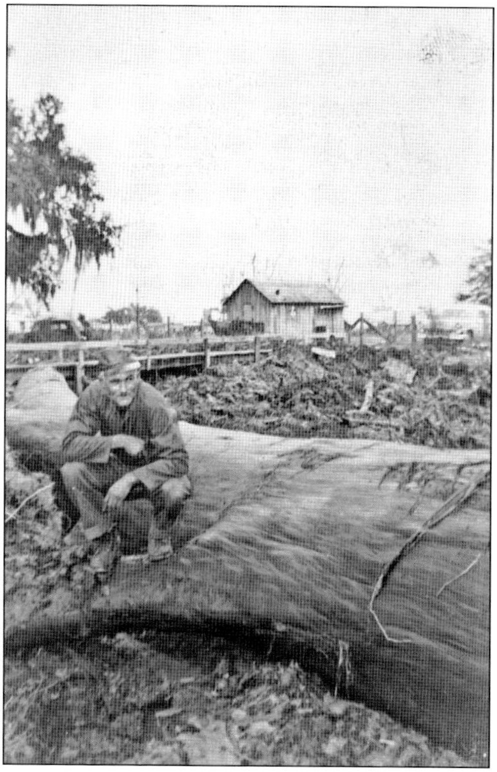

This big tree was removed to build the little bridge to go by car to Tee Bayou, known today as Sub Station Road. The little house in the background was for Clemence Aucoin Cavalier Domingue in the early 1940s. She and Joseph Dominique Cavalier had nine children. (Courtney of Wildy Templet and Hilda Templet.)

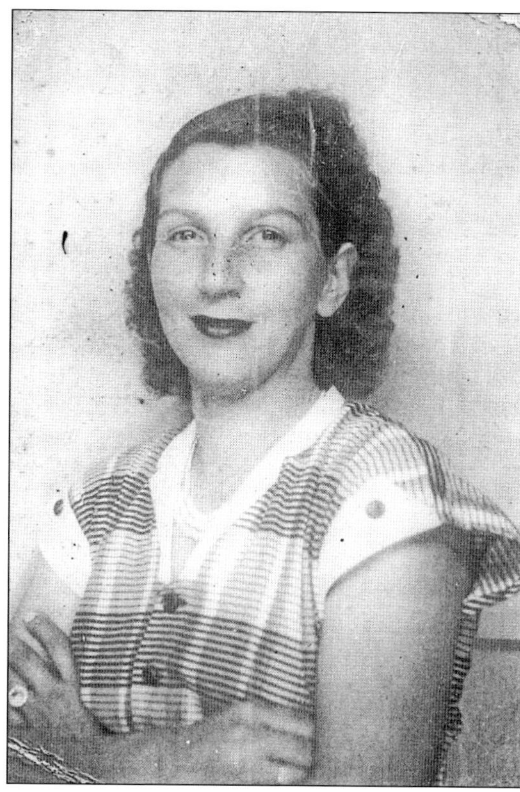

At the age of 27, Lillian Cavalier Gros Leonard poses for a picture at the Rainbow Inn. Lillian's family lived on the banks of Bayou Godell, where she was born. Joseph Domingue and Clemence Aucoin Cavalier Domingue were her parents. (Courtesy of Ann Cavalier Anderson Landry Cavalier.)

Chris Templet, the oldest son of Oleus "Junius" Templet and Dorothy "Dot" Theriot Templet, loved to fish and hunt. He helped his dad in the store and worked at Morris Crochet's farm. On August 2, 1974, at the age of 16, he was killed when putting air in a cane wagon tire. Chris died when the tire blew up and threw him against a building. (Courtesy of Dorothy "Dot" Theriot Templet.)

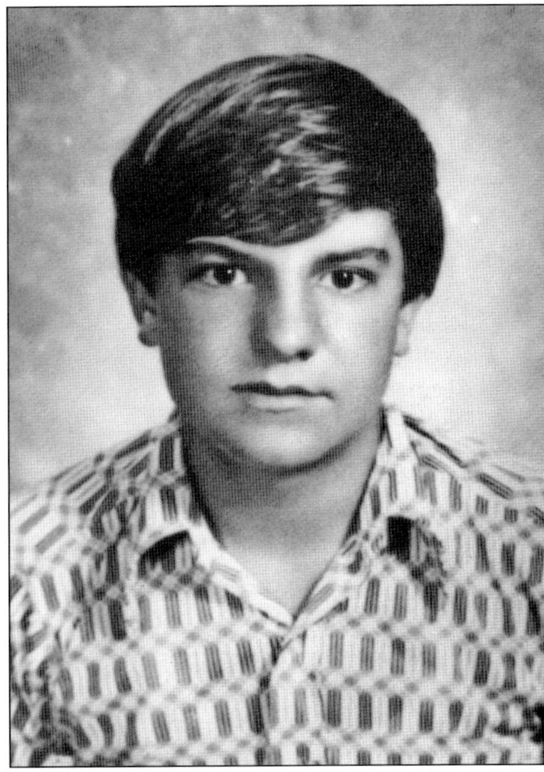

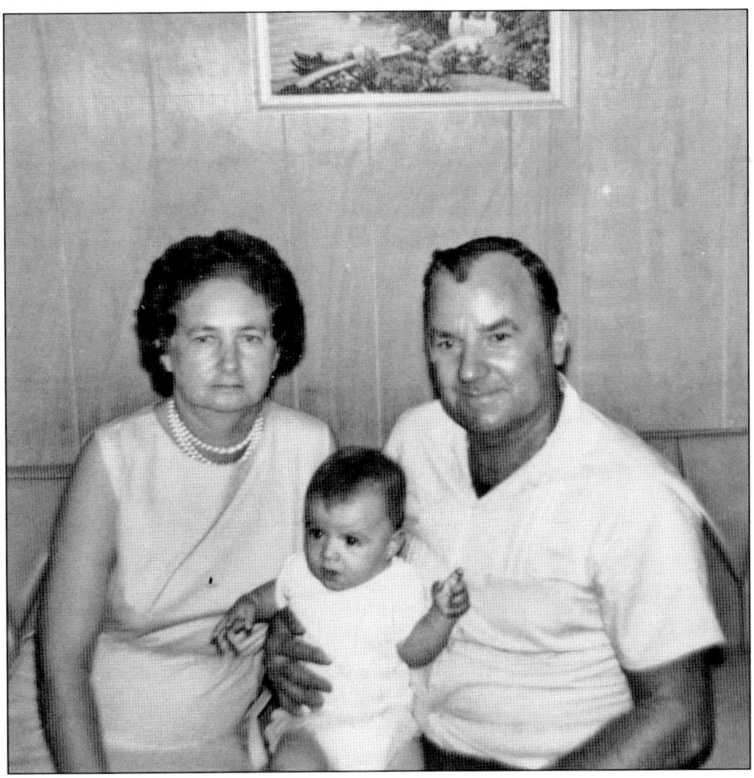

Mabel "May" Theriot and Wilbert Theriot hold their grandson Clark Domingue. Clark was born on December 4, 1964, and is about 10 months old here. (Courtesy of Clark Domingue and Loretta Cavalier Domingue.)

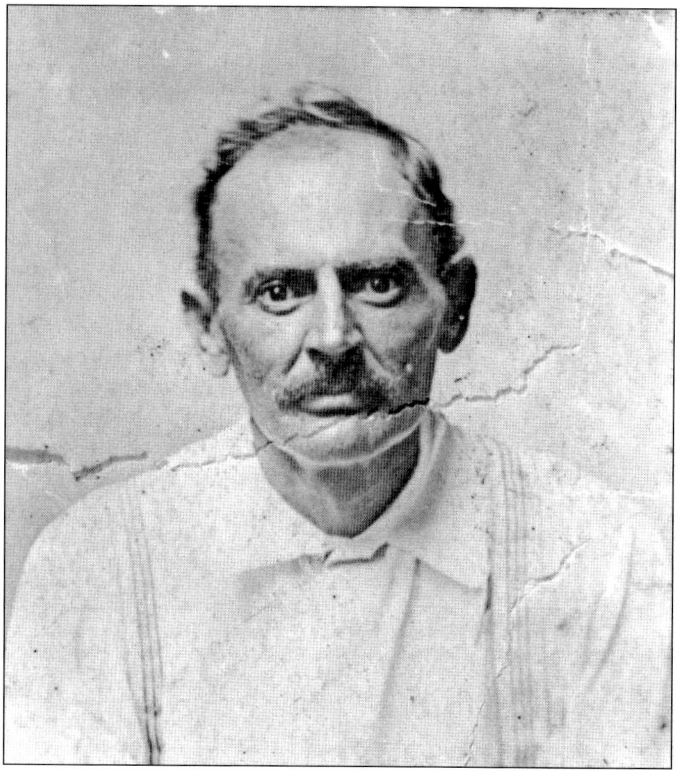

Henri Sabin St. Germain was born on December 5, 1873, in Paincourtville, Louisiana, and passed away in 1934. His parents were Joseph St. Germain and Mathilde Daigle St. Germain. He married Lavinia Oufnac. Their children were Noelie St. Germain Blanchard, Joseph St. Germain, and Delese St. Germain. (Courtesy of T.J. Blanchard.)

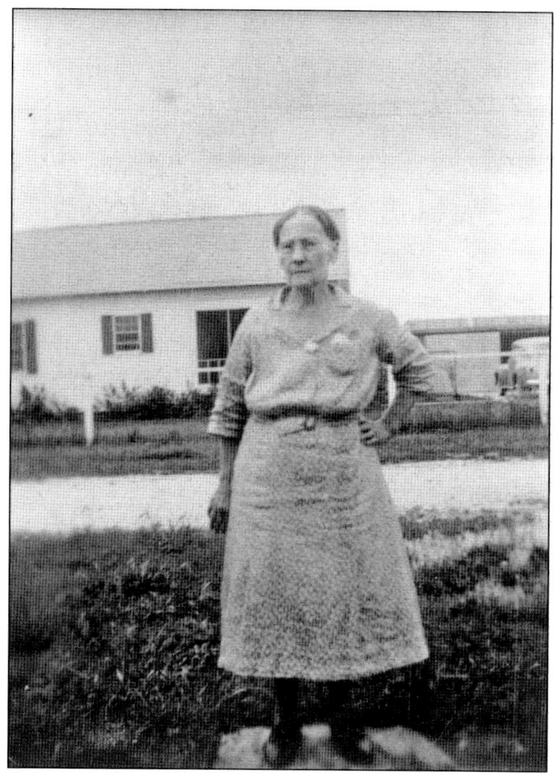

Lavinia Oufnac St. Germain was born in 1878 and died in 1961 at the age of 83. Her parents were Pierre Oufnac and Lesida Landry Oufnac. Lavinia moved with her children when her husband died in 1934. It is not known where this picture was taken. (Courtesy of T.J. Blanchard.)

Dudley Landry and Estelle Hue Landry were both 22 when this photograph was taken in 1937. Dudley and Estelle were not married at the time. Dudley was born on August 3, 1915, and Estelle was born on March 5, 1915. They were the parents of Jane Landry Gaudet. (Courtesy of Jane Landry Gaudet.)

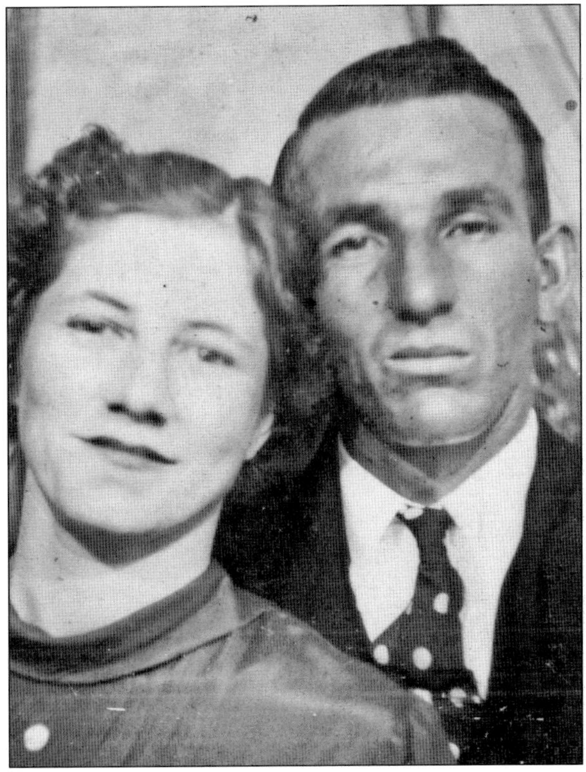

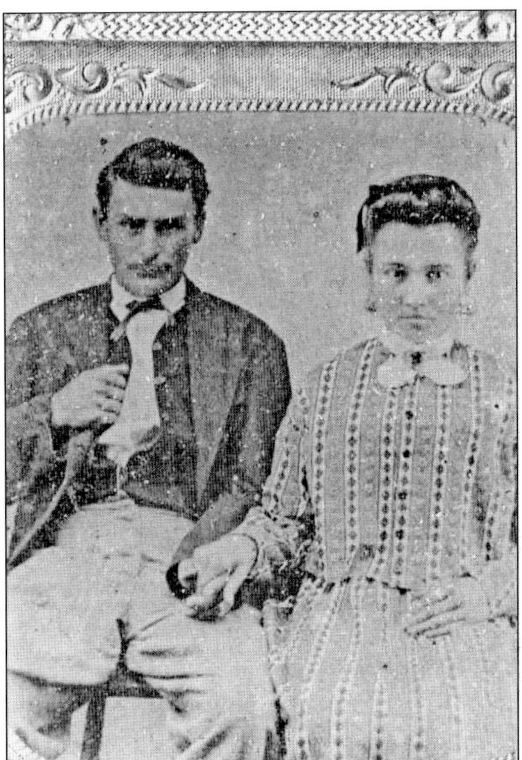

Pierre Gaudet and Christine Crochet Gaudet married on June 5, 1871, in Pierre Part. Christine was 17 years old. She was the daughter of Serevin Crochet and Euphrosine Frioux Crochet. Pierre was the son of Pierre Pedro Gaudet and Marie Delphine Stoute. They had 10 children. (Courtesy of Nadine Theriot.)

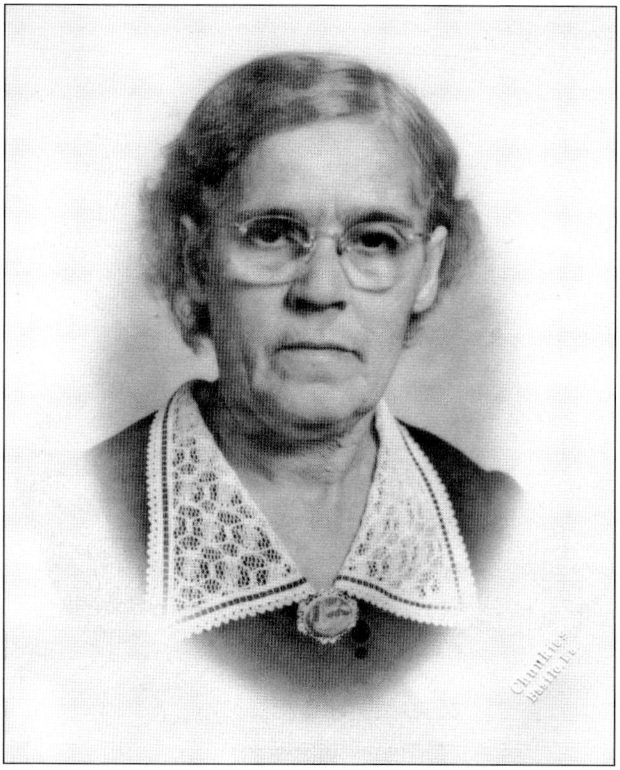

Bernadette Templet Guillot, left, was born in 1880 and passed away on June 7, 1965. She married Oibert Guillot, shown below. He was born on July 14, 1879, and passed away in 1952. They had four children, Therese Guillot Theriot, Rose Guillot Blanchard, Gerald Guillot, and Frank Guillot. (Both, courtesy of Lucille Theriot.)

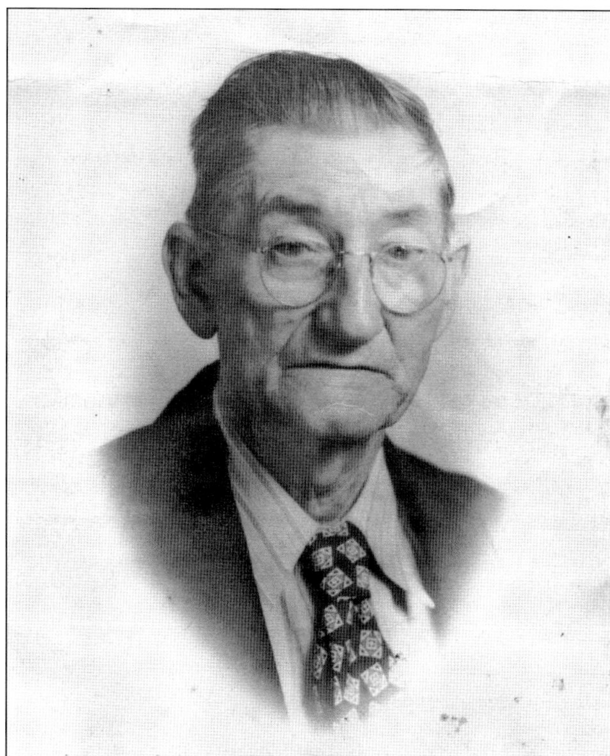

This beautiful lady is Elizabeth "Gram Beth" Domingue Gaudet. She married Pierre Gaudet on April 22, 1897, and had five children. Pierre had 15 children in all; he had 10 with his first wife Christine Crochet. Gram Beth's parents were Jean Domingue and Marcelline Cavaliere Domingue. (Author's collection.)

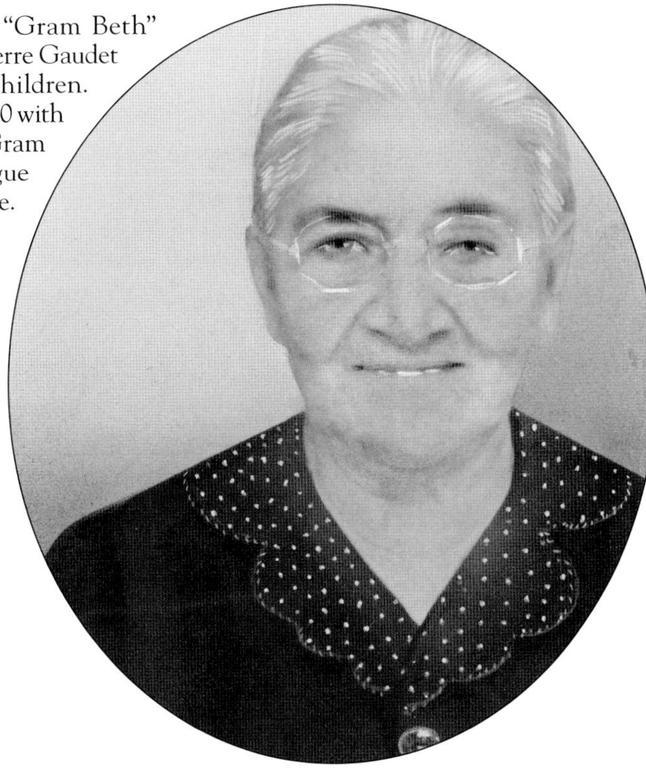

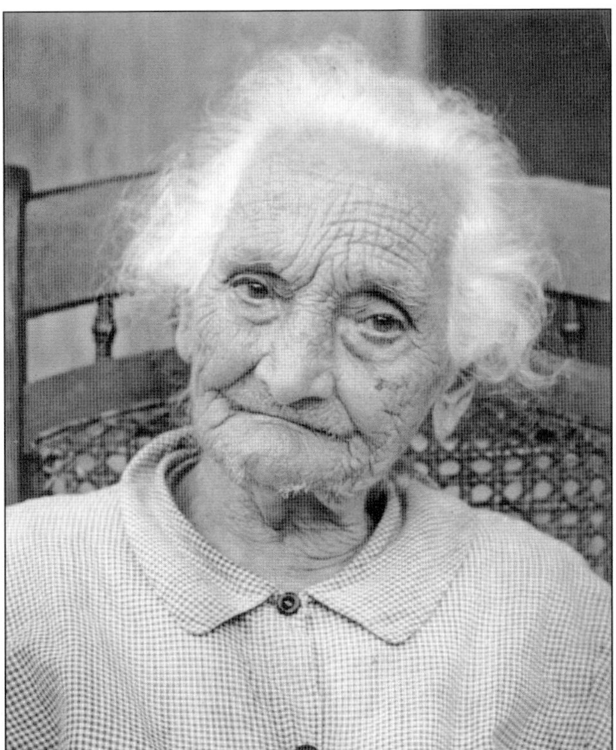

Marie Broussard Morales is pictured at the age of 83. She was born on August 11, 1867, and died in 1951 at the age of 84. She married Francis Bernoni Morales, and they had five children. Athana Broussard and Celestine Vaughn were her parents. (Courtesy of Lillian Mabile Chedotal.)

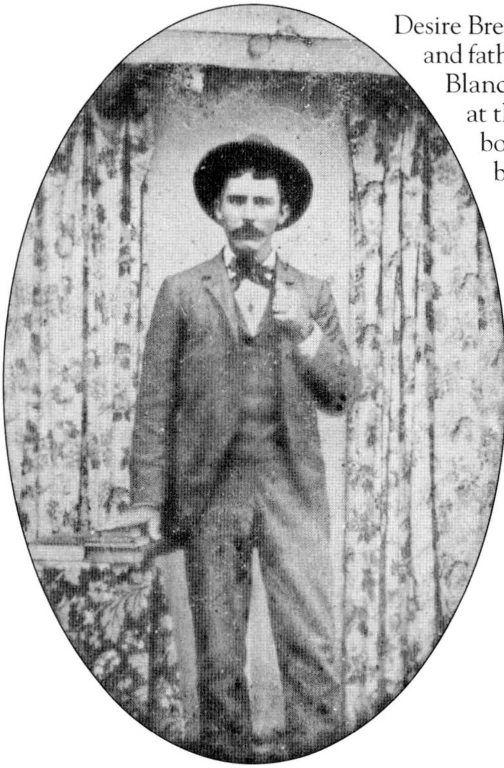

Desire Breaux Jr. was the husband of Palmire Gaudet Breaux and father to Christine Breaux Mathren and Alida Breaux Blanchard. Desire passed away on December 9, 1896, at the age of 27 after accidentally falling into a pot of boiling syrup at the syrup mill before Christine was born. (Courtesy of Nadine Theriot.)

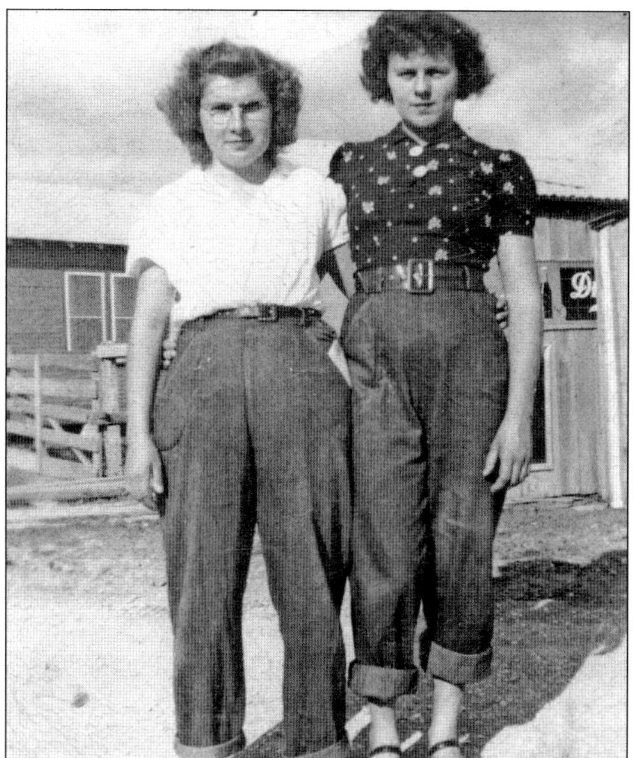

These two ladies loved to walk to Gervais Mabile's grocery store down the bay and hang out and drink a pop with their friends. Vivias Morales Blanchard is at left, and the woman at right is believed to be Lucy "T-Teen" Hebert. (Courtesy of Brenda Landry Templet and Nobert Templet.)

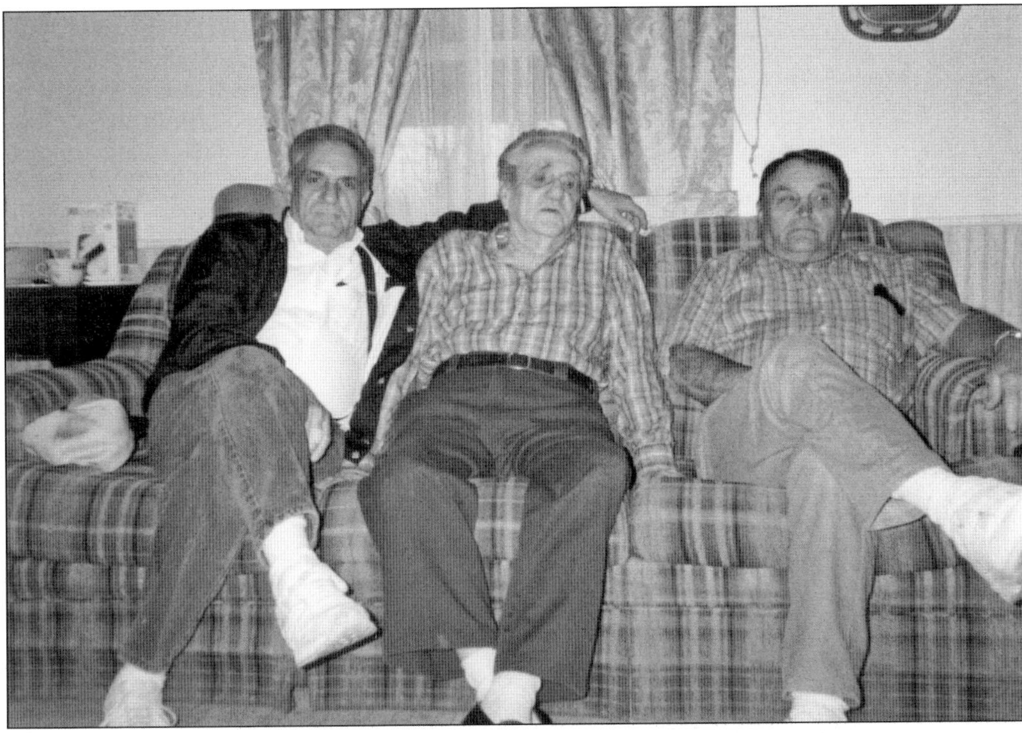

Pictured from left to right are Lent Crochet, Leonce Crochet Sr., and Leland Crochet. They are three of Oneal Crochet and Ida Gaudet Crochet's 11 children. (Courtesy of Odile Crochet Landry.)

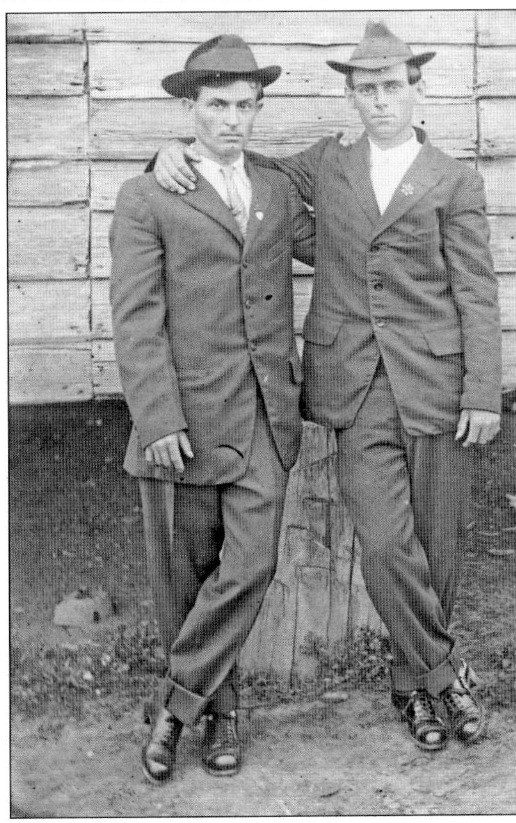

It is believed that this picture shows Bernard Hebert (left) and Zenon Templet. Zenon was born on August 10, 1893, and passed away on April 9, 1976. He married Adeline Mabile Templet on January 4, 1916. (Courtesy of Brenda Landry Templet and Norbert Templet.)

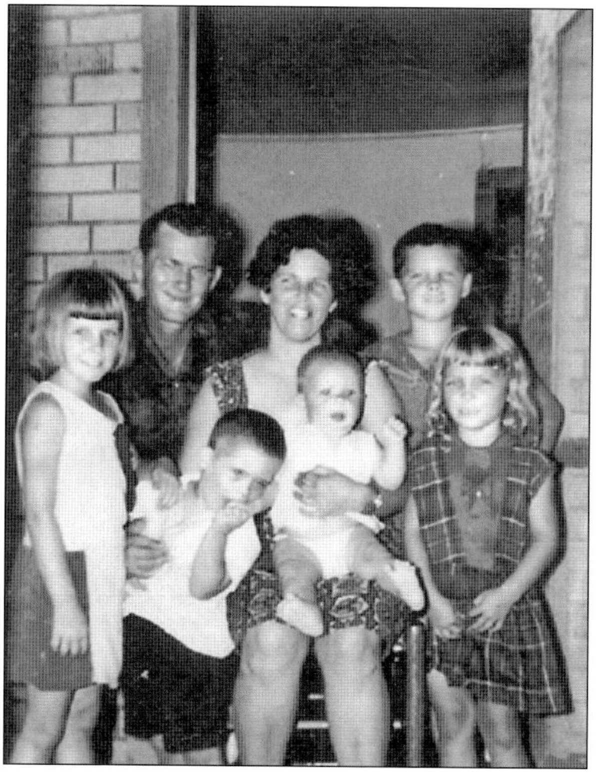

Ulysse Landry and Leabee Hebert Landry pose for a family photograph with their five children. Pictured from left to right are (first row) Patrica Landry Cavalier, Carl Landry, Thomas Landry, and Brenda Landry Templet; (second row) Ulysse, Leabee, and Peter Landry. Their house down the bay was all cypress and still stands today. (Courtesy of Brenda Landry Templet and Norbert Templet.)

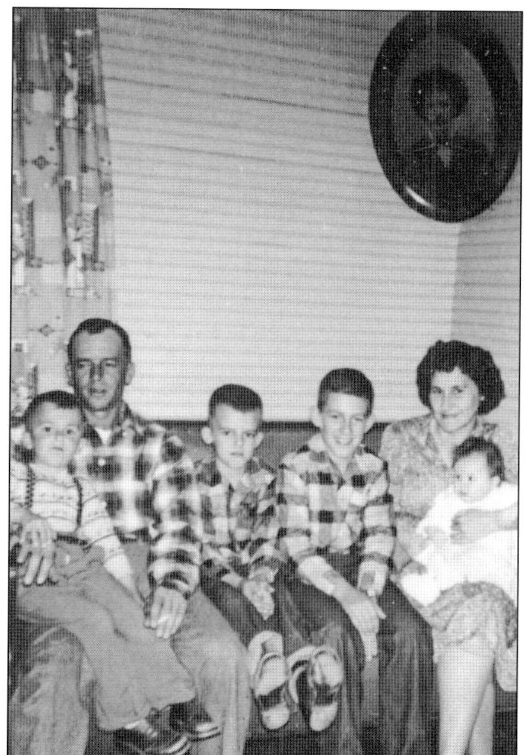

This family picture of Ned Theriot and Vernice Matherne Theriot with their four children was taken at the house of Verniese's parents, Paul Matherne and Christine Gaudet Mathern, in 1959. From left to right are Kirk, Ned, Donald, Gerald, Verniese, and Nadine Theriot. (Courtesy of Nadine Theriot.)

Ernestine Cavalier Rivere is pictured with her children around 1915. From left to right are Clahert Rivere, Flavis Rivere Simoneaux, baby Evia Rivere Pintado, and Ernest Rivere Sr. They lived in Brusly St. Vincent. (Courtesy of Alice Alleman Cavalier.)

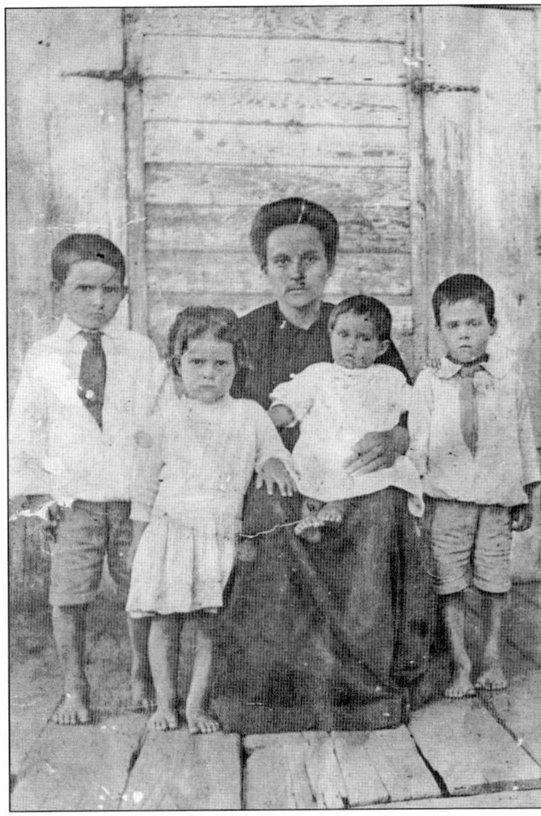

In her early 90s, Altha Mabile sits on her front porch for a picture with her children. From left to right are (first row) Carol Mabile and Altha; (second row) Roy Mabile, Leonard Mabile, Lee Ann Mabile St. Germain, and Leonite Mabile Blanchard. (Courtesy of Leonard Mabile and Regina Dupuis Mabile.)

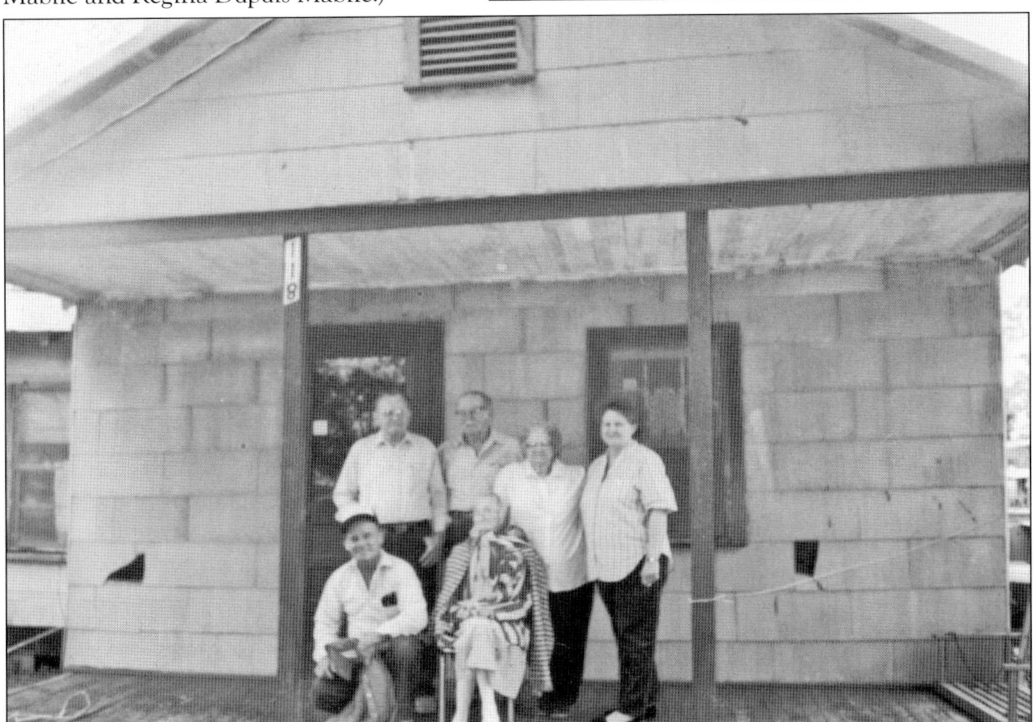

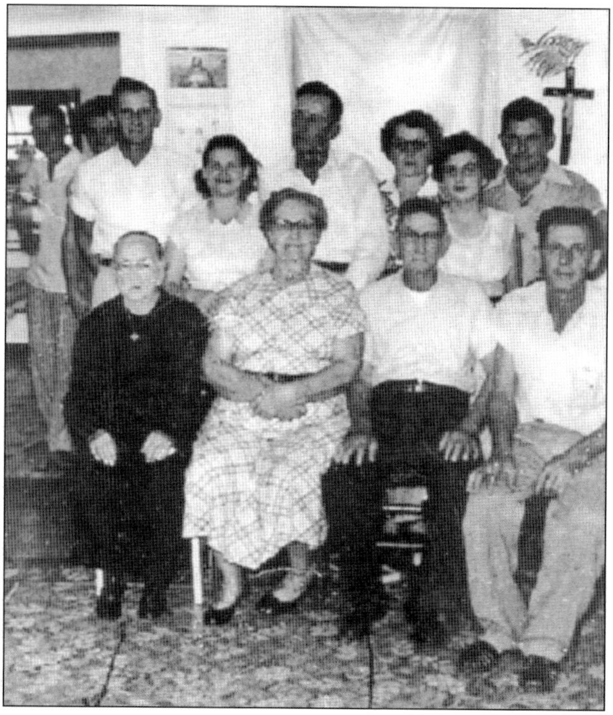

From left to right are (first row) Sidonia "Gram Jack" Blanchard, Jarville "Jack" Blanchard, Clarville Blanchard, and Louis Blanchard; (second row) unidentified, Alfred Blanchard, Leonita Mabile Blanchard, Shelby Blanchard, Alice Crochet Blanchard, Lorrian Blanchard Mabile, and Dudley Mabile. (Courtesy of Cecile Guillot Mabile.)

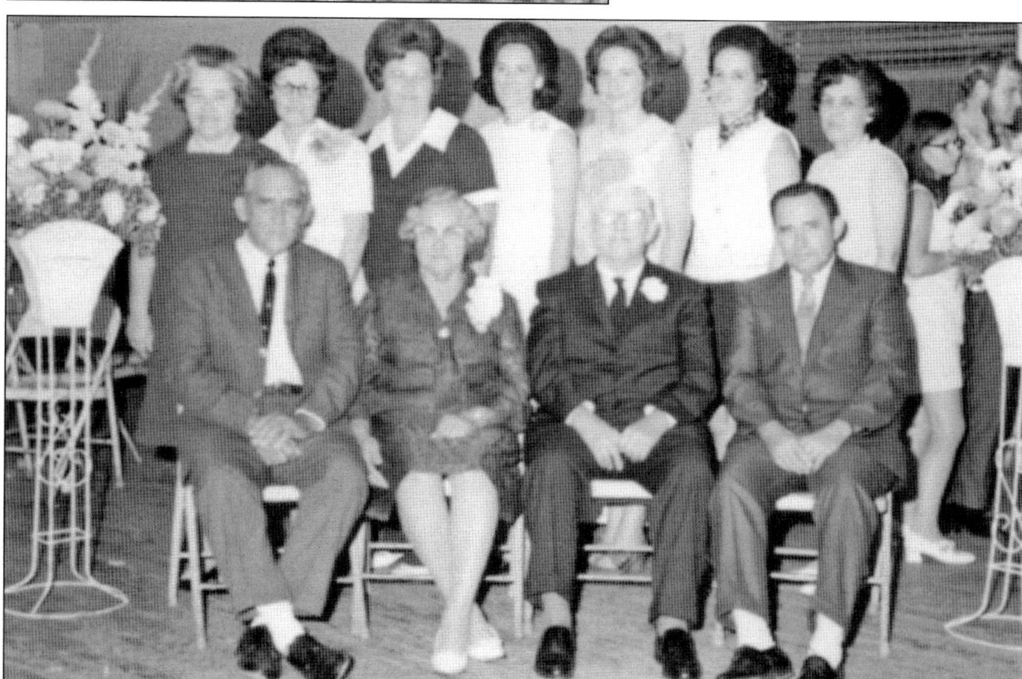

Paul Matherne and Christine Breaux Matherne are pictured with their children. From left to right are (sitting) Percy, Christine, Paul, and Lloyd; (standing) May Matherne Ragacki, Veriese Matherne Theriot, Jane Matherne Clement, Ruth Matherne Daigle, Pearl Matherne Ross, Audrey Matherne Hedges, and Melva Matherne Simoneaux. LeRoy and Virgie Matherne are not pictured. (Courtesy of Nadine Theriot.)

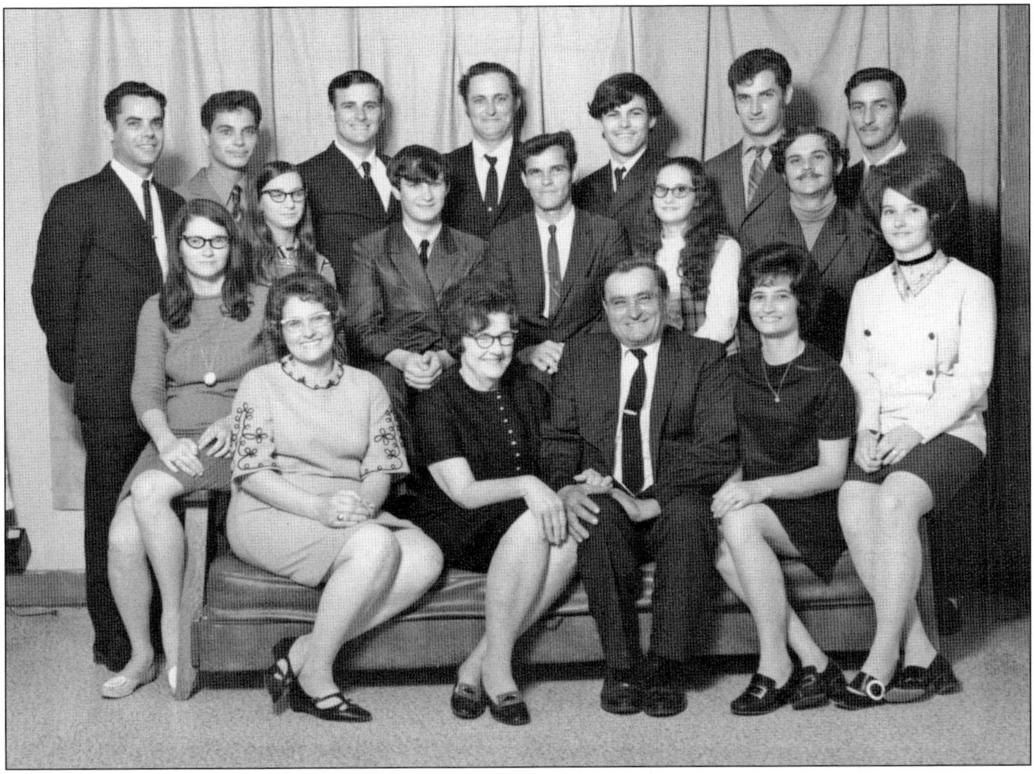

The Crochet family is, from left to right, (first row) Maude Crochet Landry, Frances Daigle Crochet, Claude Crochet, Annabelle Crochet, and June Crochet LeBlanc; (second row) Elenor Crochet Guillot, Gail Crochet Chedotal, Terry Crochet, Linwood Crochet, Robin Crochet, and Oneal Crochet; (third row) Vernon Crochet, Ernest Crochet, Earl Crochet, Charles Crochet, Reed Crochet, Patrick Crochet, and Wade Crochet. (Courtesy of Tonya Crochet Olivier.)

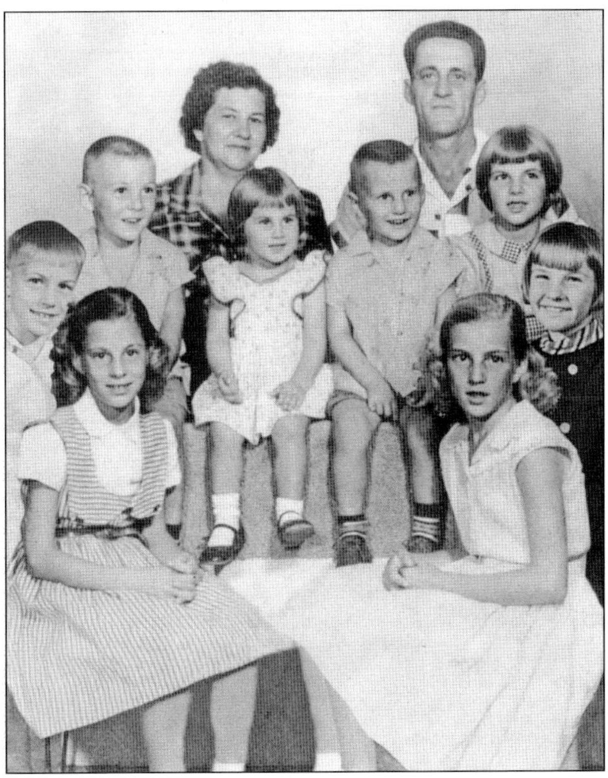

Leonce Crochet Sr. and Marie Hue Crochet's family is, from left to right, (first row) JoAnn Crochet Vaughn and Hilda Crochet Albarado Sagona; (second row) Chris Crochet and Tammy Crochet Breaux; (third row) Leonce Crochet Jr., Odile Crochet Landry, Rodney Crochet, and Barbara Crochet Sholmire; (fourth row) Marie and Leonce. (Courtesy of Odile Crochet Landry.)

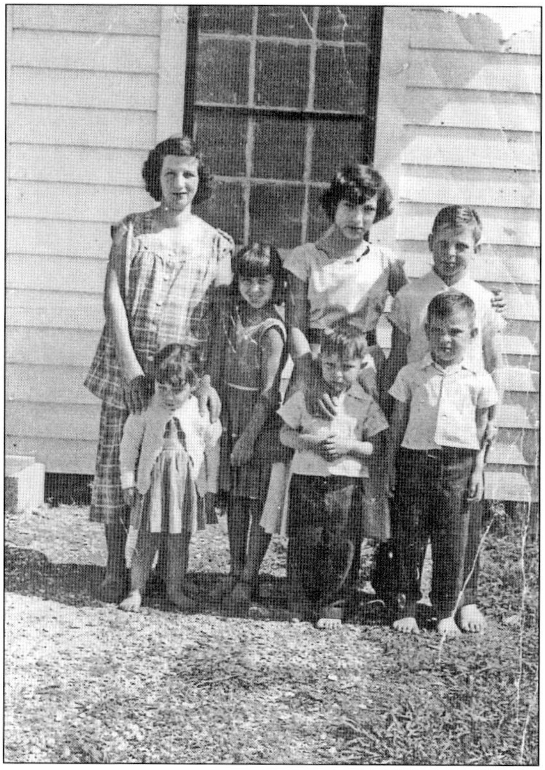

Taken on the side of Belle River Baptist Church, this picture shows the Lillian Cavalier Gros Leonard family. From left to right are (first row) Judy Gros Leonard, Rogers Gros and Haywood Gros; (second row) Lillian, Ann Cavalier Anderson Landry Cavalier, Doris Cavalier Hebert, and Harry Gros. Lillian is pregnant in the picture with Audrey Gros. (Courtesy of Ann Cavalier Anderson Landry Cavalier.)

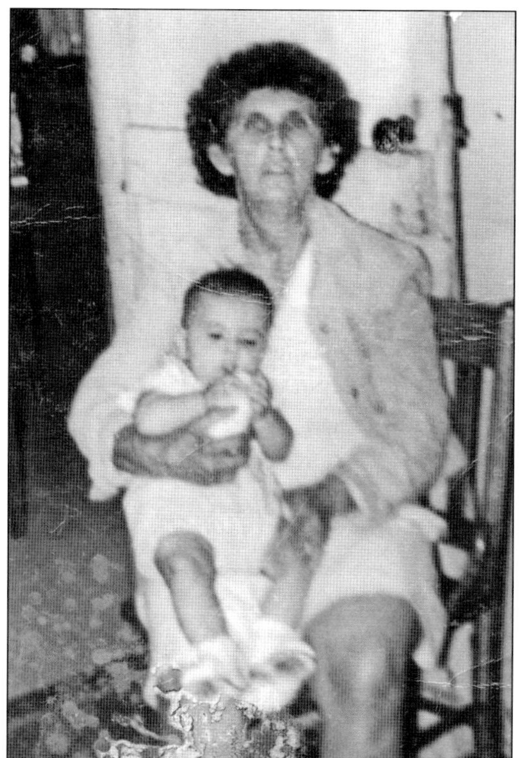

Leabee Hebert Landry lived next door to her grandmother Alicide Albarado Hebert. Alicide is holding her great-grandson Carl Landry. Carl was always sick, and she loved to rock him. He also had trouble with his feet and did not walk early, so everyone held him and spoiled him. He is about two years old in this picture. (Courtesy of Brenda Landry Templet and Norbert Templet.)

Wilfred "Buck" Cavalier and Elise Cavalier sit at the bar at Lakeview Inn down the bay. They enjoyed going to the bar to mingle with their family and friends. (Courtesy of Elise Cavalier Cavalier.)

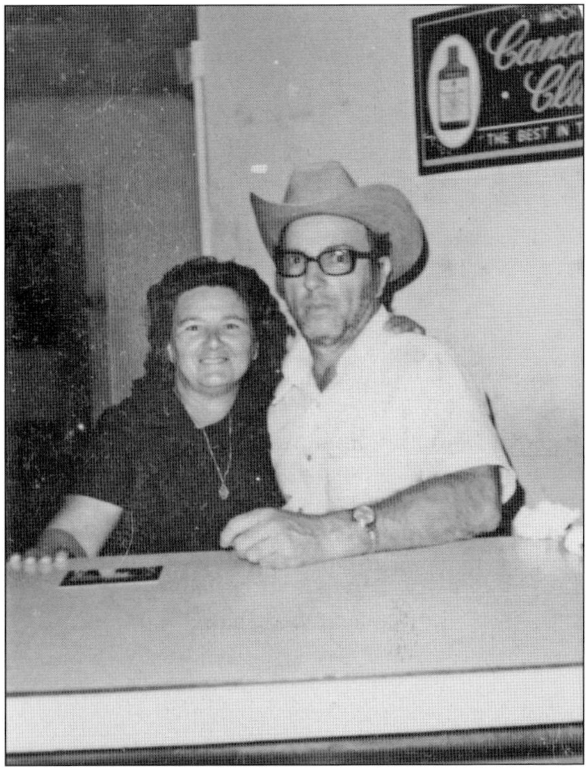

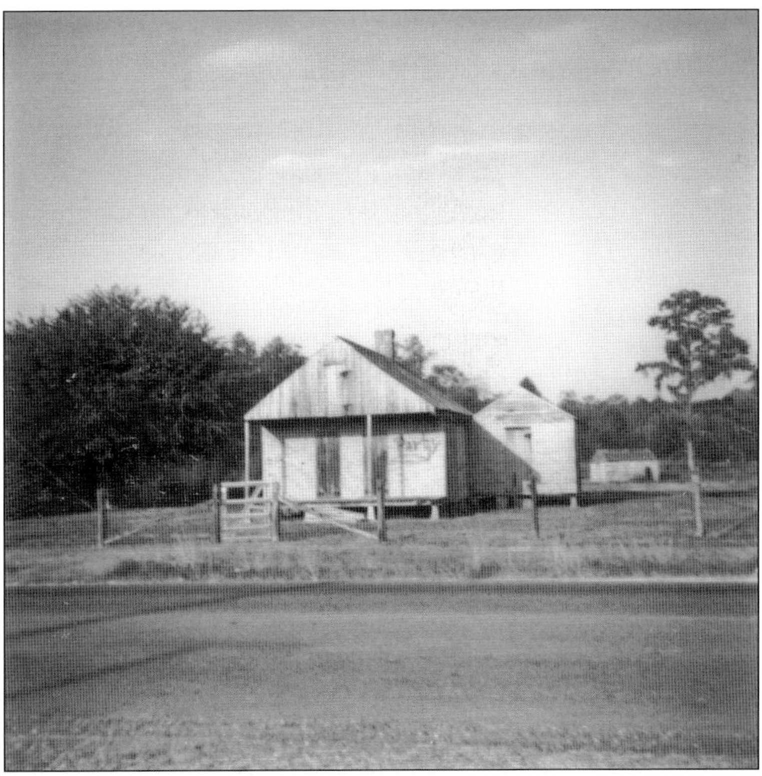

The old house of Samuel "Dut" Breaux stood along Highway 70, across from the school near the home of Louis Breaux. Dut was a bachelor and was very poor. He worked for Breaux and Daigle Store. This picture was taken in 1979. (Courtesy of Lillian Mabile Chedotal.)

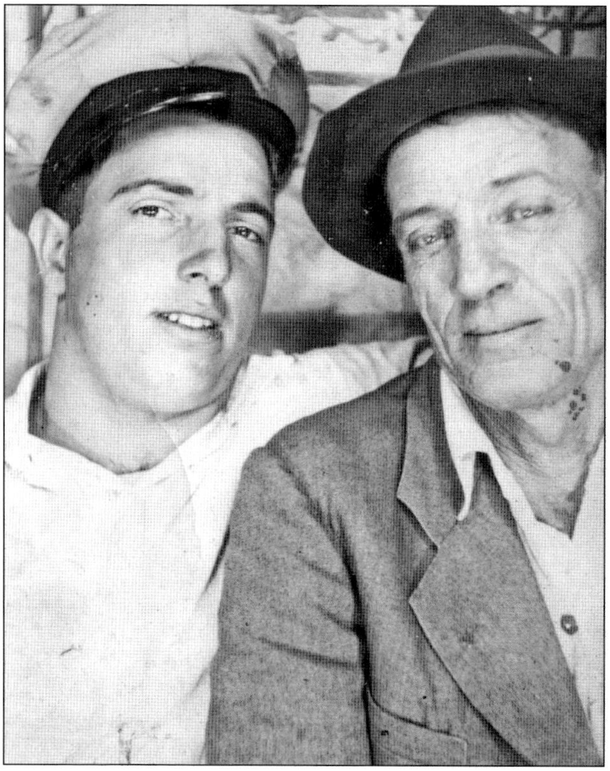

Boyd Cavalier and his son Wilfred "Buck" Cavalier left the Rainbow Inn and went across the street for this picture. They had a good time and a few drinks at the Rainbow Inn. It is unknown if Buck was married at that time. (Courtesy of Elise Cavalier Cavalier.)

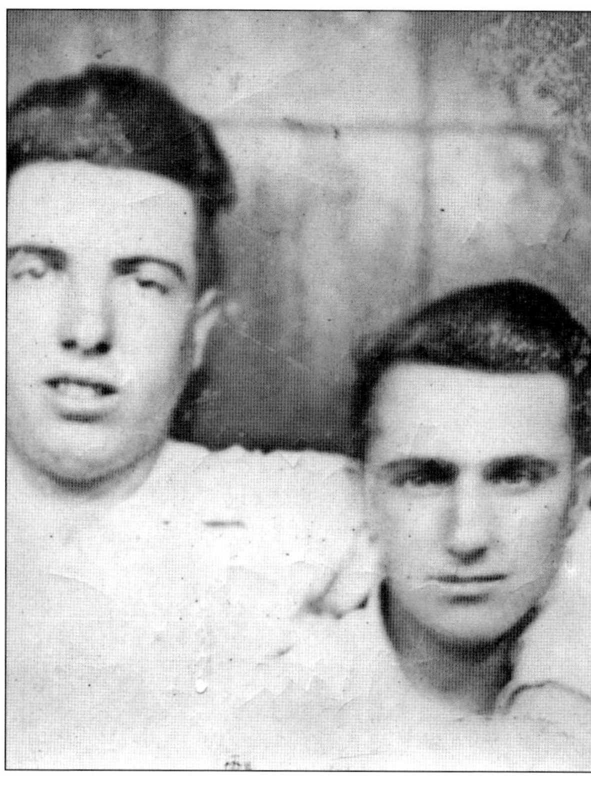

In the early 1940s, Wilfred "Buck" Cavalier (left) and Armand "Baba" Cavalier went to the Cox Theater to have their picture taken. A photographer would come about once a month on a weekend and take pictures. Buck and Baba were brothers in law. This picture was taken before Baba was married. (Courtesy of Elise Cavalier Cavalier.)

Shown here is a typical Saturday night at the Rainbow Inn. Everyone loved to grab a friend and take a picture. At right are Reuben Pierre Sedotal (left) and Frank Templet. Reuben was born on January 26, 1933, and died on December 24, 2012, and Frank was born on December 22, 1931. Below are Sam Templet (left) and Frank Templet. (Both, courtesy of Frank Templet.)

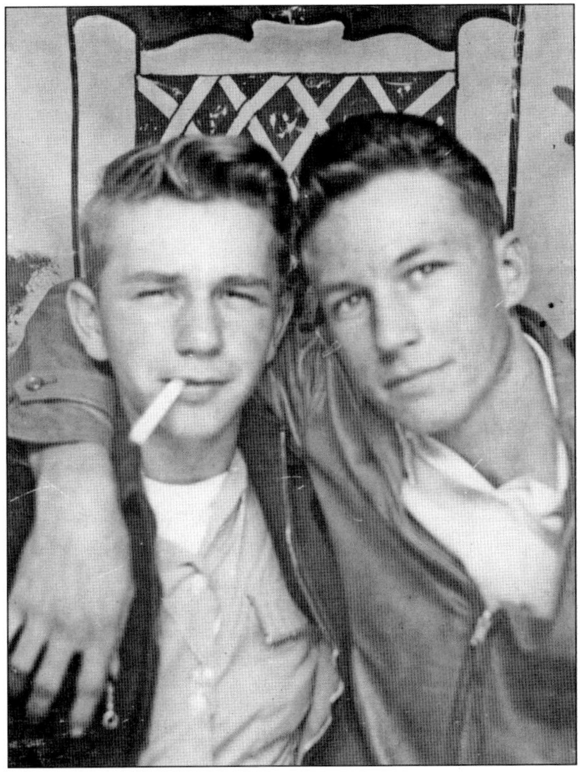

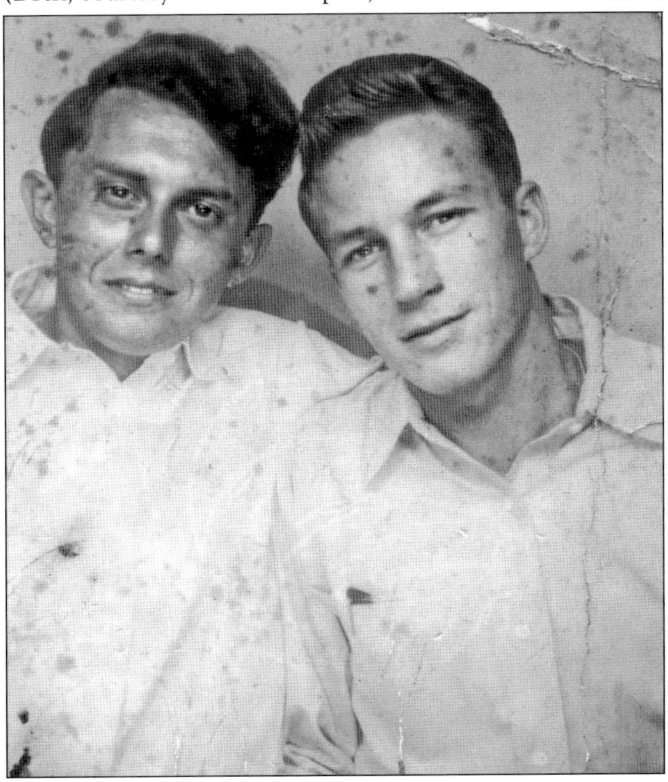

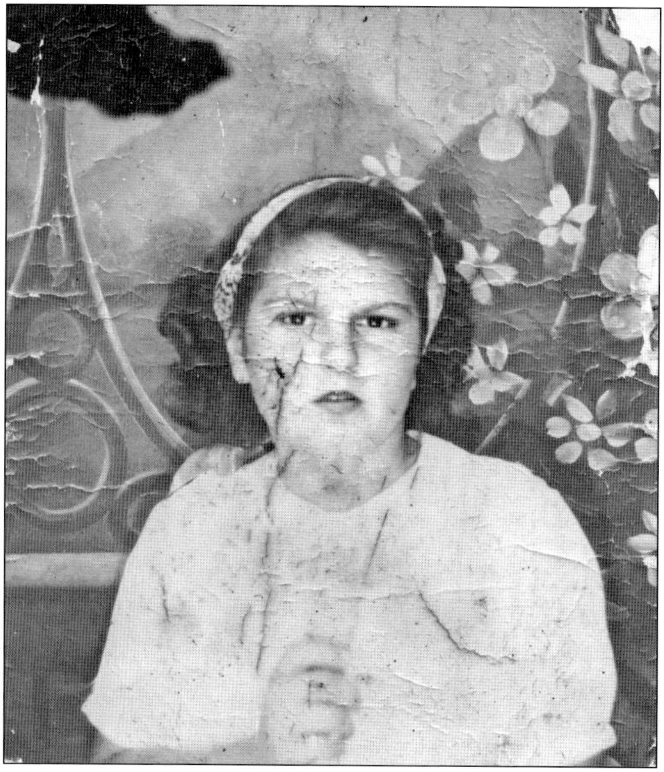

Thelma Cavalier Morales, like many others, enjoyed the photo booth. Here she poses for a photograph at the age of 14. Thelma was born on March 4, 1937, and died on February 5, 2017, at the age of 79. (Courtesy of Elise Cavalier Cavalier.)

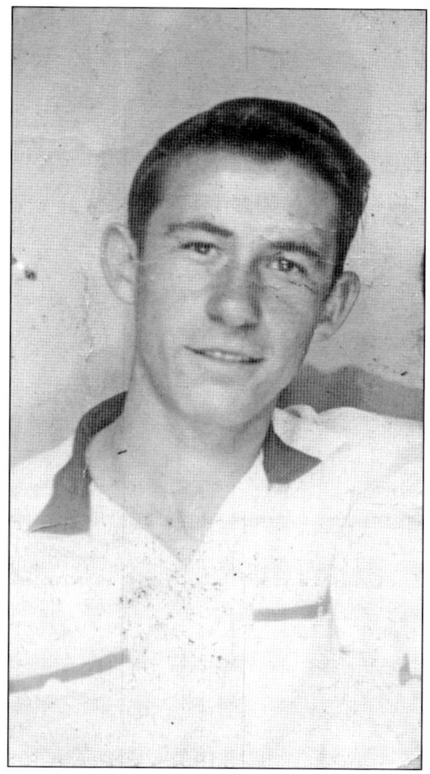

Clement Metrejean was born on May 11, 1937. He married Mathilda Martin Metrejean. Clement bought the Bonne Chance Bar from his mother-in-law, Fautine, many years ago. He and his wife still own and run the bar today. It is unknown how old he is in this picture. (Courtesy of Elise Cavalier Cavalier.)

Long ago, photographers would come and set up a place to take pictures. Most of the time, they set up at Cox's Theater. Diane Mathern Landry (left) and Elise Cavalier had their picture taken around 1956. (Courtesy of Elise Cavalier Cavalier.)

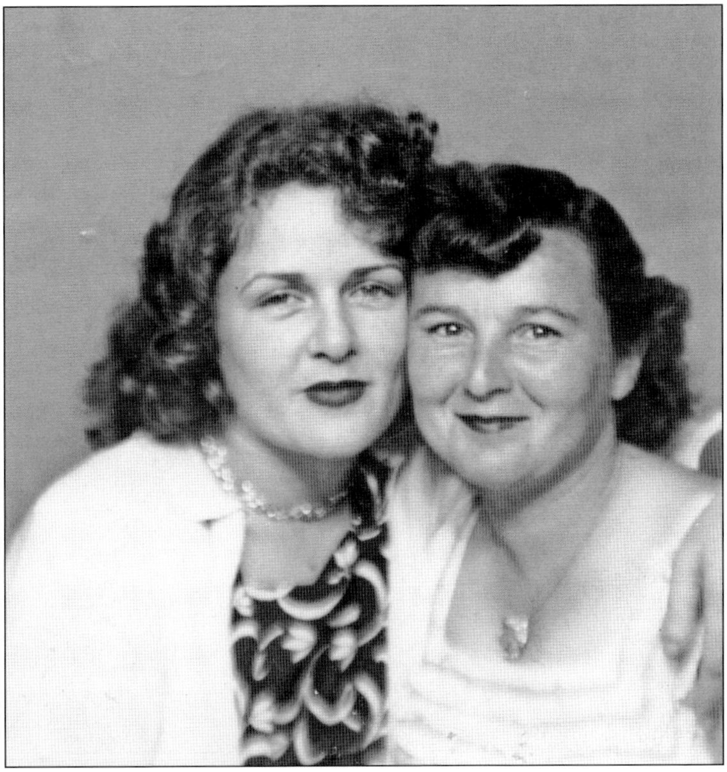

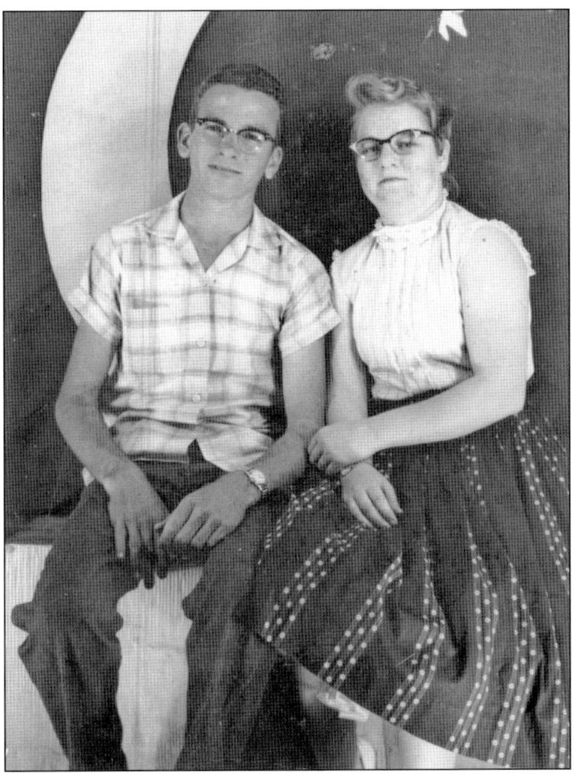

Sitting on the moon for a picture was something everyone liked to do. Pictures were often taken at the theater or next to the Rainbow Inn. In the 1950s, A.J. Theriot was 20 years old and Lucille Theriot was 19 when they took this picture on the moon. They were married on February 5, 1961. (Courtesy of Lucille Theriot.)

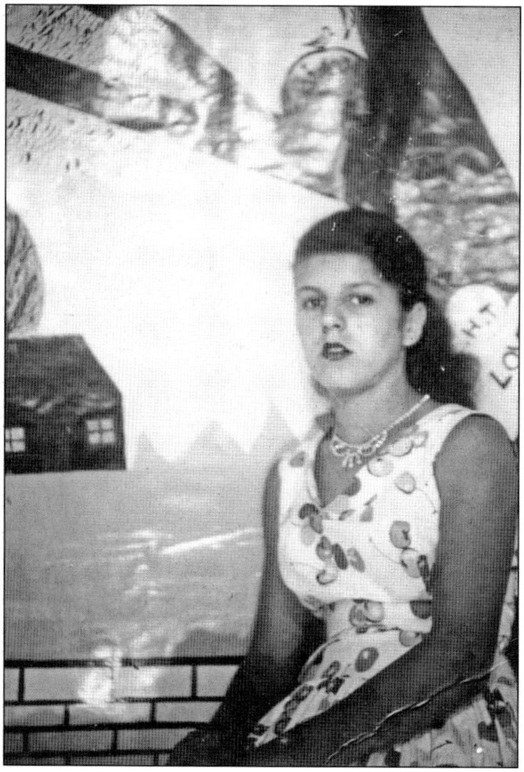

Lucy Cavalier Daigle had her picture taken by a photographer at Cox's Theater. The photographer had many different backdrops to pick from. Lucy was very young at the time this picture was taken. She married Jerry Daigle. (Courtesy of Elise Cavalier Cavalier.)

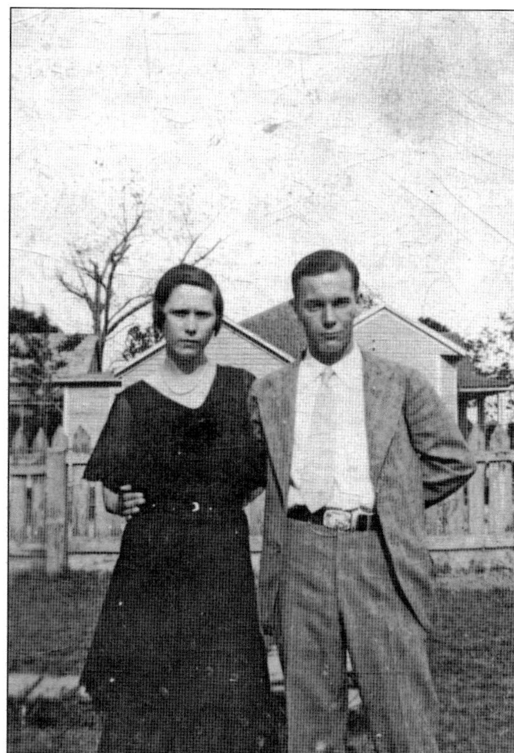

Frank Guillot is pictured with his wife, Alma Jocob Guillot. Frank was the son of Oilbert Guillot and Bernadette Templet Guillot. Alma was the daughter of Moise and Linda Cambre Jacob. Frank and Alma had one daughter. (Courtesy of Brenda Landry Templet and Nobert Templet.)

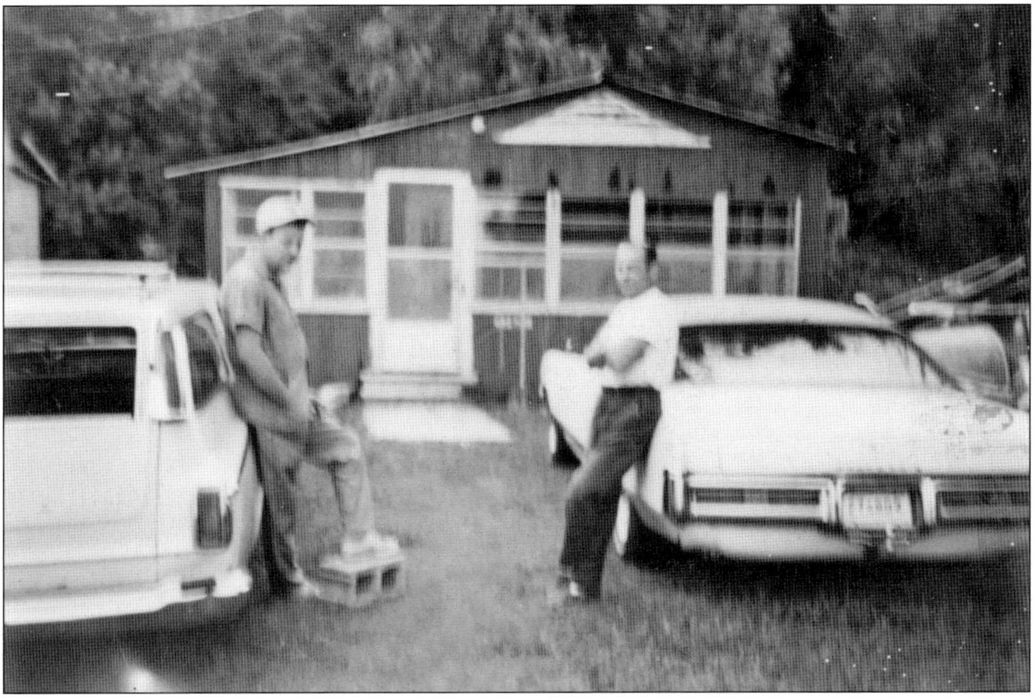

In the early 1960s, Lloyd Landry's parents owned a camp down Shell Beach Road across the street from Ed Lee's bar. It was the ideal spot for a camp. Lloyd's parents sold him the camp in the early 1970s. His family loved going to the camp. Lloyd is pictured at right. (Courtesy of Glenda Landry McGraw.)

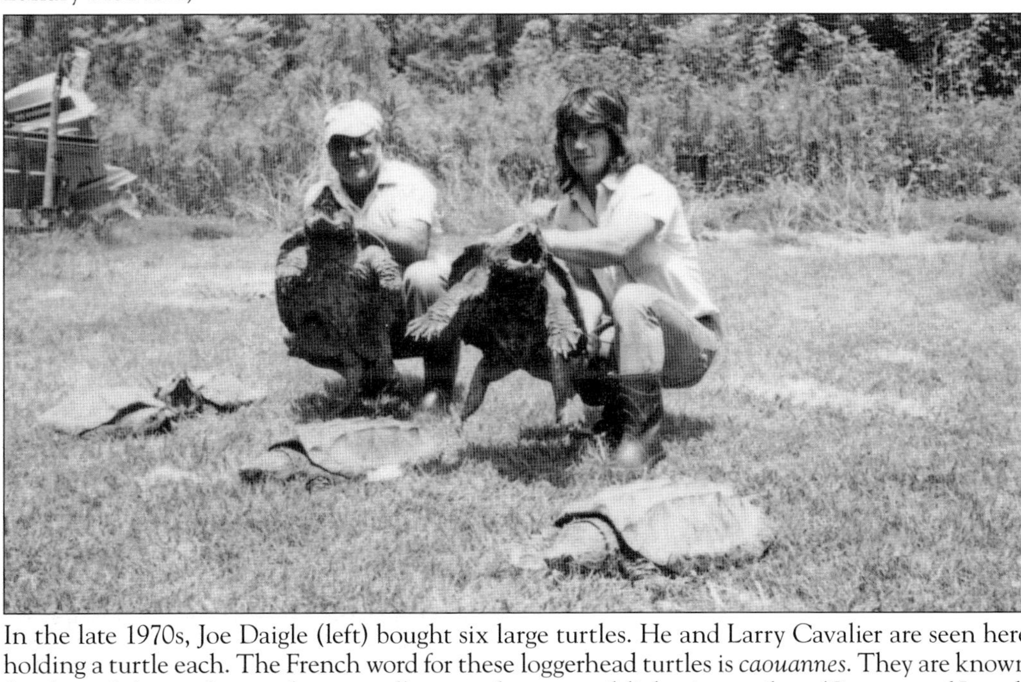

In the late 1970s, Joe Daigle (left) bought six large turtles. He and Larry Cavalier are seen here holding a turtle each. The French word for these loggerhead turtles is *caouannes*. They are known for their ability to bite and supposedly never let go until lightning strikes. (Courtesy of Joseph "Joe" Daigle and Mary Ann "Marion" Gaudet Daigle.)

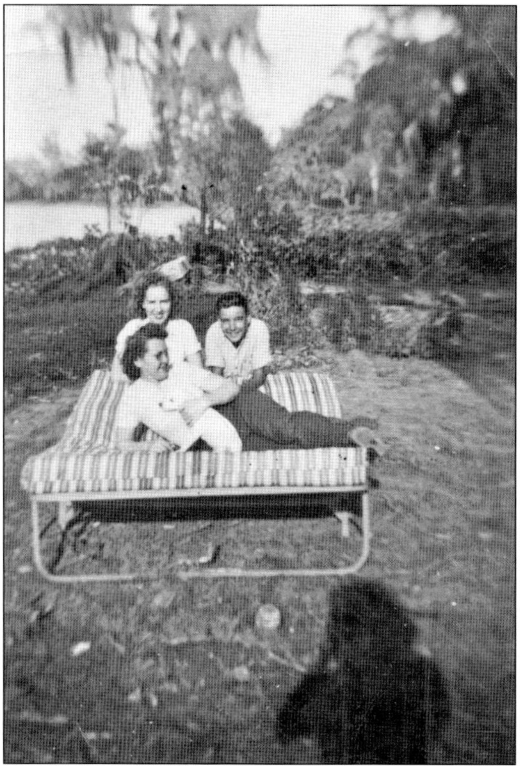

The Cavalier family is having a little camp boat fun in the spillway in Old River. Airing a mattress outside or putting the bed outside to make room in the camp for the day, Winnie St. Germain Cavalier lies on the bed, and her daughter Bessie Cavalier sits behind her with Eric Alleman Sr. (Courtesy of Alice Alleman Cavalier.)

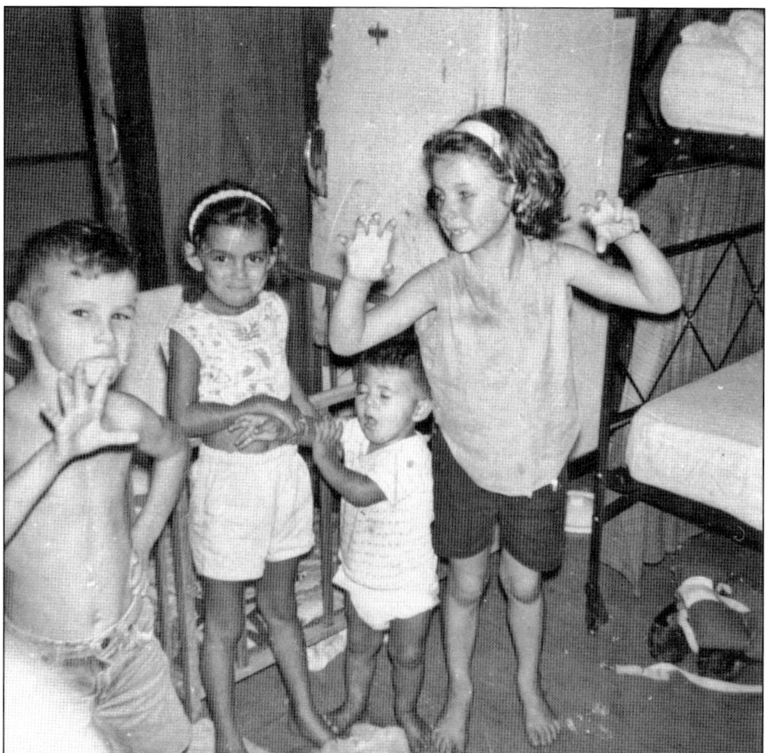

Weekend get-togethers at the camp were fun for children of all ages. Many families would camp together. This picture was taken about 1965. From left to right are Mark Hebert, Geneve Daigle Cavalier, Kevin "Crook" Daigle, and Bonnie Hebert. (Courtesy of Joseph "Joe" Daigle and Mary Ann "Marion" Gaudet Daigle.)

After a hard week working, a family barbecue was nice. Nolan "Pat" Richard loved to barbecue for everyone at the camp in Bayou Penchant. From left to right are (first row) Becky Daigle, Warren Daigle, Kevin "Crook" Daigle, Noeline "Pokeen" Dupre Richard, Nolan, Sullivan Gaudet, Gustave Joseph Gaudet, JoAnn Gaudet Leal, and Mary Ann "Marion" Gaudet Daigle; (second row) unidentified, Darryl Leonard, Joseph "Joe" Daigle, Geneve "Jeannie" Daigle Cavalier, and Brady Richard. (Courtesy of Gustave "Joe" Gaudet and Sarah Leonard Gaudet.)

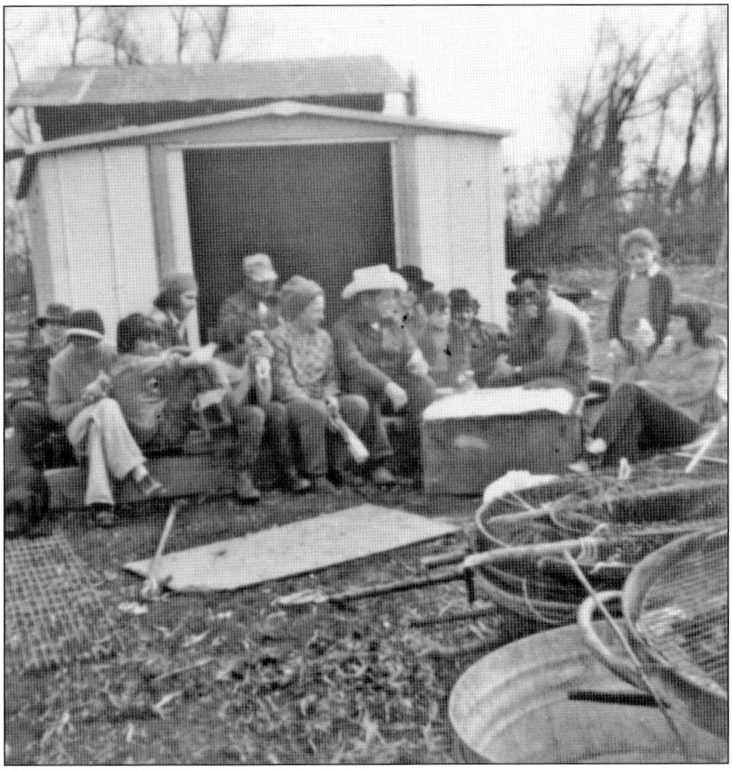

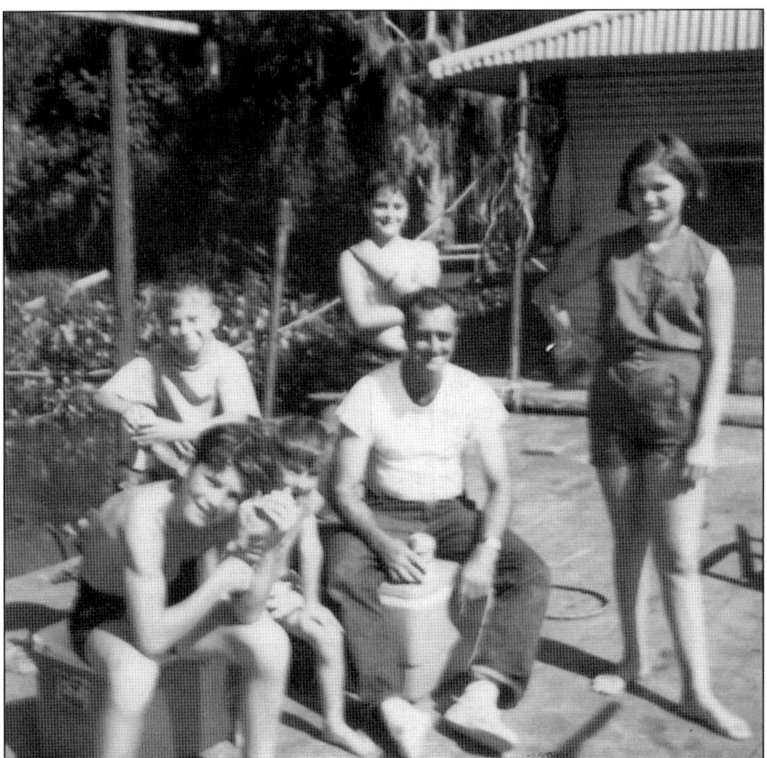

This picture was taken at the Landry camp in the spillway. The camp was always open to visitors. It is not known who the children are. Haywood Hebert is sitting on the pier having a drink and watching the children swim. (Courtesy of Wildy Templet and Hilda Landry Templet.)

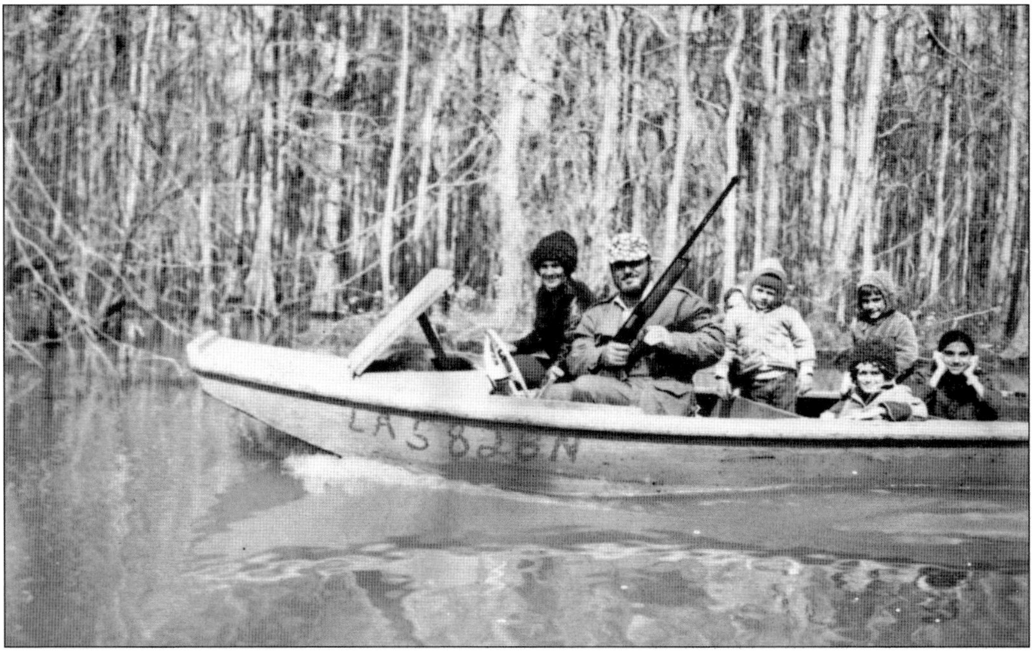

The Daigle family is on their way to the camp. Joseph "Joe" Daigle has his gun in his hand ready to get supper for the camp gang. From left to right are Mary Ann "Marion" Gaudet Daigle, Joe, Kevin "Crook" Daigle, Geneve "Jeannie" Daigle Cavalier, Warren Daigle, and Rebecca "Becky" Daigle. (Courtesy of Wildy Templet and Hilda Templet.)

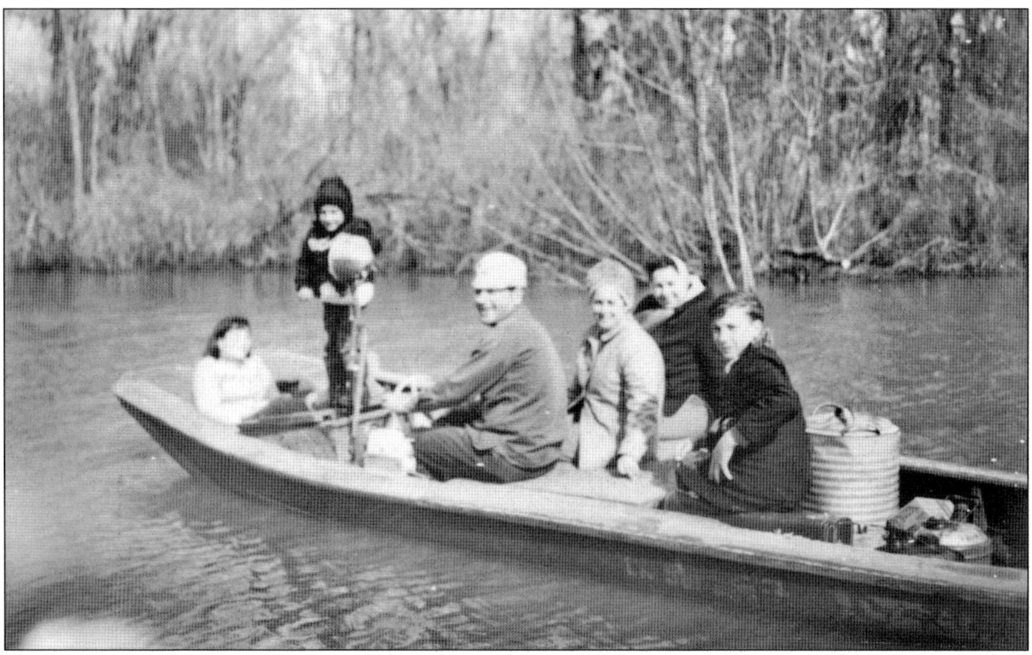

This boat is loaded for a fun weekend at the camp. From left to right are Patrica "Pat" Landry Settoon, unidentified, Odon Landry, Lois Hebert Landry, Hilda Landry Templet, and Mark Templet. It is not known what camp they are headed to, but they loved the camp. (Courtesy of Wildy Templet and Hilda Landry Templet.)

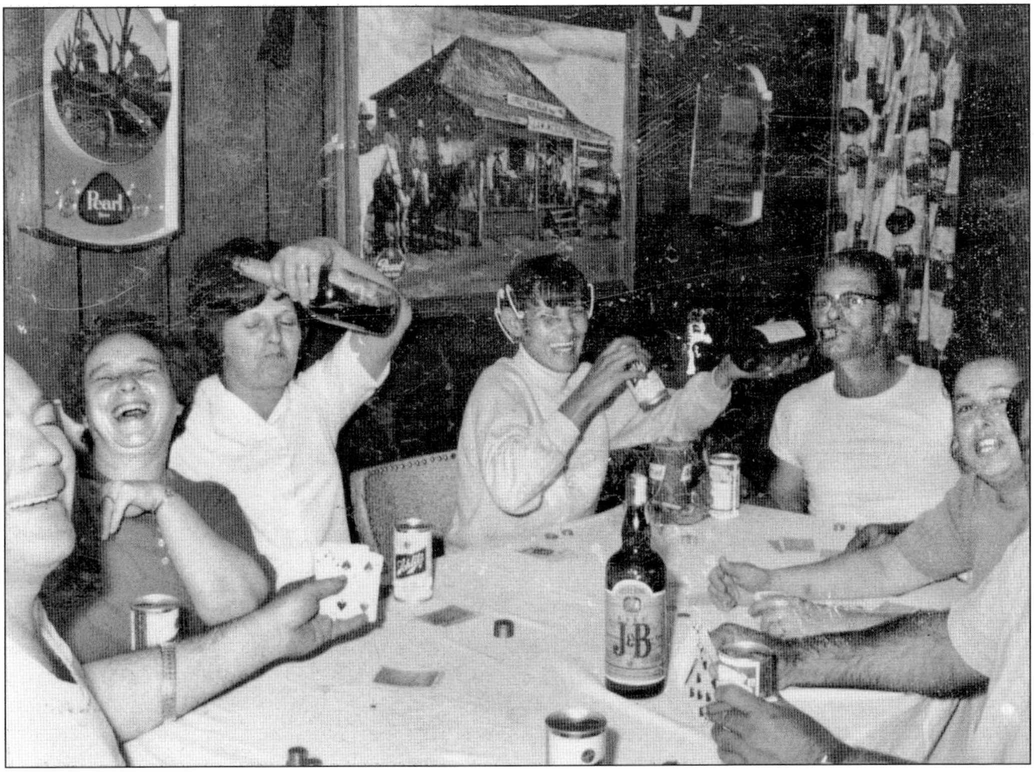

With lots of drinking and playing cards, this gang of friends always enjoyed themselves. From left to right are Odon Landry, Lois Hebert Landry, Geraldine Landry Fryou, Mary Ann "Marion" Gaudet Daigle, Gerald Fryou, unidentified, and Joseph "Joe" Daigle (just his arms visible). (Courtesy of Wildy Templet and Hilda Landry Templet.)

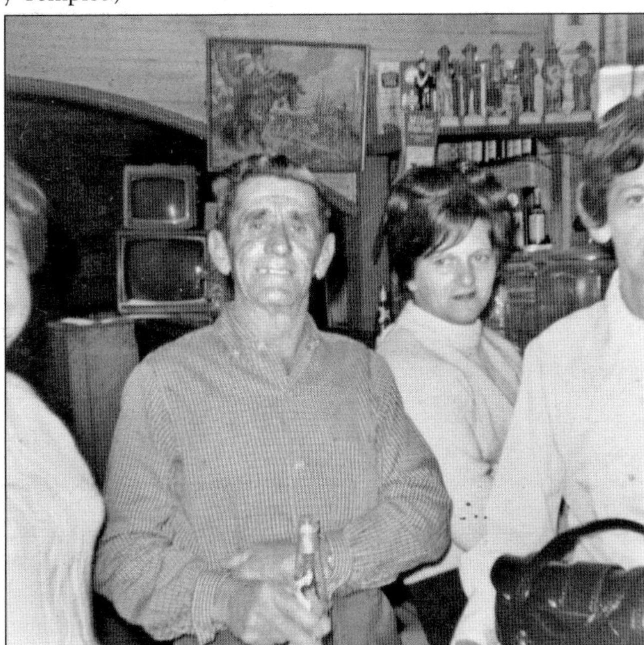

This picture was taken in May 1970. It is not known where the Landrys were, but they are having a good old time. From left to right are unidentified, Harry Landry, Geraldine Landry Fryou, and Betty Verette Landry. Geraldine has her eye on someone. (Courtesy of Wildy Templet and Hilda Landry Templet.)

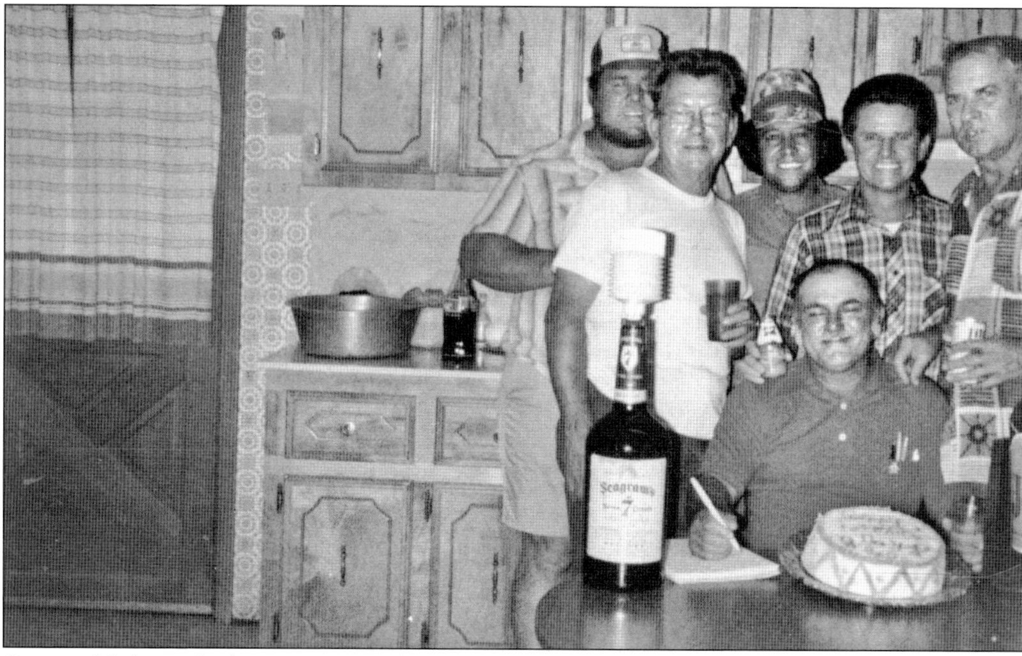

One could always find a party at Joseph "Joe" Daigle's house. Pictured is a get-together to celebrate Joe's birthday. Joe is sitting; standing from left to right are (first row) Jim Carpenter, Donald Mabile, and Randy Buras; (second row) Roy "Big Roy" Richard and Carol Richard. (Courtesy of Joseph "Joe" Daigle and Mary Ann "Marion" Gaudet Daigle.)

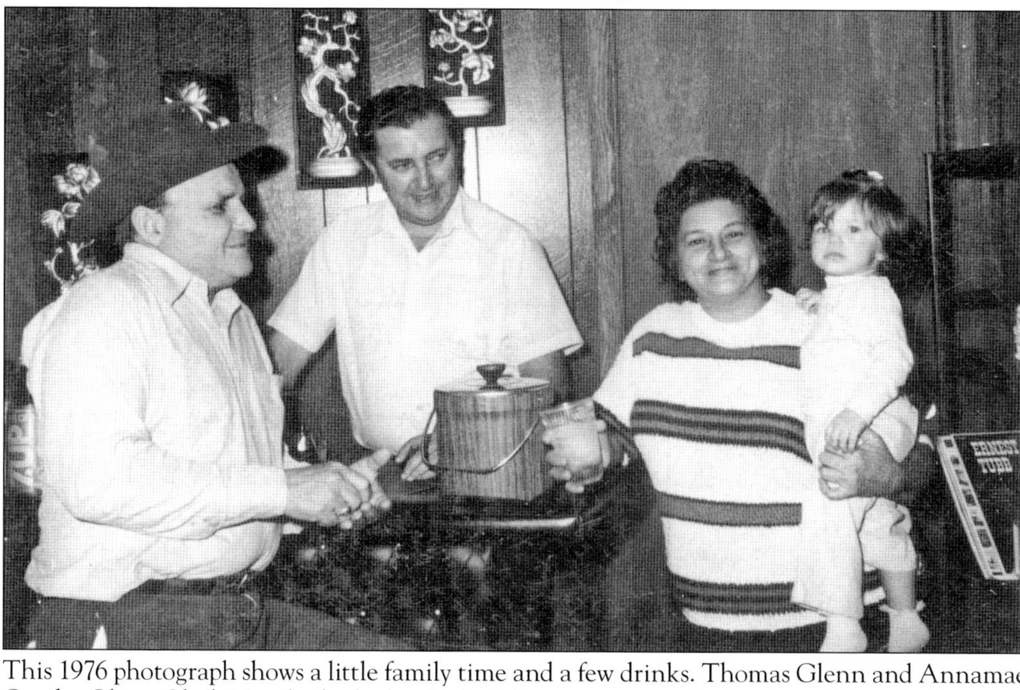

This 1976 photograph shows a little family time and a few drinks. Thomas Glenn and Annamae Gaudet Glenn Clark Morales had a bar in their house to entertain family and friends. From left to right are Andrew Metrejean Sr., Thomas Glenn, Vivian Gaudet Metrejean, and baby Monica Glynn LeBlanc. (Courtesy of Tina Glynn Cavalier and Norman Cavalier.)

Many hours of wood cutting, cleaning, and preparing goes into a pig roast. Pigs were tied on a wire, propped next to a fire in the ground, and roasted for a couple of days. As seen here in 1974, Joe Daigle and many of his friends roasted pigs. Everybody and anybody was invited to the pig roasts. (Courtesy of Tina Glynn Cavalier and Norman Cavalier.)

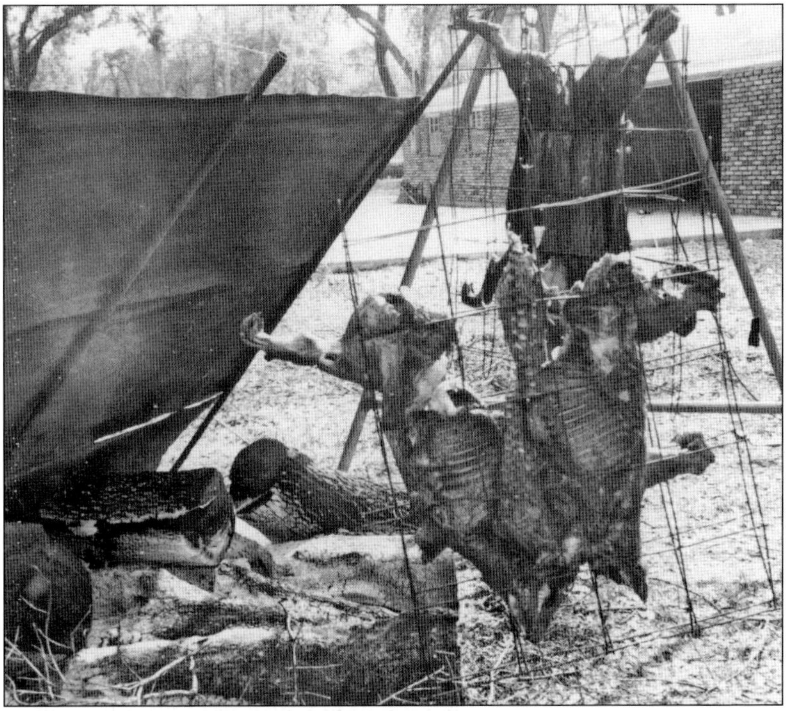

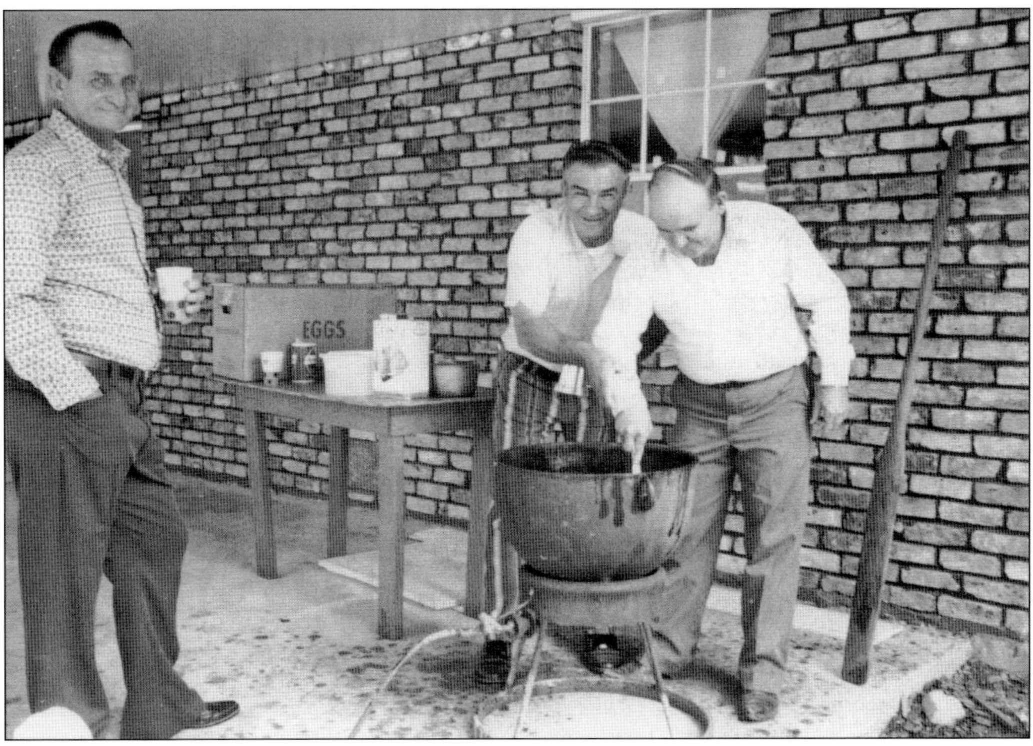

Andrew Metrejean (far right) and Milton Hebert (center) were two great cooks at Joseph "Joe" Daigle's for the pig roast. It is unknown what they were cooking. Standing by watching at far left is Eno Blanchard from Bayou Pigeon. (Courtesy of Tina Glenn Cavalier and Norman Cavalier.)

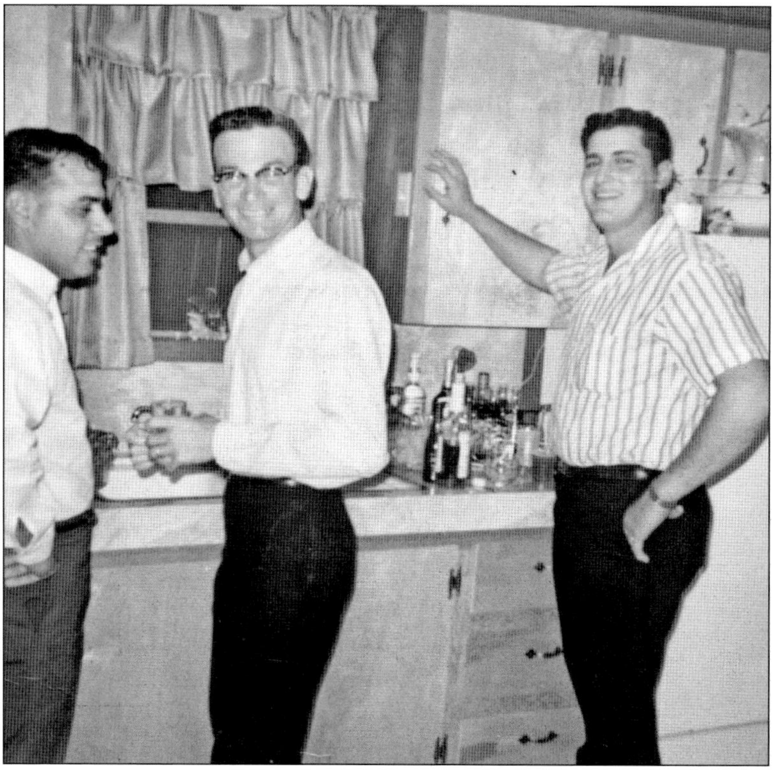

Christmas was always a fun time at A.J. and Lucille Theriot's house. They had family and friends over for a Christmas party. Having a few drinks to celebrate are, from left to right, Shelby Gaudet, A.J. Theriot, and Tony Dugas. (Courtesy of Lucille Theriot.)

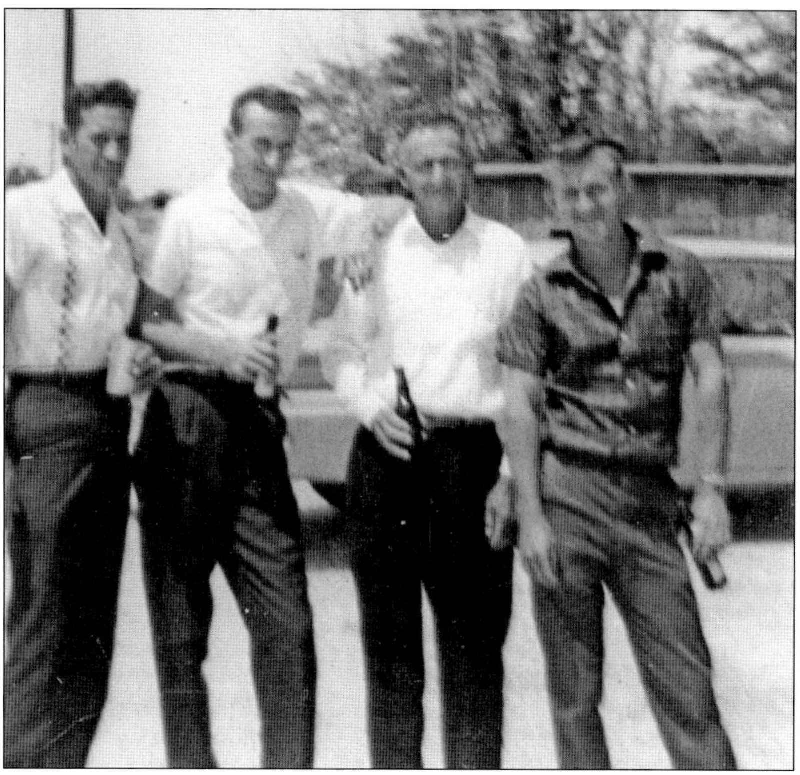

These men loved to hang out at the Live Oak Club and have a few drinks with their friends and family. From left to right are Clarence Miller, Laury Aucoin, Joe Aucoin, and Shelby Aucoin. The picture was taken in 1963. (Courtesy of Gustave Joseph Gaudet and Sarah Leonard Gaudet.)

Shelby Aucoin (left) and Joseph Gaudet are sitting on the back end of a 1961 Chevrolet Bolero. The car was a long sought-after dream for Joseph. They are in front of the Live Oak Club in Belle River. It was a beautiful day to be outside. (Courtesy of Gustave Joseph Gaudet and Sarah Leonard Gaudet.)

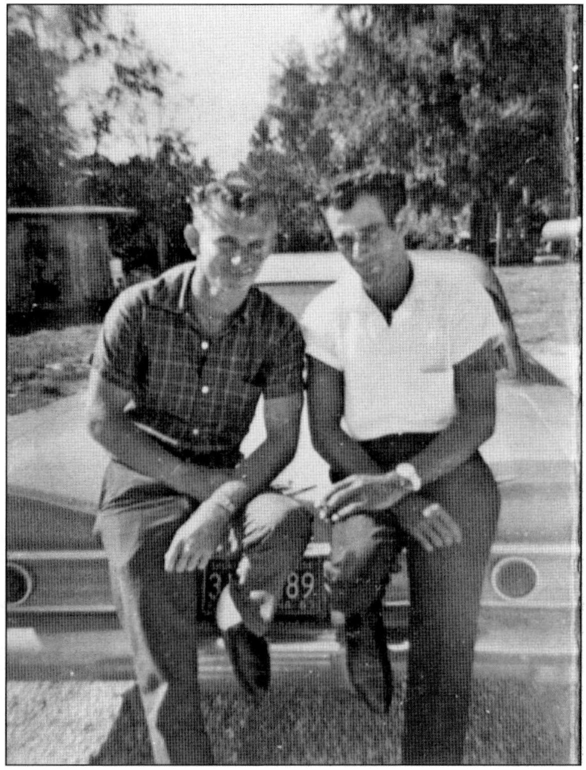

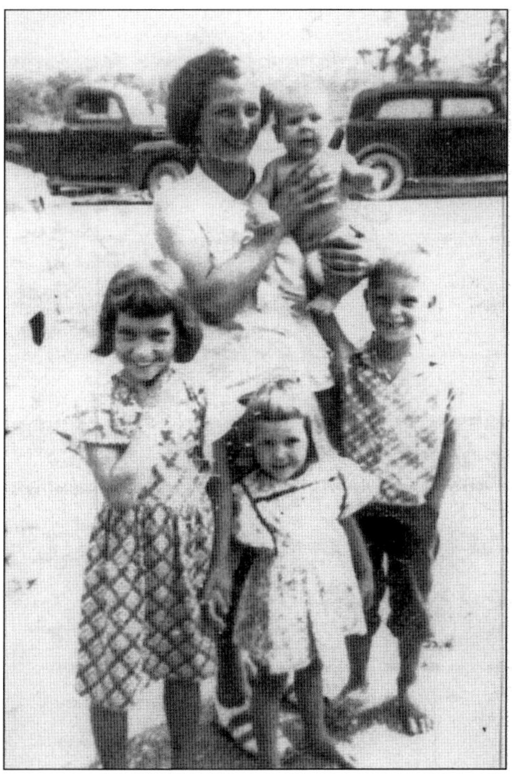

Lillian Cavalier Gros Leonard is with four of her children in front of Live Oak Inn in Belle River in the summer of 1951. From left to right are Doris Cavalier Hebert (eight), Ann Cavalier Andres Landry Cavalier (three), Harry Gros Jr. (nine months), and Norris Cavalier (three). (Courtesy of Ann Cavalier Andres Landry Cavalier.)

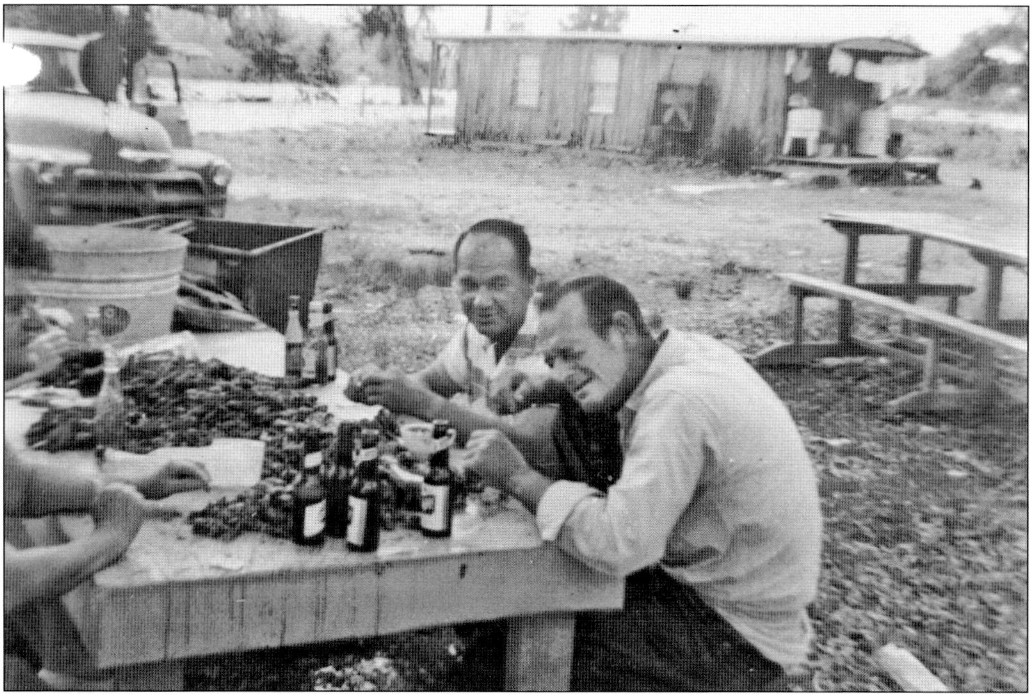

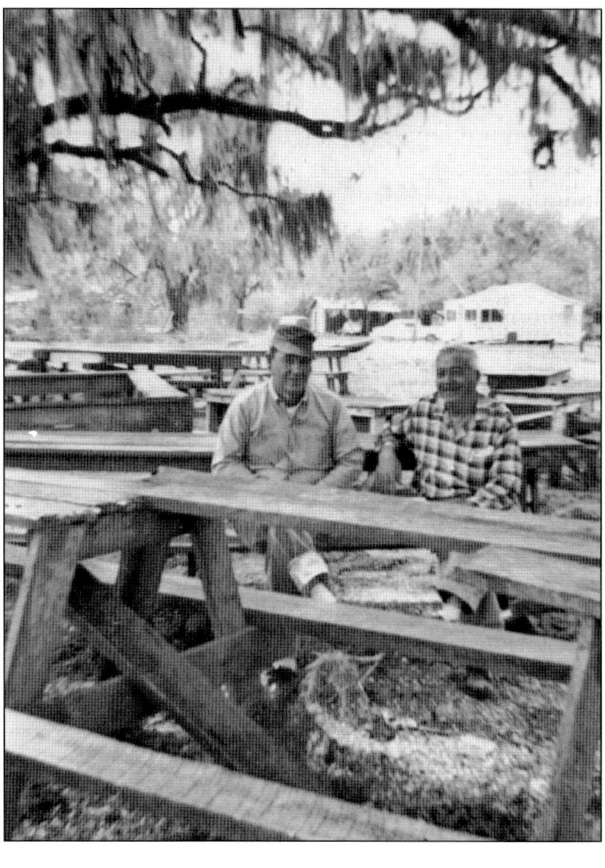

It was always nice to sit under the trees next to the Live Oak Club in Belle River. From left to right are Hilda Aucoin Leonard and her sons Rene Leonard Sr. and Gilbert "Tootsie" Leonard. They are enjoying a few beers and boiled crawfish. The little house in the background was for Maggie Lambert. (Courtesy of Gustave "Joseph" and Sarah Leonard Gaudet.)

Everyone loved relaxing under the oak trees on beautiful Lake Verret. Pictured here are Rene Leonard Sr. (left) and Tony Russo, owner of Shell Beach Bar. They had many picnic tables so families could enjoy the outdoors. Rene is 42 in this picture. (Courtesy of Gustave "Joseph" Gaudet and Sarah Leonard Gaudet.)

These two beautiful ladies are having a great time. Having their picture taken next to Cox's Theater are Agnes Cavalier Leonard (left) and Elise Cavalier. They are ready for a night of dancing and seeing friends. Elise was not married at the time. (Courtesy of Elsie Cavalier Cavalier.)

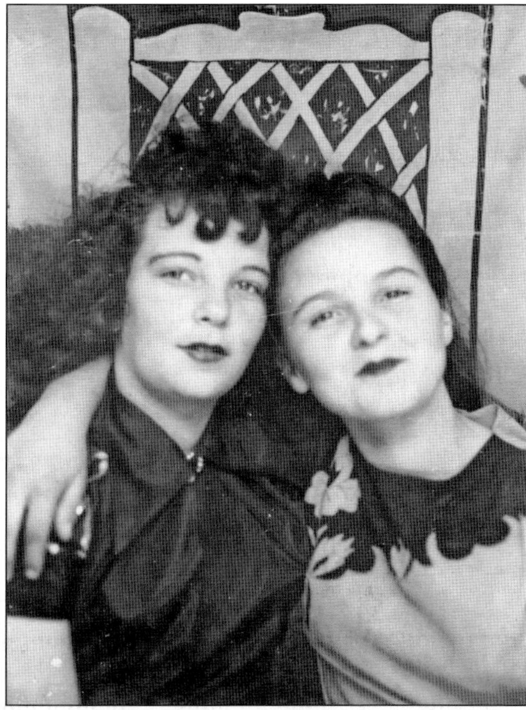

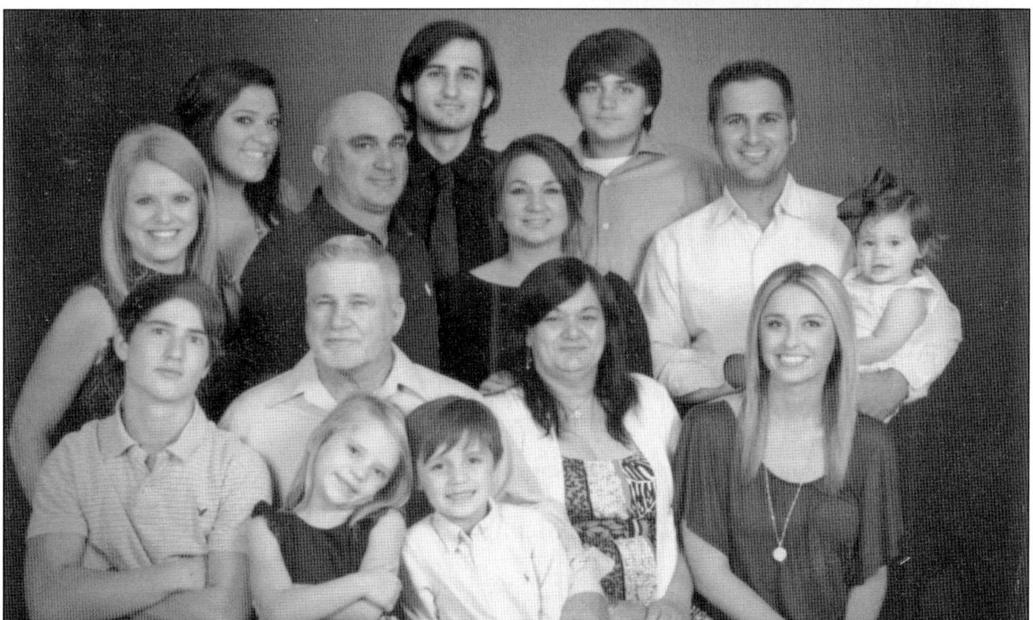

Larry Cavalier and Geneve "Jeannie" Daigle Cavalier and their children, grandchildren, and great-grandchild are pictured. From left to right are (first row) Lola Metrejean and Brant Cavalier; (second row) Brennon Cavalier, Larry, Jeannie, and Laci Brown Cavalier; (third row) Belinda Domingue Cavalier, Stafford Cavalier, Shannon Cavalier Boudreaux, Seth Cavalier, and Laityn Cavalier; (fourth row) Breanna Cavalier, Tre' Caballero, and Tyler Boudreaux. (Courtesy of Larry Cavalier and Geneve "Jeannie" Daigle Cavalier.)